English Family Life
1576–1716

For
John, Kris and Gina

English Family Life, 1576–1716

An Anthology from Diaries

Edited by
RALPH HOULBROOKE

Basil Blackwell

First published 1988

First published in USA 1989

Basil Blackwell Ltd
108 Cowley Road, Oxford, OX4 1JF, UK

Basil Blackwell Inc.
432 Park Avenue South, Suite 1503
New York, NY 10016, USA

British Library Cataloguing in Publication Data
English family life, 1576–1716: an anthology
  from diaries.
1. England. Family life, 1576–1716.
I. Houlbrooke, Ralph A. (Ralph
Anthony), <u>1944--</u>.
306.8'5'0942

ISBN 0–631–14852–3

Library of Congress Cataloging-in-Publication Data
English family life, 1576–1716.

Bibliography: p.
Includes index.
1. Family—England—History—Sources.
2. England—Social life and customs—Sources.
3. English diaries. I. Houlbrooke, Ralph A.
(Ralph Anthony), 1944–
HQ615.E54   1988   306.8'5'0942   88–7544
ISBN 0–631–14852–3

Typeset in Times 11/13pt by Photo·graphics, Honiton, Devon
Printed by T.J. Press Ltd, Padstow, Cornwall

Contents

Preface and Acknowledgements

This anthology has been designed to make available to a wider readership some of the most vivid and intimate surviving testimony concerning family life in early modern England. Diaries are widely scattered in libraries, record offices and private collections. Many of them are little known, or familiar only in inadequate editions. Basing a collection of this sort on one theme and one type of documentary source has advantages for both compiler and reader. It makes for unity, sets bounds to the editor's task, enables him to include a representative set of extracts of reasonable length, and allows different individual responses to common experiences to be compared. Certainly there are some disadvantages too. With very few exceptions, diaries have little to tell us directly about the poor, who made up the majority of the English population during this period. The selection of extracts bearing on one theme inevitably gives a partial picture of diarists' experiences and preoccupations. Many of the diaries which I have used because they throw vivid light on some aspect of family life also record a wide range of activities outside the domestic sphere.

When this project was first discussed, a collection of extracts from seventeenth-century diaries was envisaged. I subsequently decided to extend its scope to include much of Elizabeth's reign, the whole of the Stuart period, and the dawn of the Hanoverian era. Its time span now embraces both the earliest intimate diaries written in England and the exceptionally revealing journal begun by the young Dudley Ryder soon after George I's accession. In the majority of cases I have consulted the original or oldest surviving manuscripts, but I have been content to rely on certain editions of high repute, and had no choice but to depend on published versions of some diaries whose whereabouts are no longer known.

Many people have given me valuable help in preparing this book. Virginia Murphy invited me to undertake the work and discussed its progress with me on numerous subsequent occasions. Harriet Barry read my final typescript with exemplary thoroughness and made many useful suggestions for its improvement. My quest for material has been greatly assisted by the staff of the many libraries and record offices specified in the acknowledgements at the end of this preface. Mr Arthur Owen brought Isaac Archer's diary to my attention. Mr Timothy Rogers furnished me with a list of diaries in the Bodleian Library and put me in touch with Mr Stephen Butt, who generously assisted my efforts to track down Mary Woodforde's diary. Dr Michael Webb of the National Maritime Museum very kindly read for me a passage from Edward Barlow's journal, a manuscript which I could not see for myself because it was undergoing extensive repairs. Michael Hunter lent me his typescript of Samuel Jeake's diary (which he has edited together with Annabel Gregory) and allowed me to transcribe passages from it. Miss Margaret Holmes, who is editing the diary of John Richards of Warmwell, gave me valuable help and advice. Linda Pollock generously let me have a typescript of the extracts included in her anthology *Lasting Relationship: Parents and Children over Three Centuries*, thus enabling me to keep to a minimum the duplication of material she had already used. Among the many people who answered my enquiries about diaries with patience and courtesy I would like to mention particularly Lord Carbery, Lord Clitheroe, Colonel Richard Probert, Mr Matthew Festing, Mr Paul Hobhouse, Professor K. H. D. Haley, Dr A. L. Rowse, Dr David Hey, Nora de Brun and Miss S. J. Macpherson. I am indebted to Joe Bagley and Keith Wrightson for encouragement and advice.

This project could hardly have been completed without my family's assistance. My children helped me to learn how to use our word processor while I was engaged in the task of composition. My wife supported me through the vicissitudes of this apprenticeship with unfailing patience and sympathy.

Grateful acknowledgements are due for permission to print extracts to the following owners or custodians of manuscript diaries (diarists' names in brackets; full details will be found in the appendix): the Bodleian Library, Oxford (John Dee, Lady Elizabeth Delaval, Samuel Woodforde); the British Library (Katherine Austen, the Countess of Bridgewater, Elizabeth Freke, Oliver Heywood, Lady Margaret Hoby, the Countess of Warwick, Adam Winthrop); the Syndics of Cambridge University Library (Isaac Archer, William Coe); Chetham's Library (Edmund Harrold, Henry Newcome); the Viscount Daventry (Sir Richard Newdigate); Dorset Record Office (John Richards); Guildhall Library (Nehemiah Wallington); Kent Archives Office (Lady Anne Clifford); the Lamport Hall Trust (Thomas Isham); the National Maritime Museum (Edward Barlow); Mrs Margaret Oglander (Sir John Oglander); The Public Record Office (William Carnsew, first Earl of Shaftesbury); Dr Philip Riden (Leonard Wheatcroft); Dr Williams's Library (Elias Pledger, Richard Rogers); and to the following editors and publishers for permission to reproduce printed material: Associated Book Publishers (UK) Ltd (Dudley Ryder); the British Academy and Alan Macfarlane (Ralph Josselin); Michael Hunter and Annabel Gregory (Samuel Jeake); the Council of the Record Society of Lancashire and Cheshire (Nicholas Blundell); Longman Group UK Ltd (John Greene, Roger Lowe); the Warden and Scholars of New College, Oxford (Mary Woodforde), Oxford University Press (John Evelyn); Professor William Sachse (Roger Lowe); Unwin Hyman (Samuel Pepys); my thanks also to Stella Welford and Giles Woodforde for help in tracking down the Mary Woodforde diary.

R. A. H.

Rules of Transcription

Throughout the extracts spelling has been modernized ('then' has been spelt 'than' when modern usage so demands), as have punctuation, capitalization and italicization. Abbreviations have been expanded when there is no doubt of their meaning.

Numerals have usually been spelt out in full, but the practice of the original writers or editors has been followed in transcribing dates, times of day and sums of money.

Square brackets [ ] enclose editorial additions (in italic) or doubtful readings (in roman, followed by a question mark), < > enclose words or letters from the margin of the source, { } enclose interlineations, which, however, have not usually been indicated unless they introduced retrospective comment, seemed to represent a significant change of mind on the part of the writer, or did not readily fit into the existing text.

Deletions have not been indicated unless they reflect significant changes of mind on the writer's part, in which case they have been described in the notes.

A series of three dots, . . . , denote editorial omissions *within a day's entry or paragraph in a source. The omission of other entries or sections of text has not been indicated.*

Standard indentation of the first lines of day entries or paragraphs has been introduced in almost every case.

The footnotes give possible alternative readings, definitions of rare or obsolete words (normally based on the *Shorter Oxford English Dictionary*), and some original spellings (in italic) when these are especially eccentric, markedly different from those now current, or obviously based on the writer's pronunciation of the word.

Fuller information about diarists and diaries and full references for works cited in the notes will be found in the appendix.

Numbers in brackets in the main and sectional introductions refer to extracts included in the anthology.

Introduction

The ancestry of the diary can be traced far back into the Middle Ages, most clearly, perhaps, to chronicles or annals. These, like diaries, were records of events drawn up as they occurred or shortly afterwards. They were maintained at first by clerics, particularly members of religious houses, but were later undertaken by literate laymen too, especially townsfolk. Devoted first and foremost to occurrences which loomed large in the history of a particular dynasty, monastery or city, they were kept up by a succession of writers who, though often anonymous, from an early stage allowed something of their personalities and views to become apparent in occasional pungent expressions of disgust at acts of oppression or of horror at natural disasters.

By the later Middle Ages 'personal chronicles' had emerged, which described their authors' involvement in some of the events that they recorded. One of the liveliest and best known is the one written during the early fifteenth century by a citizen of Paris and usually known as the *Journal d'un Bourgeois de Paris*.[1] Alongside records of weather and prices he gave his trenchant opinions of noblemen and politicians, expressions of sympathy with the poor, and occasional descriptions of his own experiences. Accounts of certain momentous events, drawn up by people who had taken part in them, predominate among the earliest English

---

[1] Translated by J. Shirley as *A Parisian Journal, 1405–1449* (Clarendon Press, Oxford, 1968).

manuscripts to which the term 'diary' has been applied. They include the journal of Thomas Beckington's embassy to France in 1442–3 kept by an anonymous member of his suite, Sir Richard Guildford's account of his pilgrimage to the Holy Land in 1506–7, and a description of the Boulogne campaign of 1544.[2] These types of diary or journal have remained common down to the present day.

Among the medieval forerunners of the modern diary must also be included books of accounts and memoranda (*libri di ricordanze*) of the sort kept in large numbers in fourteenth-century Florence. In them, besides the records of major investments, gains and losses, are to be found family events of the first importance—births, marriages and deaths. The two categories of information were connected, for the growth of the family was accompanied by increasing expenditure and investment in education and marriage portions. In the secret record kept by Gregorio Dati (1362–1435), a silk manufacturer and merchant, the descriptions of his four marriages and the much-needed capital they brought him in the shape of dowries link his commercial activities with the more intimate domestic world. The children born of each marriage, and, all too often, their deaths, are also recorded. Dati's practice of subjecting his affairs to periodic review led him to summarize information previously entered among his *ricordanze*, notably in a brief autobiographical recapitulation which he wrote when he was about sixty-five.[3] Many English manuscripts commonly described as 'diaries' are basically account books, memorandum books, or amalgams of the two which include occasional descriptions of personal experiences. Conversely, some of the best known diaries also contain occasional summaries of accounts.

Before long, the pious extended their surveillance from economic concerns to cover their personal conduct and their

[2] N. H. Nicolas (ed.), *Journal by one of the Suite of Thomas Beckington* (London, 1828); Sir H. Ellis (ed.), *The Pilgrymage of Sir Richard Guylforde to the Holy Land, A. D. 1506*, Camden Society, old series, 51 (1851); W. A. J. Archbold, 'A Diary of the Expedition of 1544', *English Historical Review*, 16 (1901), pp. 503–7.

[3] J. Martines (tr.), G. Brucker (ed.), *Two Memoirs of Renaissance Florence: The Diaries of Buonaccorso Pitti and Gregorio Dati* (Harper and Row, New York, 1967), pp. 107–41. Cf. G. A. Guarino (ed.), *The Albertis of Florence: Leon Battista Alberti's Della Famiglia* (Bucknell University Press, Lewisburg, 1971), p. 129.

fulfilment of religious obligations. Taking stock in 1404, Gregorio Dati recognized that he had given little heed to God's commandments and made a number of resolutions concerning his future stricter observance of Christian duties.[4] The religious turmoil of the sixteenth century hastened the development of the spiritual diary as an independent genre. In the journal of Ignatius Loyola, the most interesting entries are those which describe the saint's interior life: his mental and emotional states, his movements towards decisions, his devotional tears, and above all his visions of the divine presence.[5] But the spiritual diary was developed on both sides of the religious divide, by devout Protestants as well as by the foremost saint of the Counter-Reformation.

In England the first diaries kept primarily for religious purposes date from the last decades of the sixteenth century. Such journals could perform a variety of functions, and there were considerable differences of format and purpose. First, and most obviously, they enabled individuals to keep account of their use of God's gifts, especially time itself. Secondly, they acted as registers of divine mercies and punishments, of the sinful actions which might have occasioned the latter, and of resolutions for future amendment. (Some diarists wrote down occasional meditations on their actions and experiences rather than a continuous diary.) A third function of spiritual journals was to describe the daily episodes of the struggle between God and Satan within the individual soul; the moments of temptation, apathy or depression, and the interludes of inspiration, exaltation or spiritual peace.

The comparison between the spiritual journal and the account book was one often made by advocates of the former during the seventeenth century. One of the clergymen whom John Evelyn heard on this subject drew attention to 'the infinite benefit of daily Examination; Comparing to a Merchant, keeping his books, to see whither he thrived, or went backward; & how it would facilitate our reckonings, & what a Comfort on our death bed . . .'[6] In this country the rise of Puritanism promoted the keeping of spiritual journals, but in the second half of our

[4] *Two Memoirs*, pp. 124–5.
[5] M. Gioia (ed.), *Gli Scritti di Ignazio di Loyola* (Unione Tipografico-Editrice Torinese, Turin, 1977), pp. 273–340.
[6] De Beer (ed.), *Diary of John Evelyn*, vol. IV, p. 222.

period the practice was by no means restricted to religious nonconformists: a number of diarists of this type were loyal members of the Church of England.

Autobiographies and memoirs began to be written in the period which saw the emergence of the personal diary. To judge from surviving manuscripts, the ruling class of early Renaissance Florence was the first social group to produce them in considerable numbers.[7] It is customary to insist upon the difference between diaries and autobiographies. The diarist takes the short view, the autobiographer the long: 'The diarist can see only the pattern of a day, not the pattern of a lifetime', while in the autobiography 'events are moulded and trimmed into a unified whole'.[8] The autobiographer is more selective than the diarist for a number of reasons, including lapses of memory, the fear of revealing incidents discreditable to the writer, and the wish to pick out the important from the mass of trivial events. Yet between the diary written as events occurred and the fully developed autobiography there lies no clear dividing line, but rather a range of intermediate forms.

Some diaries are based on scribbled notes transcribed at leisure.[9] Various Stuart diarists are known to have prepared substantial abstracts or abridgements of their diaries. This activity, prelude to a longer-term examination of actions, motives and experiences, was nevertheless part and parcel of the same grand design as the original diary and could not have taken place without it. (We have already seen the beginning of this process in the diary of Gregorio Dati.) Lengthy passages which bear all the marks of diary entries transcribed with very little alteration are often embedded in such abstracts. At least one autobiographical memoir, itself probably based on more detailed diaries, went through two surviving versions, between which there are significant differences.[10] All these intermediate types of writing are represented in this anthology.

[7] *Two Memoirs*, pp. 11–12.
[8] W. Matthews, *British Diaries: An Annotated Bibliography of British Diaries Written between 1442 and 1942* (University of California Press, Berkeley, 1950), p. x; A. Ponsonby, *English Diaries: A Review of English Diaries from the Sixteenth to the Twentieth Century* (Methuen, London, 1923), p. 2.
[9] E.g. Tyrer (trans. and annot.), Bagley (ed.), *Great Diurnal of Nicholas Blundell*, vol. I, pp. 7–8.
[10] Mrs Elizabeth Freke's, in British Library, MSS Add. 45718–9.

Diary-keeping during the Tudor and Stuart periods was inspired by various motives. The most fundamental was the itch to record events in a form which allowed facts and dates to be checked. The heading of a section of Adam Winthrop's diary, 'A register of the deaths of my friends, and of other things which have happened since the feast of the Nativity, anno 1596' gives a fair idea of its character as a basic *aide-mémoire*. A fuller, more descriptive diary might be the source of future amusement or edification. Sir Henry Slingsby claimed to be following Montaigne's advice in registering the 'daily accidents' which happened in his house. Montaigne had recommended his father's practice in having a diary kept. It had been 'very pleasant to look over, when Time begins to wear Things out of Memory, and very useful sometimes to put us out of doubt, when such a Thing was begun, when ended, what Courses were debated on, what conclud'd . . .' Another motive was the writer's need to account to God or himself or herself for time spent. There is an early manifestation of this need in the daily entries which the Cornish gentleman William Carnsew made in the diary which he kept in 1576–7, and some self-criticism in his admission that he spent 14 March 1576 'playinge and tryfflynge the Tyme awaye'.[11] In many diaries the intention of using the record of sins or mis-spent time as the basis of future reform is evident. The Manchester wig-maker Edmund Harrold, who despite his religious impulses spent much of his life a prey to the desires of the flesh, expressed this purpose particularly clearly near the beginning of his surviving diary in June 1712:

I've been taken up with a review of my life past since 1709, in which I find things a many to humble me, as well as raise me up. I pray God it may have this effect on me, to mend what I have in my power to mend for the time to come. Amen [(28)].

Whether or not remedial action was possible, however, the diary could act as a safety-valve, and to entrust one's experiences to this silent confidant might be therapeutic in itself, taking some of the sting out of feelings of grief, disappointment or frustration.

[11] British Library, MS Add. 37419, f. 21ᵛ; Parsons (ed.), *Diary of Sir Henry Slingsby*, pp. 54–5 (the quoted words are Montaigne's, translated); Public Record Office, SP 46/16, f. 40ᵛ.

Explicit recognition of this function can be found at the end of
an account of an acutely embarrassing *faux pas* in courtship which
Dudley Ryder, a clumsy and inexperienced suitor, committed to
his diary in June 1716. 'But', he wrote after describing the episode
in all its painful details, 'I find myself something better now I
have writ this' (13).

Many motives entered into the writing of the best and fullest
diaries. Samuel Pepys, without peer among English diarists of
this or perhaps any other period, wrote a uniquely detailed
account of his daily activities. Momentous public events probably
provided the essential initial stimulus, yet Pepys reveals himself
more intimately than the most rigorous of puritan moral
accountants. His conception of the positive side of life's balance-
sheet was sufficiently comprehensive to include, beside the steady
accumulation of material gains, a range of intellectual and sensory
pleasures, though his hearty appreciation of some of the latter
was complicated by a lurking sense of sin as well as by a
consciousness of the material waste which they often entailed.

Dudley Ryder was inspired in keeping his diary by a sort of
secular puritanism. He intended it to be first and foremost a
means of reviewing his own actions, of achieving better
understanding of himself, his temperament and his abilities, and
of recollecting what he had read. In all these ways it would
enable him to use his time more effectively.[12] But Ryder's was
far from being an exclusively introspective record; he also
described the conversations in which he took part, the characters
of his acquaintances and the exciting political events which he
witnessed.

It is seldom clear why diarists should have chosen a particular
moment to start writing. Some did however leave an explanation.
Two nonconformists, Henry Newcome and Elias Pledger, were
inspired by the examples set by other diarists. Thomas Isham
started his Latin journal of events in and around his Northamptonshire home in 1671 at the suggestion of his father, who promised
him six pounds a year for carrying out this useful exercise (52).
(The Ishams were one of those families, like the Woodfordes and
the Blundells, in which the keeping of diaries and kindred records

---

[12] Matthews (trans. and ed.), *Diary of Dudley Ryder*, p. 29.

seems to have become something of a tradition.) By the mid-seventeenth century the practice was certainly sufficiently widely commended in devotional literature and the biographies of eminent men to bring it to the notice of a very large readership.

What made people continue writing diaries once they had begun? Of the diarists of this period, it was perhaps Henry Newcome who best answered this question, in testimony which will find an echo in the experience of many would-be diarists:

And though sometimes I intermitted this course for some days or months, and after I came into the country sometimes it was neglected, yet I could not be quiet till I had taken it up again. And though sometimes it was very sapless and empty, and I have thought it was to little purpose to keep it unless I put more in, yet I remember this thought oft prevailed with me to keep it up, that I knew not but that in time I might have something remarkable to set down, . . .[13]

The gentry are the social group best represented among the authors of surviving Tudor and Stuart diaries, though a number of the more substantial spiritual journals were the work of puritan clergy. But the prerequisites of diary-keeping, especially the ability to write, and a desire to order one's temporal or spiritual affairs, were by no means restricted to the gentry and clergy. Given the high level of literacy in towns, and the influence of Puritanism in many of them, it is perhaps surprising that we know of relatively few urban diarists, despite the fact that Pepys, the greatest diarist of all, belonged to this group. But what survives may not fully reflect the actual social spread of diary-writing during our period. The chances of survival were much higher in the muniment rooms of country houses than in towns, where dynastic continuity was far rarer, and residential mobility much greater.

But even when all allowances have been made for the casual destruction of manuscripts over the centuries, it seems highly unlikely that diaries were ever kept by more than a tiny minority of people even in those social classes in which the habit was most widespread. Why did some people keep diaries and not others? It is tempting to seek the answer to this question in some distinctive set of psychological traits, yet the sheer variety of

[13] Parkinson (ed.), *Autobiography of Henry Newcome*, vol. I, p. 14.

personalities revealed by diaries, ranging from the complacently extrovert to the anxiously introspective, makes this line of enquiry seem unpromising.[14] Nor was diary-writing dependent upon any particular set of personal circumstances. An element of physical or psychological separation did however play an important part in many, though by no means all, cases. War and travel, by lifting men out of the rut of their everyday lives and exposing them to extraordinary events, acted as exceptionally powerful stimuli to the desire to record individual experiences. Religious commitment was often seen as a pilgrimage, and those who undertook it often felt themselves distinguished by God's call from the indifferent majority. Some diarists had suffered estrangement from those who should have been closest to them in their family lives; in other cases the writer's own drive and ambition, or the aspirations of relatives, had set him on a course of upward social mobility which removed him from the milieu in which he had been born. In all these instances separation helped to create in diarists either a need for a confidant to share their preoccupations or the sense that their experiences were out of the ordinary and worth recording.

The fact that a number of early diaries give an unrivalled picture of their writers' attitudes and preoccupations has made them particularly attractive sources for those historians who have attempted to penetrate our ancestors' mental worlds. A number of biographies have drawn on diaries, notably Sir Arthur Bryant's three-volume study of *Samuel Pepys* (1933–8).[15] A. L. Rowse used the diary of William Carnsew of Bokelly to evoke the life of an Elizabethan country gentleman in a few colourful pages of his classic work on *Tudor Cornwall: Portrait of a Society* (1941); Wallace Notestein employed many other diaries laid under contribution in this anthology as sources for a memorable series of portaits of *English Folk: a Book of Characters* (1938) and *Four Worthies* (1956).[16] In recent years the growth of interest in the development of the family has drawn social historians to diaries in the course of their attempts to investigate the most intimate

---

[14] Compare Ponsonby's view in *English Diaries*, pp. 38–9.
[15] *Samuel Pepys: . . . The man in the making; . . . The years of peril; . . . The saviour of the navy* (Cambridge University Press, 1933, 1935, 1938).
[16] All three published in London by Jonathan Cape.

relationships. It was on a diary covering in some detail the exceptionally long span of forty years that Alan Macfarlane based his innovative study of *The Family Life of Ralph Josselin* (Cambridge University Press, 1970). This is noteworthy for its systematic analysis of evidence relating to such topics as childbirth, the care of young children, the age of departure from home, the making of marriages, and the relative strength of ties between members of the elementary family, neighbours, and more distant kinsfolk. Efforts to assess the quality of relationships between parents and children have depended particularly heavily on diaries. Many were exploited in the best essays in the collection *The History of Childhood* (Souvenir Press, London, 1976), edited by L. de Mause. Diaries, together with autobiographies, also formed the basis of Linda Pollock's *Forgotten Children* (Cambridge University Press, 1983), a study which not only effectively demolished many ill-founded hypotheses previously advanced but also set out evidence for a high degree of continuity in parental attitudes towards children between the sixteenth and nineteenth centuries.

Pollock's book was conceived as a contribution to an energetic debate on the history of the family in Western Europe, and in England in particular, which has revolved round certain major issues. The most important questions concern the pace of change. Some historians argue that the Western family has undergone a fundamental transformation in the last few centuries;[17] others, while readily admitting that changes have taken place, believe that they have been, at any rate until recent years, much slower and less profound than in most other human institutions. The various changes whose importance nobody denies include the dramatic falls in both fertility and mortality during the last century and a half, resulting in smaller families and much-enhanced life expectancy for their members. But wide divergences of view persist as to whether these changes are likely to have improved family relationships.

A once controversial question, whether family households were considerably larger and more complex before the industrial

---

[17] The most influential exposition of the view that radical changes occurred during our period is to be found in L. Stone, *The Family, Sex and Marriage in England 1500–1800* (Weidenfeld and Nicolson, London, 1977).

revolution, may now be regarded as resolved: most of them were not. But whether they were more 'porous', more subject to the influence of kin or neighbours, remains a controversial point. Perhaps the most intractable questions concern the possible effects of broader social, political and religious developments on family relationships. Have they brought about a substantial shift from authority and distance within the family to affection and engagement, and if so, when did it take place? Sceptics, and the proponents of slow and uneven change, have pointed out that authoritarian attitudes are by no means incompatible with affection, called in question the influence of prescriptive models of behaviour, and asserted that the variety in the quality of relationships existing at any one time, the product of differences in individual temperaments as well as social and economic circumstances, has, save perhaps in the very long term, out-weighed the significance of change.

The passages chosen for this anthology will show that diaries can throw some light on these questions. But most diaries also have certain limitations as sources for the social historian. The most important of these is the selectivity of even the fullest of them, and the key to a proper assessment of a given diary's usefulness as a social document lies in identifying the diarist's foremost concerns and the principles of selection which governed his or her choice of things to write down. Many of the most conscientious diarists, for example, were pious people whose dominant preoccupation was their standing with God. Ralph Josselin was most eloquently descriptive in times of danger, particularly sickness and childbirth. It was then that he scrutinized the course of events with the sharpest anxiety, expecting to discern in the outcome evidence of divine goodwill or displeasure. The greater part of what we can learn from his diary about his children's pastimes is contained in entries describing their narrow escapes from hazards. We are indebted for the information that Josselin himself loved playing chess to the fact that, after the death of his infant son Ralph, he expressed the fear that his devotion to the game might have offended God.[18] His careful descriptions of his children's illnesses and the obvious sorrow he felt in face of their deaths leave no doubt that Josselin was an

[18] Macfarlane (ed.), *Diary of Ralph Josselin*, p. 114.

affectionate and solicitous parent, but his diary says relatively little about the children's development, hardly anything about his daily relations with them. It seems likely, for instance, that Josselin considered most of his children's misdemeanours and the reprimands or punishments meted out to them too trivial to be noted down, and most early diaries probably have limited value as sources for the history of upbringing and discipline. Dr Macfarlane believes that Josselin's marriage can be classified as a 'joint-role relationship',[19] yet although his diary contains some few allusions to his co-operation with his wife in accomplishing tasks or reaching decisions, Josselin wrote very little of their common activities or of the extent to which he relied on her help or advice. The pleasures of conversation, shared pastimes and physical love found no place in Josselin's description of his days. Despite his obvious affection for them, the fears and trials Josselin suffered on account of his wife and children stand out more clearly and vividly than the pleasures they afforded him.

Most other diarists resembled Josselin in their reticence about aspects of their lives which seem interesting to the modern reader. Whether their main concern was to chart the course of their relationship with God, account for their use of their time, or simply chronicle the exceptional events of their careers, much of what they took for granted went unrecorded. Very few diarists of this period reveal themselves to us in so many aspects of both their interior and their outward lives that we feel we know them thoroughly. Samuel Pepys, the greatest English diarist of his age, is the outstanding exception. In his diary the important and the trivial, the fine and the coarse, the magnanimous and the mean, rub shoulders in a unique panorama of reported experience.

Nearly all diarists remained silent about certain areas of their lives; but these areas varied greatly from one diarist to the next. The delight of diaries lies in their sheer variety: perhaps no other type of source bears so clearly the stamp of its authors' individuality. Each diary has something different to tell us, either because of some special concern unique to its writer, or because the impact of an exceptional event on the humdrum round raised the curtain of reticence for a moment. Thus Lady Margaret

---

[19] A. Macfarlane, *The Family Life of Ralph Josselin, a Seventeenth-Century Clergyman: An Essay in Historical Anthropology* (Cambridge University Press, 1970), p. 110.

Hoby's diary, for example, while telling us next to nothing about
her feelings for her husband, provides an unrivalled picture of
the daily activities of a country gentlewoman (15). William
Carnsew's gives us the spectacle, extraordinary in our eyes, of a
country squire reading useful books aloud to his adolescent sons
(56); John Dee's records the rhythm of his wife's menstruation
(30); Nehemiah Wallington's preserves the authentic sound of early
seventeenth-century childish talk (42); Isaac Archer's describes a
son's reflections on reading the intimate journal of a father with
whom he had had an exceptionally complex and difficult
relationship (69). Instances could be multiplied. All enhance our
appreciation of the range of past experience.

But awareness of the variety of diarists' preoccupations and
personalities, and of their being exceptional by virtue of the very
fact that they kept diaries, must also arm us against the temptation
to base excessively broad generalizations about early modern
family life on this type of source. Two examples will serve to
illustrate the more obvious dangers. The best accounts to be
found in seventeenth-century diaries of the relations between
fathers and their adolescent sons were penned by puritan ministers
(57, 58, 61). In each case the father had serious problems with
at least one of his sons. The transition from childhood to
adulthood may have been a difficult phase of life in that period
as in this, yet uncritical reliance on this group of diaries for our
picture of seventeenth-century adolescence would be unwise.
Perhaps these puritan fathers maintained an anxious surveillance
which made it unusually difficult for their sons to establish
themselves in the outside world, or alternatively made them
particularly likely to kick over the traces. This is speculation.
But in any event there is no reason to think that the pattern of
experience in these families was typical of the population as a
whole. It is also true that with some notable exceptions the most
vivid sustained accounts of married life in diaries of this period
contain much friction and unhappiness. Is this a true reflection
of the nature of marriage in Stuart England? Or were unhappily
married people more likely than others to write diaries to which
they might confide their frustrations? Does the explanation lie in
the fact that suffering is easier to describe than felicity, so that
contented spouses are more likely to remain silent about their
experiences?

Some of the most interesting accounts of married life are to be found in diaries kept by women.[20] The public spheres of political and economic life were dominated by men, and it is therefore in the intimate records of the family—letters, autobiographies and diaries—that we find the most authentic and articulate expressions of female opinions and points of view. Nine of the sources used here—just over a fifth of the total—were written by women. Even among diarists, women were a fairly small minority, but the rich variety of what they wrote makes up to some extent for its comparative paucity. This variety is the more striking in view of the fact that nearly all the female diarists represented here belonged to the upper classes: the ability to write fairly fluently was more restricted among women than it was among men. The lives of most married women of gentle birth centred on the domestic domain. Yet what a world of difference there was between the busy life of Lady Margaret Hoby, with her responsibilities in the local community as well as the household, and the leisured existence of Lady Anne Clifford, with its spells of almost palpable ennui (15–16). Some of the most graphic descriptions of the experience of childbirth and the most touching evocations of the world of childhood, are, not surprisingly, to be found in women's diaries (35, 41, 47–8). But the distinctive aspect of women's situation which left the clearest mark on a number of the diaries used here was their subordination to men—fathers or husbands. About half our female diarists suffered frustrations and tensions as a result of the conflict between their duty of obedience and their own wishes, or obligations which they thought to be even more important. Recorded reactions to the pressures of male authority ranged from Lady Margaret Hoby's carefully considered answer to an unspecified husbandly 'demand' to the frankly avowed resentment of Mrs Freke (15, 26). For one brief phase of life, social convention permitted a partial reversal of roles, casting men as suppliants or 'servants'. The unique pleasures of flirtation and courtship, which could be deliciously amusing if one's heart was not engaged, are captured in the exceptionally frank testimony of Lady Elizabeth Livingston (4).

[20] A sensitive and useful discussion, together with an annotated list of diaries, will be found in S. H. Mendelson, 'Stuart women's diaries and occasional memoirs', in M. Prior (ed.), *Women in English Society, 1500–1800* (Methuen, London, 1985), pp. 181–210.

The aim of this anthology is to illustrate from early English diaries a variety of individual perceptions of the different facets of family life. It follows the life-cycle of the elementary family through its successive phases and then, in its concluding section, turns briefly to the wider network of more distant kindred. Relationships, not the material conditions of life, are its central concern. Two initial objectives were to make the selection representative of a large cross-section of society and also to use little-known texts in preference to those already widely familiar. The majority of diary-writers, however, belonged to the ranks of the gentry and the professions, while some of the most familiar diaries, especially Pepys's, are also the most richly informative. The different criteria for inclusion have not proved fully compatible, and a number of compromises have had to be made. But in the resulting selection representatives of both sexes, a considerable age range, and many different social and occupational groups find a place, as do extracts from diaries both famous and little known.

The distinction between the diary and other types of record must not be too sharply drawn. Forty-three sources have been used here, of which more than half may be described as diaries without serious qualification. They are registers of their authors' activities maintained regularly, though not necessarily daily, over an extended period. To a second category belong the books of reflections, prayers and resolutions occasioned in the pious by certain significant actions and events. A third group comprises sources which, like the old Florentine *libri di ricordanze*, contain a heterogeneous collection of memoranda and accounts. Finally, a number of abstracts or partially revised versions of diaries or original memoranda have also been laid under contribution. Lying on the shadowy frontier between the diary and autobiography, such writings nevertheless contain numerous passages which seemed to retain enough of their original form to warrant their inclusion. All these sources share the most important quality of the diary: they preserve details of events, feelings and preoccupations which would have been lost had they not been captured without delay.

I

Courtship and Marriage

Something of the great variety of patterns of courtship and matchmaking which existed in seventeenth- and early eighteenth-century England is illustrated here. Most people in the late teens and early twenties probably enjoyed a considerable degree of freedom in forming their own attachments to members of the opposite sex, but had to accept a fairly long spell of celibacy after sexual maturity during the period of service or apprenticeship which preceded economic independence and marriage. Roger Lowe (2) was in just this situation. He was involved with a number of girls, and was in love with at least one of them, Mary Naylor, before his eventual marriage to Emm Potter in 1668. Among the upper classes the arranged marriage remained common. One such match, in which he played a key role on behalf of Lord Sandwich, was vividly described by Samuel Pepys (3). Some of the other examples of courtship described here lay somewhere on the spectrum between the freedom enjoyed by Roger Lowe and the control evident in the Carteret–Mountagu match (3). Dudley Ryder (13), a member of a prosperous middle-class dissenting family, was free to make a fool of himself in his infatuation with Sally Marshall, yet the shrewd advice of his sympathetic but hard-headed father, upon whom he was financially dependent, helped him to contain his passion. Lady Elizabeth Livingston's reflections (4,5) bring to life the contrasting experiences of agreeable flirtation and passionate attachment in the hothouse atmosphere of the Restoration court. She believed that it was wrong to 'steal a marriage' without her father's consent, but that, had her lover remained constant, she could eventually have won paternal agreement to her own choice. In the event she accepted, with an exceedingly bad grace, an arranged marriage.

In general, men had more liberty in courtship than women. The young Lancashire women of Roger Lowe's acquaintance enjoyed considerable freedom in their social lives. But uncertainty about Mary Naylor's father's attitude towards their association compelled the couple to be circumspect in deciding when and where to meet (2). In negotiating their marriages, Samuel Jeake (8), Nicholas Blundell (10), and Walter Calverley (11) all had to deal with the parents of their prospective brides. Yet girls might have strong ideas of their own about the choice of a husband which were by no means necessarily in tune with those of their parents. This is apparent not only from the case of Lady Elizabeth Livingston (5), but also in Sir John Oglander's rueful admission that it was his daughter Bridget's importunity which had induced him, against his own wishes, to give way to her chosen match (1). In 1685, Elizabeth Evelyn, perhaps precisely because she was aware of her father's intention of 'bestowing her very worthily', decided to 'steal' her marriage rather than risk his refusal (9). In the seventeenth century there was an unresolved tension between the long-established principle that a marriage must rest on the free consent of the parties and the sentiment, especially common among the upper classes, that parents were the best judges of suitable matches for their daughters. John Evelyn's account of Elizabeth's marriage reverberates with shock and outrage and shows that this affectionate but authoritarian father was determined to punish disobedience by means of reduced material provision.

The experience of 'romantic love' was widespread during this period, and it is illustrated by a number of these passages, especially those describing the frustrated passions of Elizabeth Livingston and Dudley Ryder (5, 13), and the entry in which Roger Lowe recorded his secret tryst with Mary Naylor and their pledge of mutual fidelity (2). Even in an arranged marriage, a show of gallant wooing by the prospective bridegroom might be considered desirable, as Pepy's account of the Carteret–Mountagu match demonstrates (3). But what these extracts also show is the importance of material considerations in the minds of some men who were free to choose their brides. The marriage settlement bulks large in Nicholas Blundell's account of the weeks leading up to his wedding in 1703 (10). Walter Calverley's memoranda about his marriage to Julia Blackett in 1707 are dominated by his sometimes resentful recital of the attendant expenses and financial negotiations (11), while Samuel Jeake was prepared to drive quite a hard bargain with the mother of his intended bride (8). A combination of sentiment and calculation is apparent in Roger Lowe's record of his dealings with young women in 1663 (2).

Weddings among the gentry and prosperous yeomanry were commonly occasions for feasting and celebration which might continue for several days.[1] That of the seaman Edward Barlow came close to this pattern (7), but its comparatively small scale reflected the slender means of Barlow and his bride. In general, however, the best accounts of nuptial festivities are not to be found in diaries, and the weddings most fully described in these passages were for various reasons somewhat atypical. In the case of the Carteret–Mountagu marriage, the day ended with the customary bedding of the newly married couple, but all the proceedings were conducted with a gravity and decorum which betray the influence of puritan notions of seemliness (3). Pepys was clearly surprised by them, even though he found them 'delightful'; most aristocratic weddings would no doubt have been a great deal more 'merry and jovial', to borrow his words. The simplicity and privacy of Samuel Jeake's wedding (8) seem to have been somewhat exceptional even by puritan standards, and may have resulted from Jeake's innate gloom and shyness, and the extreme youth of his bride, as much as from his religious opinions.

---

[1] See e.g. G. Parfitt and R. A. Houlbrooke (eds), *The Courtship Narrative of Leonard Wheatcroft, Derbyshire Yeoman* (Whiteknights Press, Reading, 1986).

1 THE MARRIAGE OF SIR JOHN OGLANDER'S YOUNGEST DAUGHTER, 1649

⟨Last of October, <u>1649</u>⟩ Know all men that I, Sir John Oglander, Knight, do acknowledge that the match between Sir Robert Eyton's[1] son and my daughter Bridget was never with my approbation or good liking. It was her importunity that induced me to give way unto it, and she was resolved to have him whatsoever became of her, and gave me so much under her hand before marriage. I confess I never liked Sir Robert, or his estate, a swearing, profane man. I beseech God to bless them and to make her happy, which I much doubt. She was both lame and in years,[2] which moved somewhat with me, though most with her. Melius est obliuisci, quod non potest recuperari.[3]

The marriage of my last daughter (as I fear she is the worst matched of them all) cost me very dear—more than any of the others. For Sir Robert and his son and one Mr Manly came[4] to me after[5] Michaelmas with seven horses and hay and oats [*sic*] (hay then being at 12*d* the tod) and continued six weeks, which was out of my way 50*li*; then I gave in moneys 1500*li*, and 100 more at six years' end, besides half year's diet, and to let them have money besides, otherways they would have done full ill. Besides, she hath many things her mother and I gave her, and more I fear she will take away. I pray God bless them, for it is a match of her own making, and I never approved of the old or young man, or of the estate.

London, National Register of Archives, no. 9841 (photocopy), account book begun in 1642, ff. 61–2.

---

[1] Or Eaton.
[2] Her precise age is uncertain.
[3] It is better to forget that which cannot be recovered.
[4] Or possibly *coome*.
[5] Or possibly *affor*.

2   ROGER LOWE AND MARY NAYLOR, 1663

[*May*] 5. – Tuesday. . . . At my coming home I called at Roger Naylor's and partly engaged to come bear them company that night; I coming down to shop and stayed awhile, and then went again and privately engaged to Mary to sit up awhile to let us discourse, which she promised, and the main question was because we lived severally that we would not act so publicly as others, that we might live privately and love firmly, that we might be faithful to each other in our love till the end: all which was firmly agreed upon. This was the first night that ever I stayed up a wooing ere in my life.

[*June*] 8. – Monday. I went to Roger Naylor and Mary cried to me, said she would have nothing to do with me, was highly displeased at me; but in the conclusion she was well pleased, would have me go with her day after to Bamfurlong, and she would go before; and to signify she was before, she would in such a place lay a bough in the way, which accordingly she did, and I found it upon

9, Tuesday, upon my going to Bamfurlong and at house I found her. As we came home we went into a narrow lane and spoke our minds walking to and fro, and engaged to be faithful till death. . . .

21. – Lord's day. . . . At night I came to Sushey, and there I met with Margaret Wright, Mr Sorrowcold's maid. She needs would have me with her home. I went and she made much of me. I came from thence to Roger Naylor's and there they were at supper. I went with Mary and other wenches to a well, bottom of Town Field.

[*July*] 8. – Wednesday. I was in a sad condition of mind, for Roger Naylor was from home and Mary would not assent to have me come thither, but I went and she was something displeased. She went to give calf drink; I followed her and there we speak to either, which was very satisfactory to both, and the other day after she came to shop, and was very glad to see me. Said she, 'Am not I a wise wench to engage myself thus?' At those times my affections[1] ran out violently after her, so as that I was never contented one day to an end unless I had seen her, and chiefly my affections were set upon her virtues and womanly qualities.

13. – Monday. . . . I was sent for to Bamfurlong to Anne Greensworth to write letters to London and Preston, took my leave, and came to Roger Naylor's house, the Cabinet that received the choice of my affection. Her father was not at home. She gave me an handkerchief because I was hot, to dry me with. . . . The other day I came home, and when comen I went to Roger Naylor's, and there Mary was put in fright with her father concerning me, for which she reserved the telling of it till another time, but it was matter of much trouble to me. I was sent for to Bamfurlong and I went, but it was with a sad heart, for I sincerely loved her—and now what a grief is it that such amicable friend as love is, such a friend as is desired everywhere and without which a common weal, nay, a family would not subsist, yet that this friend that we two have made choice of above all other, yet that there should be such actors and abettors against it as her father and others! Some cry 'Murther O!', others cry 'Let him remain silent in the cabinet of our hearts', and indeed that's our resolution till malice and spite have said their worst and best, and then we'll advance this our friend to the highest protection: till then we will be silent.

[*August*] 30. – Lord's day. Mary Naylor frowned on me all day and I was very much troubled to know the reason and cause of it, so . . . at my return homeward I went into house and found her alone and willed her to tell me the reason of her frowning, but she would not; but I was very much troubled at it. But I commit all to God, for my trust is him. I had before this time presented my service to Ellin Marsh of Ashton, who had a house and living, and kept a private mediator to intercede for me, from whom and by whom I received answer that she would give me the meeting ere long, only I must be secret, to which I promised I would. The Lord work for me which way may be most for his glory and my comfort and direct me what best to take in hand and order all my affairs.

---

[1] *effections* (his usual spelling).

[*September*] 1. – Monday. Roger Naylor was gone to Chester, and I went down and Mary and I went into parlour and talked two hours at least, and she cried to me and seemed to be very sad, and the reason was because of fear of her friends, lest they would never respect her; so she would have us part. I was indifferent, though sadly troubled, but ere we parted she was very merry because she had eased her spirit to me. So we parted, but it was with a further resolution of faithful and constant affection.

18th. – I was in a great perplexity by reason of Mary Naylor, who was too strange to me in her affections.

22. – Tuesday. . . . This night Mary Naylor came to me and spake kindly to me, to my great satisfaction. . .

24. – Thursday. . . . This afternoon I went down to Roger Naylor's, and Mary and I talked together. After she and I were parted James [*Naylor*] and I went to Leigh,[2] and when I came home there was a direct N and half of M providentially made upon my breeches, plain to view in any man's sight, made of mire with leaping. I looked upon it to be from providence, and foretold something in my apprehension. The smallest of God's providences should not be passed by without observation.

29. – James Naylor invited me to their house. I went and found Mary alone and very pleasant. This night I sang in shop by a candle the chief verses of the 71 psalm with alacrity and heart cheerfulness.

[*October*] 5. – Monday. Mary Naylor sent for me to their house. We talked together concerning our private matters, and this morning she promised never to marry any except myself.

21. – Wednesday. . . . Ann Barrow sent for me to John Naylor's. I went and we conferred together of time and place, when and where James and I must meet her. But in this discourse I entreated for myself to be the next in succession if in case they two should break off, to which she did not say no, neither yea. . . .

23. – Friday. Roger Naylor went from home, and I went to house and Mary and I sat together in parlour, and it satisfied me very much.

---

[2] *Leashe.*

29. – Thursday, . . . At this time I did love Mary extremely, and was sad I could not see her notwithstanding.

30. – Friday. She came to me and was very loving which did very much satisfy me.

[*November*] 2. – Monday. I went down to Roger Naylor's and Mary was not so favourable to me as I conceived she should be, and I was troubled very sore.

13. – Friday. Jane Wright, Mr Sorrowcold's maid, came to town and we were very merry together. I accommodated her with ale, and so we parted. I was at this time in a very fair way for pleasing my carnal self, for I knew myself acceptable[3] with Emm Potter, notwithstanding my love was entire to Mary Naylor in respect of my vow to her, and I was in hopes that her father countenanced me in the thing.

[*Lowe's courtship of Mary Naylor nevertheless petered out shortly after this. He was badly upset when he heard on 22 November that Mary's brother James had threatened to tell their father Roger all about Mary's association with him, so it appears that the elder Naylor had not after all accepted his design. After 23 November he made no mention of Mary till the following May, when they had a quarrel. He married Emm Potter in March 1668.*]

Sachse (ed.), *Diary of Roger Lowe*, pp. 20–4, 27–8, 34–7, 42–3, 45.

3 SAMUEL PEPYS HELPS TO ARRANGE A MARRIAGE FOR THE DAUGHTER OF HIS PATRON, LORD SANDWICH, IN 1665

[*February*] 3. . . . . Then took coach and to visit my Lady Sandwich; where she discoursed largely to me her opinion of a match, if it could be thought fit by my Lord, for my Lady Jemimah with Sir G. Carteret's eldest son. But I doubt he hath yet no settled estate in land—but I will inform myself and give her my opinion. . . .

[*Pepys recorded further discussion of the match with Lady Sandwich in March. It was not however until 23 June, when they met at Whitehall,*

---

[3] *exceptable.*

*that Sandwich himself broached the matter to Pepys after a long
conversation about naval affairs.*]

[*June*] 23. . . . From that discourse my Lord did begin to tell me
how much he was concerned to dispose of his children, and
would have my advice and help; and propounded to match my
Lady Jemimah to Sir G. Carteret's eldest son—which I approved
of, and did undertake the speaking with him about it as from
myself; which my Lord liked. So parted, with my head full of
care about this business. . . .

[*Later the same day Pepys visited Sandwich again to receive further
instructions, and agreed that the idea should first be put to Carteret by
an intermediary; Pepys suggested Dr Timothy Clarke, a physician-in-
ordinary to the royal household, of which Carteret was Vice-
Chamberlain.*]

24. *Midsummer Day.* Up very betimes, by 6, and at Dr Clerke's
at Westminster by 7 of the clock, having overnight by a note
acquainted him with my intention of coming. And there I, in
the best manner I could, broke my errand about a match between
Sir G. Carteret's eldest son and my Lord Sandwich's eldest
daughter—which he (as I knew he would) took with great
content; and we both agreed that my Lord and he, being
both men relating to the sea—under a kind aspect of His
Majesty—already good friends, and both virtuous and good
families, their alliance might be of good use to us. And he did
undertake to find out Sir George this morning, and put the
business in execution. . . .

[*Pepys visited Clarke again that afternoon.*]

So to Dr Clerke, and there find that he hath broke the business
to Sir G. Carteret, and that he takes the thing mighty well.
Thence I to Sir G. Carteret at his chamber, and in the best
manner I could, and most obligingly, moved that business; he
received it with great respect and content and thanks to me, and
promised that he would do what he could possibly for his son,
to render him fit for my Lord's daughter. And showed great
kindness to me, and sense of my kindness to him herein. . . .

25. *Lord's Day.* . . . At noon dined. And then I abroad by
water, it raining hard, thinking to have gone down to Woolwich;
but I did not, but back through bridge to Whitehall—where after
I had again visited Sir G. Carteret and received his (and now his

Lady's) full content in my proposal, I went to my Lord Sandwich; and having told him how Sir G. Carteret received it, he did direct me to return to Sir G. Carteret and give him thanks for his kind reception of this offer, and that he would the next day be willing to enter discourse with him about that business. Which message I did presently do, and so left the business, with great joy to both sides. My Lord, I perceive, intends to give 5000*l* with her, and expects about 800*l* per annum jointure. So by water home and to supper and bed, being weary with long walking at Court. . . .

[*July*] 5. . . . And so to Whitehall to Sir G. Carteret, who is come this day from Chatham; and mighty glad he is to see me, and begun to talk of our great business of the match—which goes on as fast as possible. But for convenience, we took water and over to his coach to Lambeth, by which we went to Deptford, all the way talking—first, how matters are quite concluded with all possible content between my Lord and him, and signed and sealed—so that my Lady Sandwich is to come thither tomorrow or next day, and the young lady is sent for—and all likely to be ended between them in a very little while—with mighty joy on both sides, and the King, Duke, Lord Chancellor, and all mightily pleased. . . .

14. . . . So . . . in the evening . . . I by water to Sir G. Carteret, and there find my Lady Sandwich and her buying things for my Lady Jem's wedding. And my Lady Jem is beyond expectation come to Dagenhams, where Mr Carteret is to go to visit her tomorrow; and my proposal of waiting on him, he being to go alone to all persons strangers to him, was well accepted and so I go with him. But Lord, to see how kind my Lady Carteret is to her—sends her most rich jewels, and provides bedding and things of all sorts most richly for her—which makes my Lady and me out of our wits almost, to see the kindness she treats us all with—as if they would buy the young lady. . . .

15. [*Pepys accompanied Philip Carteret to Dagenham.*] . . . But Lord, what silly discourse we had by the way as to matter of love-matters, he being the most awkward man I ever met withal in my life as to that business. Thither we came by time it begin to be dark, and were kindly received by my Lady Wright and

my Lord Crew;[1] and to discourse they went, my Lord discoursing with him, asking of him questions of travel, which he answered well enough in a few words. But nothing to the lady from him at all. To supper, and after supper to talk again, he yet taking no notice of the lady. My Lord would have had me have consented to leaving the young people together tonight to begin their amours, his staying being but to be little. But I advised against it, lest the lady might be too much surprised. So they led him up to his chamber, where I stayed a little to know how he liked the lady; which he told me he did mightily, but Lord, in the dullest insipid manner that ever lover did. So I bid him goodnight, and down to prayers with my Lord Crew's family. . . .

16. *Lord's Day.* . . . And having trimmed myself, down to Mr Carteret; and he being ready, we down and walked in the gallery an hour or two, it being a most noble and pretty house that ever for the bigness I saw. Here I taught him what to do; to take the lady away by the hand to lead her; and telling him that I would find opportunity to leave them two together, he should make these and these compliments, and also take a time to do the like to my Lord Crew and Lady Wright. After I had instructed him, which he thanked me for, owning that he needed my teaching him, my Lord Crew came down and family, the young lady among the rest; and so by coaches to church . . .

Thence back again by coach—Mr Carteret having not had the confidence to take his lady once by the hand, coming or going; which I told him of when we came home, and he will hereafter do it. So to dinner. My Lord excellent discourse. Then to walk in the gallery and to sit down. By and by my Lady Wright and I go out (and then my Lord Crew, he not by design); and lastly my Lady Crew came out and left the young people together. And a little pretty daughter of my Lady Wright's most innocently came out afterward, and shut the door to, as if she had done it, poor child, by inspiration—which made us without have good sport to laugh at.

---

[1] Anne Lady Wright was the sister of Lady Sandwich and widow of Sir Henry Wright. Dagenhams was her seat; Lord Crew her father.

They together an hour; and by and by church time, whither he led her into the coach and into the church; and so at church all the afternoon. . . .

So home again and to walk in the gardens, where we left the young couple a second time . . .

17. Up, all of us, and to billiards—my Lady Wright, Mr Carteret, myself and everybody. By and by the young couple left together. Anon to dinner, and after dinner Mr Carteret took my advice about giving to the servants, and I led him to give 10*l* among them, which he did by leaving it to the chief manservant, Mr Medows, to do for him. Before we went I took my Lady Jem apart and would know how she liked this gentleman and whether she was under any difficulty concerning him. She blushed and hid her face awhile, but at last I forced her to tell me; she answered that she could readily obey what her father and mother had done—which was all she could say or I expect.

So anon took leave and for London. . . . In our way Mr Carteret did give me mighty thanks for my care and pains for him, and is mightily pleased—though the truth is, my Lady Jem hath carried herself with mighty discretion and gravity, not being forward at all in any degree but mighty serious in her answers to him, as by what he says and I observed, I collect.

. . . to Deptford, where mighty welcome, and brought the good news of all being pleased to them.

Mighty mirth at my giving them an account of all; but the young man could not be got to say one word before me or my Lady Sandwich of his adventures; but by what he afterward related to his father and mother and sisters, he gives an account that pleases them mightily. . . .

[*Pepys mentioned briefly two further encounters between the young couple before their wedding on 31 July. On the day, Pepys and the Carteret parents arrived at the church late because they found no coach awaiting them at the Thames ferry.*]

31. . . . So that when we came, though we drove hard with six horses, yet we found them gone from home; and going toward the church, met them coming from church—which troubled us. But however, that trouble was soon over—hearing it was well done—they being both in their old clothes. My Lord Crew giving her—there being three coachfuls of them. The young lady

mighty sad, which troubled me; but yet I think it was only her
gravity, in a little greater degree than usual. All saluted her, but
I did not till my Lady Sandwich did ask me whether I had not
saluted her or no. So to dinner, and very merry we were; but
yet in such a sober way as never almost any wedding was in so
great families—but it was much better. After dinner, company
divided, some to cards—others to talk. . . .

At night to supper, and so to talk and, which methought was
the most extraordinary thing, all of us to prayers as usual, and
the young bride and bridegroom too. And so after prayers,
soberly to bed; only, I got into the bridegroom's chamber while
he undressed himself, and there was very merry—till he was
called to the bride's chamber and into bed they went. I kissed
the bride in bed, and so the curtains drawn with the greatest
gravity that could be, and so good night.

But the modesty and gravity of this business was so decent,
that it was to me, indeed, ten times more delightful than if it
had been twenty times more merry and jovial. . . .

Latham and Mathews (eds.), *Diary of Samuel Pepys*, vol. VI, pp. 29, 135–8,
148, 157–61, 176.

4 LADY ELIZABETH LIVINGSTON REBUKES
HERSELF FOR FLIRTING, *c.*1667–8

. . . Another way of vain consideration is when we do an action
that is really no way evil in itself, but yet is like to be of evil
consequence; we seldom think of what may happen. The present
time is generally as much as we will be got to consider, and
that, God knows, but rarely neither. Yet we must think upon
the days that are to come or else fall into many snares.

Therefore in the first place 'tis good to avoid all secret actions
that are, though innocent in themselves, yet of such a nature as
would make us ashamed if known; for there may a time come
when we shall be surprised by an unlucky question, and then
'tis odds but we shall preserve our secret by a lie. Therefore I
resolve never more to hear a young man talk of love to me
(though I keep that unruly passion out of my own heart) unless

he is approved on by my parents, and is also at liberty to dispose of himself, ⟨At this time I condemned myself for having heard the Conte Dona speak to me of love⟩ for when I listen to discourses of that nature from one that is in the power of others, I give them encouragement to sin by offering me a heart that is not their own to give away, and may justly hereafter be reproached by him when he finds a hopeless love increase; whilst all the while I meant nothing but harmless mirth, finding a diversion to hear him talk like one of the lovers I have read on in romances.

Again I have not considered wisely when I suffer a vain curiosity to know the secret thoughts of those who pretend to be in love with me so far to prevail as to engage me in little subtleties to find out the truth. This can proceed from nothing but a pride I have to be admired, and a desire to be well assured that what they seem to be is not counterfeit; and for this end with a particular knot of friends who are young like myself, and fond of mirth, I foolishly throw away much time in plotting how to discover what we would know, which two of my friends have undertaken to find out.

But in fine I considered not; there can no way be taken to satisfy my curiosity, but he will find out I wish to know that his thoughts and words agree; or else they must invent some lie or other to save me from being suspected to have set them on to watch his inclinations, so what was begun innocently enough ends in sin.

Therefore we ought diligently to search our heart to the bottom, deeply considering the paths we tread in, that we may walk warily, lest hereafter we say with a sorrowful spirit—

'O that I had considered the end as well as the beginning of my actions; then should I have increased in favour with God and man.'

Oxford, Bodleian Library, MS Rawlinson D. 78, ff. 226–8.

5 LADY ELIZABETH LIVINGSTON'S REFLECTIONS ON HEARING OF THE MARRIAGE OF LORD ANNESLEY, HER ERSTWHILE SUITOR, TO LADY ELIZABETH MANNERS, 3 DECEMBER 1669

Though at my cousin Essex Griffin's house I released all my Lord Annesley's vows to me, yet I was still fool enough to think t'was impossible he could be prevailed withal to break them.

But now sure the extrem'st ill fate of my whole life is past, since the man who wholly possessed my heart has proved himself false and unworthy of it, and I have lived to see him that I loved above all things in this world (excepting my conscience and my honour) guilty of such crimes that I tremble to think what rewards he will one day receive for them.

Never could any man more earnestly profess to love than he, nor I believe scarce did ever any real passion appear more moving than his dissembled one did; for what can I call it else, how can I conclude that he ever truly loved me, who had so little value for my good name in the world as to hazard the loss of it by his sudden change; for had not God in much mercy even miraculously preserved my reputation, for onc (almost) in this censorious world that would have had charity enough not to suspect my virtue when they saw that four or five days' time of absence had banished me from my lover's heart, hundreds would have condemned me. For his sake, I will never trust sighs, tears, nor vows any more, nor believe that 'tis possible by any obligations in the world to make a man that does not truly fear God faithful or just; my Lord Annesley ['s] last actions has plainly declared that he is neither.

For his sake I did not scruple to displease my best friends; for his satisfaction I offered to avoid for ever the conversation of one of them who he believed to be his enemy.

Rather than break the promises solemnly made betwixt us, which (if I know myself at all) I would have lost my life rather than have broke, I refused to be married to a man of great merit whose rank in the world is equal to his, and his fortune far greater. In fine I gave him all the innocent marks of a most

tender affection that he could reasonably[1] wish for. 'Tis true he
never could persuade me to steal a marriage with him, which he
said could proceed from no cause but want of love, which he
much mistook; I had other principles than his, and never could
be prevailed withal by him not to think it a crime ever to marry
without the consent of both his parents and mine. All I could
do for him was to promise (if he continued constant) I never
would give myself to any other. We were both young enough,
I told him, to wait till that consent could be gained. He seemed
out of his wits almost for my saying that word 'if he continued
constant', and by a hundred extravagant expressions endeavoured
to make me repent the having had one minute's doubt of him.
Amongst other things I remember well that he begged of God
(if ever he could be capable of breaking his vows to me) that
the church[2] in which he was to be married to another might fall
upon his head and crush him to pieces, and if that judgement
failed that he might never live a happy day with his wife, that
their discord might be known to all the world, that at last he
might not die a common death but some remarkable way, by
which God's heavy judgement might be visible upon him, and
that as for his race, if he left any behind him, he wished they
might all be miserable as well as himself. After all these wicked
curses upon himself, he swore he loved me beyond expression,
and that he could not bear with my manner of temper, my
having a doubt of his truth; for he was sure there was nothing
(except the murder of his father) which he would not do to be
ever mine. His extravagant expression[s] made my blood chill,
and I blamed him very much for them. At the same time I
cannot but own I was guilty of tasting a secret pleasure when I
thought of all his flights of passion, which made me foolishly
believe he never could have changed.

And yet when the time was come that my cousin Essex Griffin
and her lord (encouraged by their example) had persuaded me
to break my resolutions and resolve upon a private marriage,
Lord Annesley was no more the same man; and now I have lost
him for ever, and that too in so short a time after the repeating

---

[1] *reasonable.*
[2] *chruch.*

of his vows that this is a blow which would go near to break a harder heart than mine.

I was not at all impatient for a change in his father's resolutions, not at all doubting but, if the king's power had not,[3] time and perseverance in our love would most certainly have done it, and that much sooner too than he hoped; and therefore most rash as well as unjust was he to break his vows rather than for a short while to endure the threats of an incensed father, which had they been put in execution, would certainly have proved sorrows much lighter for him to groan under than those he will [feel?] (if not in this world to be sure in the next) for having broke his faith.

How often has he wished himself eternally damned if ever he were guilty of such a crime, and I now do as earnestly wish him true repentence here, which may prevent his torments in another world, for revenge is a mistaken sweet that never shall have place in my heart.

I am sometimes strangely amazed when I consider how immediately after I left him, Lord Annesley proved false. Had he seen and loved the lady he has married before I lost his heart, he would have had some little (though but an ill) excuse, for some beauties are so dazzling that they conquer young men by surprise; but that was not his case. Had he been naturally of a covetous temper, and so far dreaded the effects of his father's anger that he resolved to sacrifice both his love and his honour rather than risk the loss of his estate for my sake, I might have expected to be forsaken when an estate came once to be put into the balance with me; but by those offers he made at the time our marriage was treated of to accept of a far less maintenance during his father's life time with me than he would have done when other marriages were proposed to him, and by his pressing me when my Aunt Stanhope had broke off that treaty to venture the marrying of him privately without any settlement at all, I had reason to believe covetousness was not his vice, which indeed is more likely to be an attendant of old age than youth.

The very day that Lord Annesley and I parted, he had so much

---

[3] According to Lady Elizabeth's account, Charles II had promised to use his influence with Lord Anglesey, Annesley's father, to gain his consent to the marriage.

grief in his face, and spoke to me with so much reason and generosity of all his father's threatenings, that I left him without the least suspicion or uneasiness of mind.

After loving me passionately for three years together without knowing whether ever he should be able to touch my heart or no, he was well assured that he had gained it, and might well believe that a kindness which was not got with ease would always last, and therefore 'twas natural enough for him to have resisted his father's will with an unshaken resolution, when he proposed to give him to another; and 'tis incredible that in the short space of only four days' absence he should become thus perjured and ungrateful.

Such changes are so little ordinary and so very surprising that I could never cease wondering at these things, did I not consider that nothing can happen without the permission of a just God whom I have offended, and who has taught me by the sorrows which I feel how unworthy I have been to desire with such unreasonable earnestness anything in this world which I was not sure God had allotted for me, and to place my heart, which God alone has right to, upon a frail, deceitful creature, by whom I am punished for that sin and folly. . . .

Oxford, Bodleian Library, MS Rawlinson D. 78, ff. 253–9.

6   JAMES JACKSON'S MEMORANDA ABOUT HIS SON DICK'S WEDDING, 1671

March 20th 1670[*1671*]:

Memorandum the day [*and*] year abovesaid an agreement made betwixt my son Richard and Frances Chamber and thereupon contracted in the presence of John Chamber of Blackdike, George Ostell and Thomas his son, Henry Currey and James Jackson and Ellas Chamber her mother.

May 30th 1671.

	li	s	d
Dick's cloak. 8 yards and a half at ii*s* ii*d* per yard:	0.18.		5
6 yards of baize for lining at i*s* iiii*d* per yard	0. 8.		0
one set of mohair buttons	0. 2.		2
half an ounce of silk	0. 1.		0
neck button	0. 0.		6
black thread	0. 0.		2
More for his suit. per cloak.	1.10.		3
2 yards and a quarter at 6*s* 8*d* per yard	0.15.		0
buttons to his doublet	0. 0.		8
silk vi*d*, galloon[1] vi*d*, [collar?][2] iiii*d*	0. 1.		3
His suit.	0.16.		11
Two hats. A dun castor[3] for Frances ix*s* vi*d*. All	0.13.		0
paid out for all to him that day	3. 0.		2
For Frances gown.			
x yards of Rosetta at ii*s* iiii*d* a yard comes to	1. 2.		6
half a pound of whalebone	0. 1.		0
½ an ell of buckram	0. 0.		8
3 yards of galloon	0. 0.		9
silk ½ an ounce	0. 1.		0
Ferreting Ribbon[4]	0. 1.		8
paid pro Dick: ii*li* xix*s* vi*d* Summa toto:	1. 7.		7
paid pro Frances: i*li* vii*s*			

---

all   iiii*li* vi*s* vi*d*   all upon account iiii*li*. vii*s*.ix*d*

Memorandum July iiiith 1671 was my son Richard and Frances Chamber married at Abbey Church and Mr Bolton preached twice next Lord's day following.

Carlisle, Cumbria Record Office, microfilm no. JAC 257, section TL/702.

[1] A narrow, close-woven ribbon or braid, of gold, silver or silk thread, used for trimming clothes.
[2] *collo*ʳ.
[3] *Dun castor:* a greyish-brown beaver hat.
[4] *Firrittin Ribbin:* a stout cotton or silk tape.

7 THE MARRIAGE OF EDWARD BARLOW,
SEAMAN, 1678

And lying in the Downs expecting a fair wind again, about ten days after our coming there, that there came down from London a young woman of my acquaintance and one that I had known some time and was then a servant maid in a friend's house at London, whom I had a great love for. And through the kind respects I then bore to her I had promised her to make her my wife, although she was but a servant and had little or nothing more than her clothes to her back, and I confess I had not much more than herself; and had I stayed longer at London I had married her there, but things falling out to the contrary, she came down to Deal for the same purpose. And being come down sent me word, and I going ashore, and being come together we soon concluded of the matter. And having some acquaintance in the ship, we agreed to send for a licence to Canterbury for our marriage together. And having procured one, which cost me eighteen shillings, on the [*blank*][1] of January we were married in the parish church of Deal in Kent by the minister of the same, before some acquaintance and several witnesses. And returning from the church, which was a small mile out of the town, at the King's Head in Deal we had our wedding dinner, being accompanied with several persons of good repute and credit, as the commander of His Majesty's ship, Captain Wiltshire, and two or three more commanders, and our own commander, Captain Jones, and several of our merchants, which were going passengers with us, and a gentlewoman, also going for the island of Jamaica. And being all very merry, having music and wine plenty, and good victuals enough, being willing to make one merry and joyful day of it, not knowing when I should have another; and it was to prove, I did hope, one of the best day's work as to my future happiness in this world, for I had met with a good wife, which every man doth at his first marriage. But it is an old saying 'A good Jack makes a good Jill' and 'The proof of the pudding must be in the eating.'

Greenwich, National Maritime Museum, MS JOD/4.

[1] Barlow's marriage to Mary Symans took place on 21 January: see Lubbock (ed.), *Barlow's Journal*, vol. II, p. 309n., referring to Deal parish register.

8 THE MAKING OF SAMUEL JEAKE'S MARRIAGE,
1680–1

[*1680*] ⟨June 7 Monday⟩ Resolved to seek Mrs Elizabeth Hartshorn of the age of 12 years and 8 months in marriage, with the consent of her mother Mrs Barbara Hartshorn of Rye. And this day about 3h p.m. went to her house to mention it; but prevented by company from a convenient opportunity.

⟨8 Tuesday⟩ About 1h p.m. I went again, and finding Mrs Barbara Hartshorn alone had a fit opportunity to propose it immediately, which was accepted; and the portion argued, I insisting upon £1200, she first offered £500 in money, and the house she lived in (one of the best in the town), which she rated at £200; and at last said she would make her a fortune to me of £1000, viz. £700 in money, £100 in household goods and the house valued at £200, which was above the moiety of her whole estate, except her jointure of £40 per annum during life, and she having a son to provide for besides.

Note a congeries of Jupiter, Mars, Venus and Mercury in conjunction in Gemini in trine to the ascendant.[1]

⟨9 Wednesday⟩ In the morning I acquainted my father with what I had proposed etc. for his consent: for I had not acquainted him with it before. In the evening I was at Mrs Hartshorn's, and had some further discourse, amongst which she told me that should she ask advice, none would advise her to give so much, and that she would not make the like offer to any other person in the world.

⟨11 Friday⟩ About 1h p.m. I went thither again, and stayed about four hours; but we came to no conclusion. In the evening I came to a resolution in my own thoughts, and had my father's consent to proceed as I pleased; and having a fit opportunity of waiting on Mrs Hartshorn to her own house, I told her about 9h p.m. that I had advised with my father, and perceived him satisfied; and that I did comply with those terms she had proposed, and declare myself to be her most humble and most obedient son and servant for ever, which she respectfully accepted with expressions of satisfaction.

---

[1] Jeake's text is accompanied by diagrams illustrating the positions of planets at the time of important events in his life.

⟨14 Monday⟩ About 1h 30′ p.m. I went to Mrs Barbara Hartshorn's, having her consent to propose it to her daughter Mrs Elizabeth Hartshorn, for whom I had an affection from her infancy. My first motion was as I remember to this effect: 'My Dear Lady, the deep impression your person and virtues have made upon my mind oblige me to become your servant, and I beseech you Madam be pleased to believe the greatness of my affection, to which be pleased to return me the favour of having a place in your heart.' 'Sir' (said she) 'it is so weighty a business that I am not capable of returning you an answer without a long time of consideration.' The rest of our discourse may be superfluous and impertinent to memorize, being continued till 4h p.m. After which I went to walking with her mother and her and Cousin Mary Key, and returning, stayed there till past 8h p.m. Note the cluster of planets in Gemini as before hinted and the Moon in the midst here carrying the influence of Jupiter and Mars to Venus and Mercury, Venus and Mars being lords of the 1st and 7th. This seemed to show a successful time for such addresses.

⟨16 Wednesday⟩ About 6h p.m. I went to Mrs Barbara Hartshorn's, and having her approbation before, had now the declared consent of her daughter.

⟨28 Monday⟩ Having drawn up the terms of the marriage and settlement and shown it to my father, I went in the evening to carry it to Mrs Hartshorn; which when she had perused she told me she liked nothing in it, and insisted upon the repayment of £500 if her daughter died without issue. Which I not granting, she seemed so much averse that I thought she repented of what she had offered, and she was very pressive for me to take my leave of her daughter that night, which I desired her not to importune, for I were resolved not to do. I returned home somewhat concerned. And she came after to me, with many pleasing and persuasive words to return part of the portion as aforesaid.

⟨29 Tuesday⟩ About 7h a.m., being sent for by Mrs Barbara Hartshorn, I went thither. She told me she perceived I was troubled, and that she would not have me concerned: she then mentioned the repayment of £200 and I mentioned the repayment of £300 if I died without issue. But without coming to any conclusion, I was sent for home, and she, perceiving my concern, told me she would resolve me by night. As soon as I was gone she sent for Mr Michael Cadman and showed him the rough draft which I had left with her, acquainting him of the difference between us: he thought that what I had drawn up in writing was reasonable and that she ought not to insist on the repayment of any part of the portion. Whereupon she sent him to me to tell me that if I had no other discouragement, then she did accept of the propositions I had made according to the paper which I had drawn up, wherein was contained a reservation of £40 per annum to her during life, in case her daughter died without issue, etc. This assurance he came and gave me about 10h a.m. I replied that I had no other discouragement, and that I did return her my thanks that she was pleased to consent, and went to her house with him to make my acknowledgements.

[*July*] ⟨12 Monday⟩ About 2h p.m. (the writings concerning the marriage being sealed just before by Mrs Barbara Hartshorn and myself) I was betrothed or contracted to her daughter Mrs Elizabeth Hartshorn in the presence of my father and her mother, Mr Michael Cadman and Mr Thomas Miller, in form following: viz., taking her by the right hand, I said 'I Samuel take thee Elizabeth to be my betrothed wife, and promise to make thee my wedded wife in time convenient: in token whereof is this our holding by the hand.' Then loosing my hand, she took me by my right hand, repeating the same words *mutatis mutandis*.

[*August*] ⟨31 Tuesday⟩ I removed with my father to the house which was Mrs Hartshorn's, and which I was to have in part of the portion, and first began to keep house there. . . .

[*September*] By reason of my melancholy in this month and the next, being perhaps the most violent I ever were afflicted with, and which made me pass some whole nights without sleep, there arose great displeasure and difference between me and my intended mother-in-law and wife. But in the beginning of November it pleased God out of his abundant mercy to cheer and raise my spirit without any known occasion; but as the seed sown springeth up we know not how, even so the merciful God day after day made my spirit cheerful and lively. So that by degrees I recovered easily my repute again with them.

[*1681*] ⟨February 11 Friday⟩ Perceiving myself sufficiently again in favour with my mother-in-law, I moved her about 3h p.m. for the consummation of my marriage with her daughter; which

without any reluctancy she granted, and it was appointed to be celebrated on March 1 next. And in the interim all things providentially concurred to favour it with happy omens.

⟨March 1 Tuesday⟩ About 9h 35′ a.m. I was married to Mrs Elizabeth Hartshorn at Rye by Mr Bruce, in the presence of Mr Thomas Miller, Mr Nathaniel Hartshorn and the sexton, we going though in the day time, yet so much incognito that there was no concourse or notice taken either of our going or coming. The day was cloudy, but calm. The sun shone out just at tying the nuptial knot, and also just at his setting. Devirg[*ination*] 3 Thursday night.

Hunter and Gregory (eds), *An Astrological Diary*, pp. 149–54.

9 'STEALING A MARRIAGE': THE MARRIAGE OF ELIZABETH EVELYN IN 1685 DESCRIBED BY HER FATHER

[*July*] 27   This night when we were all asleep went my daughter Elizabeth away to meet a young fellow, nephew to Sir John Tippet (Surveyor of the Navy, and one of the Commissioners), whom she married the next day, being Tuesday, without in the least acquainting either her parents, or any soul in the house. I was the more afflicted and astonished at it in regard we had never given this child the least cause to be thus disobedient, and being now my eldest, might reasonably have expected a double blessing. But it afterward appeared that this intrigue had been transacted by letters long before, and when she was with my Lady Burton in Leicestershire, and by private meetings near my house. She of all our children had hitherto given us least cause of suspicion; not only for that she was yet young, but seemed the most flattering, supple, and observant; of a silent and particular humour, in no sort betraying the levity and inclination which is commonly apparent in children who fall into these snares, having been bred up with the utmost circumspection, as to principles of severest honour and piety. But so far, it seems, had her passion for this young fellow made her forget her duty, and all that most indulgent parents expected from her, as not to consider the consequence of her folly and disobedience 'til it was too late. This affliction went very near me and my wife, neither of us yet well composed for the untimely loss of that incomparable and excellent child which it pleased God to take from us by the smallpox a few months before. But this farther chastisement was to be humbly submitted to, as a part of the burden God was pleased to lay farther upon us; in this yet the less afflictive, that we had not been wanting in giving her an education every way becoming us. We were most of all astonished at the suddenness of this action, and the privateness of its management; the circumstances also considered and quality, how it was possible she should be flattered so to her disadvantage: he being in no condition sortable to hers, and the blessing we intended her. The thing has given us much disquiet: I pray God direct us how to govern our resentments of her disobedience, and if it be his will, bring good out of all this ill.

August 2   So had this affliction discomposed us, that I could not be well at church the next Lord's day, though I had prepared for the Blessed Sacrament. I hope God will be more gracious to my only remaining child, whom I take to be of a more discreet, sober and religious temper, that we may have that comfort from her, which is denied us in the other.

This accident caused me to alter my will, as was reasonable; for though there may be a reconciliation upon her repentance, and that she has suffered for her folly; yet I must let her see what her undutifulness in this action deprives her of, as to the provision she else might have expected, solicitous as she knew I now was of bestowing her very worthily.

[*On 16 August Evelyn heard that Elizabeth had fallen ill with smallpox. Mrs Evelyn went to her daughter and stayed with her for most of the time till her death just under a fortnight later. Evelyn visited her twice: on 22 August, when he found her 'very sensible and penitent for her fault' and again on 28 August, the day before her death, 'to see, and comfort her'.*]

De Beer (ed.), *Diary of John Evelyn*, vol. IV, pp.460–2.

10　NICHOLAS BLUNDELL'S RECUSANT
MARRIAGE, 1703

[*February*] ⟨28⟩ I went to Scarisbrick to discourse my cousin Robert Scarisbrick about my going to Heythrop. I lodged there.

[*This oblique reference is the first in Blundell's diary to the projected match. He was hoping to arrange a marriage with Frances, daughter of Marmaduke, third Lord Langdale, and granddaugher of Lady Webb. Heythrop Park in Oxfordshire was the residence of Sir John Webb.*]

[*March*] 3 . . . I writ to my Lady Webb and sent Walter Thelwall with it the next day to Heythrop.

13 I writ letters all day to Lord Molineux, Lord Langdale, Mr Philmot etc.

18 . . . I went through Ormskirk to Scarisbrick and showed them my Lady Webb's letter.

19 I sent Thomas Howerd to Liverpool to the post with a letter for the Lady Webb.

28 I writ to Lord Langdale, inclosed it to Cousin Eyre the lawyer and sent it to the post by Pater Gillibrand.[1]

[*April*] 4 I received a letter from Lord Langdale. I sent Henry Bilsbury to Croxteth; he brought word Lord Molineux was come home.

5 I went with Pater Gillibrand to wait of Lord Molineux at Croxteth when he returned from London.

6 Aunt Frances had account from Mr Bloore by orders of Lady Webb that I might wait of Mrs Frances Langdale as soon as I pleased.

11 Mr Edward Molineux came to wish me a good journey to Heythrop.

12 I went to Liverpool to have a black coat made by Edward Porter for my journey to Heythrop. . .

13 I began my journey towards Heythrop, dined at Warrington and lodged at Holmes Chapel.

17 I came from North Leach to Heythrop, found the family all there, and also my Lord Langdale.

---

[1] *Gelibrond*: Rev. William Gillibrand, S. J., chaplain at Little Crosby, where Blundell lived.

19 I discoursed Lord Langdale in his chamber and Lady Webb in the dining room. I made my[2] first address to Mrs Frances Langdale.

21 Lady Webb discoursed me in the garden. I discoursed Mrs Langdale in the kitchen garden. . . .

22 . . . Lady Dowager Webb read the heads of agreement of marriage to be between Mrs Frances Langdale and me Nicholas Blundell in presence of Lord Langdale and Sir John Webb.

23 Mr Trinder the lawyer came to Heythrop for instructions to draw articles of marriage.

24 Mr Trinder drew up the heads of articles of marriage.

25 Mr Trinder brought to Heythrop the heads of articles of marriage fairly transcribed, which were agreed to by Lord Langdale, Lady Webb and myself. . .

26 I writ my first letter from Heythrop to Cousin Henry Eyre. . . .

28 . . . I presented my diamond ring to Mrs Frances Langdale.

[*May*] 2 I walked to Mr Ireton's with Mrs Frances Langdale and Pater Gillibrand.

3 I went from Heythrop through Oxford to Waterperry.[3]

5 I writ at Waterperry to Mrs Frances Langdale and sent it by Oxford post.

[*The next nine days' entries describe Blundell's journeys to and from London and his stay there, in the course of which, in company with his cousin Henry Eyre, he twice met Mr Trinder, the lawyer who had drawn up the articles of marriage.*]

15 I came to Heythrop from Waterperry with Pater Gillibrand.

16 I walked in the kitchen garden with Lady Webb Senior and gave her an account of my London journey.

17 I walked with Mrs Frances Langdale to Fairford. . .

20 . . . I presented my gilt coffee spoons.

23 . . . Lord Gerard was with Mrs Frances Langdale and me discoursing in the hall.

24 . . . Mr Trinder came to Heythrop after he had been

---

[2] *by*
[3] The seat of Sir John Curzon.

drawing up writings at London. Pater Gillibrand transcribed the articles of marriage twice, to be sent to Lord Langdale.

26 Lord Langdale came to Heythrop from the north.

29 The two Lady Webbs and Lord Langdale went to see Little Master at nurse. Mrs Frances Langdale and I stayed at Heythrop. I writ to Bishop Giffard[4] by request of F.L.

30 Much intercession made to my Lord Langdale to make him to sign a single draft to me for the payment of the second thousand pound.

31 . . . I went a second time to London; lodged at Oxford with Mr Trinder. . . .

[*June*] 1 I came with Mr Trinder from Oxford, dined at Wycombe,[5] and so came to London.

3 I went with Mr Trinder to Mr Pigot. I paid Mr Person for a wedding ring.

5 I received the foul draft of my marriage deed from Mr Pigot and delivered it to Mr Trinder to be engrossed. . . .

9 I visited Bishop Giffard . . . They began to engross my marriage deeds.

11 I dined with Lady Curzon; tried on my wedding suit there and in other places.

12 My marriage deeds were examined in Cousin Henry Eyre's chamber by him, Mr Trinder and their clerks.

13 I began my journey from London towards Heythrop, dined with my Landlord of the Red Lion in Wycombe and lodged in Why-field.

14 I came from Why-field to Heythrop by 10 of the clock; found Lady Gerard there.

15 Lord Langdale, Lady Webb, Sir John Webb, etc. heard the marriage deeds read; all we at Heythrop concerned therein subscribed them before four witnesses.

16 Lady Dowager Webb acquainted me the marriage was to be the day following.[6] Lady Dowager Webb signed the deed for payment of £100 per annum to Mrs Frances Langdale.

[4] Right Rev. Bonaventure Giffard, Bishop of Madaura; appointed Vicar Apostolic of London district, 14 March 1703; see Tyrer and Bagley, *Great Diurnal*, vol. I, p. 36 n. 41.

[5] *Wickham*. See ibid., p. 349, for identification of this place as Wickham, Berks. But that seems too far west. This must be High Wycombe.

[6] The very short notice was probably a precaution taken for the safety of the officiating Catholic priest: see ibid., p. 37, n. 42.

17 I was married to Lord Langdale's daughter by Mr Slaughter, a clergyman.

20 Mr Burcher of Barnsley sent a How-do-you to my wife and me.

21 I went with Sir John Webb to Parson Burcher's and gave him half a guinea as marriage dues.

22 I went with the two Lady Webbs, my wife, etc. to Mrs Bedulf's in Bolton in Wiltshire.

25 My chariot came to Heythrop to carry my wife home to Crosby.

27 Parson Burcher and his wife came to take leave of my wife and me.

28 I began my journey from Heythrop towards Crosby with my wife. . . .

[*July*] 2 . . . I brought my wife home to Crosby.

Tyrer (trans. and annot.) and Bagley (ed.), *Great Diural of Nicholas Blundell*, vol. I, pp. 31–8.

11   WALTER CALVERLEY'S MARRIAGE, 1706–7

⟨On⟩ Sunday 21° July 1706 I went towards Newcastle and dined at Mr Fawkes in my way this day, and got thither on Tuesday night, and whilst I stayed, lodged at Mr Thomlinson's, being two nights, and on Wednesday dined and supped at Lady Blackett's, and Thursday afternoon set forwards for home, and gave Mr Pemberton a visit in my return, and got home on Saturday night.

⟨A⟩nd after that I went about twice or thrice more before we came to conclude of the match, but made not long staying either time, and still dined at my Lady Blackett's, and she sent her coach for me to dinners. And about the beginning of October 1706 the match was agreed upon and I signed proposals in order to a settlement for marriage.

⟨And⟩ in beginning of November after, I went over and took Samuel Hemingway with me to assist about matters, and the settlement, drawing etc., and stayed most of a three weeks; and the draft was made very long, but not then fully agreed to, though we had counsel of both sides, and several meetings both of Mr Wilkinson, Mr Thomlinson and the counsel, and at some of them I was also present myself. They made use of Mr John Ord for drawing the writings, and Mr Barnes counsel for my Lady, and I had Mr John Cuthberts, the recorder of Newcastle, for my counsel. But the matter was not then concluded, upon account of some scruples about the young lady's portion, when it would be due and payable, but was left off (though in great forwardness towards finishing) till my Lady had sent to London and taken advice about the portion, which she did later end of same November, and had opinion that it was payable upon marriage. But because some doubt was made by Mr Poley about the interest, and that Mr Vernon seemed to advise for a decree to confirm matters, etc., I applied myself to Mr Thornton, who, to make the payment more secure, advised two or three years' time to be set for payment of it, with interest, and if not paid in that time, the settlement to be void, or else that the trustees should stand seized to such uses as I should afterwards appoint, and then upon payment I might make a deed with uses according to the settlement, or else my Lady might in that time (if thought fit) obtain a decree for mortgaging etc.: of which I writ to my Lady, but she would not consent to it, though by one of Mr Thomlinson's letters I had thought it would have been agreed to, and sent Samuel over afterwards towards Christmas, but he returned without effecting anything. So, rather than the match should break, I consented to take my Lady and Mr Wilkinson's promise for the payment of the portion and security for the interest in the meantime with security for my Lady for the other matters. And according to that resolution I sent Jack Hare over with a letter at Christmas 1706, with which my Lady was pleased. And afterwards, the 30th December 1706, I went over and got to Newcastle 1º Januarij after, and concluded the settlement and all things pursuant. And on Monday the 6º Januarij ejusdem the settlement was got ready engrossed, and also the bonds from my Lady and Mr Wilkinson, and were examined towards night at Mr Wilkinson's, and afterwards about eight in the evening executed at my Lady's. There was a lease for possession which first I executed, and then the settlement and counterpart were executed by me, Lady Blackett, Mr Wilkinson and Mrs Julia Blackett (none of the other trustees signing or being present or acquainted with it that I knew of). And my Lady executed the two bonds to me about the jewel and the 500*l*, and I executed to her the bond for payment of the interest for the 500*l* to her during life, and she and Mr Wilkinson also executed the bond to me for payment of the interest for the portion till the principal should be paid, which was agreed to be six per cent, but I was but to pay five per cent to my Lady because hers was for life, but the other to me might make as short as they would. And the jewel to be delivered at my Lady's death being but put down at 250*l* value in the bond, I would not have it so, but said would be contented with what value she put down, whereupon she ordered it to be made of value of 300*l* or thereabouts (though it had been valued to me at 350*li*); and for the other jewel given by my Lady made me sign a receipt on the back of the deed as for 250*l* received and acknowledgement of 750*li* more secured by my Lady for the 1000*li* mentioned in the deed which was to be given by her, though in fairness I ought but to have given a receipt as for 150*li* for the value of the jewel then already given, and the value of the other to be delivered at death should have been put in 350*li* as was intimated to me to be of that value.

⟨The⟩ witnesses to these writings were Mr Thomlinson, Mr Ord, and Samuel Hemingway.

⟨And⟩ on Tuesday the 7° Januarij 1706/7 I was married to Mrs Julia Blackett (the eldest daughter of Sir William Blackett) in St Andrew's Church in Newcastle by Mr Thomlinson, before my Lady, Sir William Blackett, Mrs Elizabeth Blackett, and Mrs Frances Blackett, brother and sisters to the young lady, my nephew Thompson Wade, Mr Wilkinson, and others, about eleven in the forenoon. And I gave Mr Thomlinson as for marrying me a purse with [*blank*] guineas, intending to be for the trouble also which I had given him in lodging at his house for all the times before, and other kindnesses etc. And my Lady was at cost of entertaining all friends and relations upon this occasion. But I gave them gloves; and when I came first away to Esholt about 3° Februarij 1706[7], I distributed to the servants in the house about sixteen or seventeen guineas. And I reckon it had cost me before in five or six journeys and on the road etc. about 140*li*, besides other charges hereafter mentioned.

⟨I ga⟩ve Mr Cuthbert, the counsel, in November 1706, three guineas about the settlement, which he only perused and amended, and had no more trouble save the perusing of the bonds, which Samuel Hemingway drew, about the jewel and other matters. My Lady paid for the settlement about 18*li*, and, memorandum, when 'twas first drawn, they had my writings to peruse, which [*I*] took over with me for that purpose.

⟨I and⟩ my mother were at cost of a fine set of dressing plate for my wife, came to 116*li* and odd moneys. And I paid for a pair of ear rings for her 130*li* and a bill for gloves bought at London, 15*li* 6*s* 6*d*, and for a new coach bought of one George Whitelatch, 82*l* 7*s*. and for velvet for lining it etc., 30*li* 7*s*; in all, 374*li* 15*s* 3*d*, towards which I first of all gave my Lady bills for 250*li* before marriage. And after marriage, before I came first away from my ⟨Lady⟩'s about 25° Januarii 1706[7], paid my Lady the residue, 124*li* 15*s* 3*d,* out of 500*li* which I received towards the marriage portion of my wife. And memorandum I gave a receipt for it to the trustees in part of the 6000*li* and got home to Esholt about 5° Februarii 1706[7].

⟨And⟩ memorandum I was at charge also for more gloves at Esholt, and it cost me for my own wedding clothes, and a long wig etc. and several liveries near 300*li*, besides above 50*l* I laid out about buying in new coach mares on this occasion to the others I had before. . . .

⟨Memorandum⟩ on the 20th Februarij 1706/7 I went over to Newcastle again, and stayed there till 17th March, after what time I set forward with my wife in our own coach, and got to Esholt on the 20th same March. . . .

. . . Thursday, 11° September 1707. Made an entertainment at Esholt to all the neighbouring gentlemen and their ladies, and ⟨on⟩ Saturday after, being 13° same September 1707, had my tenants and neighbours and wives at another entertainment provided on purpose.

⟨Both⟩ the said entertainments were upon the account of my wife's first coming to Esholt.

British Library, MS Add. 27418, ff. 96ʳ, 97ʳ, 99ʳ, 100ʳ, 103ʳ.

12 DUDLEY RYDER'S THOUGHTS ABOUT THE PROSPECT OF MARRIAGE, 1715–16

[*1715*] *Thursday, June* 30. . . . Walked about the parlour and prayed to God that he would turn the current of my affections towards himself. This as soon as I had done praying put me upon reflecting upon myself. And I could not but conclude that the most prevailing passion or view that I had was a love of esteem. There is indeed another thing that goes hand in hand with that and this is the prospect and hope of an agreeable woman for my wife. To these two I think all my other ends may be reduced.

[*1716*] *Friday, April* 20. . . . At 8 o'clock Mr Whatley came to see me and stayed with me till 10 o'clock. . . . At length we came to talk of matrimony, and I said though I had often upon consideration thought that the miseries and inconveniences that attended that state were much greater than the advantages of it and a man runs a vast hazard in entering upon it, yet at the same time I could not suppose myself capable of being completely happy here without it. I cannot but be uneasy to think that my life shall terminate with myself. The having children is a kind of continuance and prolonging life into future ages and generations.

Thursday, August 30. . . . Met Cousin Joseph Billio. We went to the coffee-house together. . . . We talked about matrimony and agreed in this that the sorrows and cares and burdens to which it exposes a man don't seem to be sufficiently balanced by the joys and pleasures one can expect from it. I wish I could reason myself into an easy state of mind under the thoughts of never being married, but I find a strong inclination towards it, not from any principle of lust or desire to enjoy a woman in bed, but from a natural tendency, a prepossession in favour of the married state. It is charming and moving, it ravishes me to think of a pretty creature concerned in me, being my most intimate friend, constant companion and always ready to soothe me, take care of me and caress me. . . .

Matthews (ed.), *Diary of Dudley Ryder*, pp. 45, 224, 309–10.

13 RYDER COURTS SALLY MARSHALL, 1716

[*1716*] *Tuesday, April* 3. Rose between 5 and 6 in order to accompany my sister part of the way to Bath. I had before pleased myself with the thoughts of having by that means the company of a very pretty lady, and I found my expectation not in the least disappointed. The lady was Mrs Marshall. She had something so very agreeable in the cast of her countenance and features of her face as touched me very sensibly when I first saw her. I therefore kept as close to the coach side as possible and took all the opportunities I could of looking into the coach and talking to her, and indeed I had more assurance than ever I had before, for I ventured to talk to her very soon. But my eyes were always fixed upon her and the more I looked the more I felt myself moved and pleased with her looks, and it was something of a pleasure to me now and then to meet her eyes and catch them turned upon me. I had the vanity to think that she was pleased with me at first, but soon my joy upon that account was turned into uneasiness and a great many little accidents, the motions of her eyes or change of her looks or words made me think her approbation at best but very fitful. I think I never felt my heart more sensibly moved in my life than I did with the sight of her. She has some inexpressibly sweet in her countenance. She never said much but had as I thought a most agreeable modesty. I and Brother went with the coach to dinner at Slough. All the way I took every opportunity I could to look at her and talk to her and express a tender concern and peculiar regard for her. I could not help wishing I was going to the Bath with her and told her so. At Slough I had her company nearer and was more and more charmed with her and did what I could to entertain her with discourse, but I was, as I am always, very deficient that way. . . .

Tuesday, May 1. I have been thinking of going down to the Bath to see my sister, who is there now. Indeed what excites me to it the more is the prospect of seeing Mrs Marshall who went down with Sister. I think I never saw a woman who pleased me better and had something so very agreeable in her.. . . [*Ryder arrived in Bath three weeks later.*]

Sunday, May 27. . . . Stayed at home after sermon all the rest of the afternoon with Mrs Marshall and Sister and Mr Powell was with us. His company is strangely agreeable to them and Mrs Marshall seems to have a peculiar love of it. I found myself very deeply affected with her, and I could not help at night telling my sister of it. My sister took it all in jest and I could not get her to talk with me in earnest about it, but I think I never was more deeply in love in my life. But indeed what makes me the most uneasy of anything with it is that I am conscious I am not agreeable to her. Nothing aggravates my circumstances so much as the acceptance Mr Powell meets with from her and the joy with which she receives him. I am far from having a mean opinion of Mrs Marshall. I admire her extremely, her beauty, good nature and good sense, but these I believe would not have that effect upon me which they have and make me so very uneasy if it was not that she favours Mr Powell much more than me and delights in his company while she neglects mine. And yet he is not a rival properly, for he seems very indifferent about her himself. It was some kind of consolation to me and struck me with pleasure when he told me, talking about her, that he would not give 6*s* for a kiss of her. How hard and unhappy is our fate that love must be bestowed where it is so little valued. And yet I don't know neither. If I was as much beloved, perhaps I should not be so much in love. . . .

Friday, June 1. [*Ryder, together with Samuel Powell and the ladies, went on an excusion by chaise to see the house and gardens at Dyrham Park near Bath.*] . . . At one side of the gardens there is a wilderness of high large trees in which there are a great many agreeable shades.

In one of them we made our dinner of some cold things we brought and sat down upon the grass for two or three hours. In this time Mrs Marshall showed a great disregard of me and love for Mr Powell; particularly she refused me a kiss when she gave him one immediately after. This put me into such a confusion and uneasiness that I could not bear it and was forced to take a walk by myself among the trees. Nor could I prevent the tears gushing out, that I was forced to be absent almost an hour. During this time Mr Powell and the ladies were very uneasy what was become of me, but I came at last and my eyes I believe betrayed what I had been doing. . . .

Sunday, June 3. I went to meeting both parts of the day. My thoughts run upon Mrs Marshall. I wanted an opportunity to talk to her and discover something of my passion. At last she came into Sister's room and I longed for an opportunity to speak to her and Sister went out, but her maid was in the closet. However, I could not help taking the opportunity of speaking to her, of begging of her to forgive all the rudeness I have been guilty of in her company, especially that in the garden, but she put it off and said she did not know anything of the matter. I was so confounded that I could scarce speak a word to her and I was fain to sit mute and silent, speaking only a word now and then. I find I have run myself further into the mire, and the more I endeavour to get out the more I get in. I think I never felt so great a pain in my life before; I could almost have been willing to die, my anxiety and trouble was so great. But I find myself something better now I have writ this. I will endeavour to drive her out of my thoughts. To bed at 12.

Wednesday, September 12. [Just over three months after the end of the Bath holiday, during a dinner-time discussion of his financial affairs at the Marlborough Head Tavern, Ryder's father outlined the provision he had made for his sons in his will.] . . . He then told me he would ask me one question and desired me to answer him ingenuously and plainly. I said I would. It was whether I had not a kindness for Mrs Marshall (which my mother guessed I had). The colour came in my face and [*I*] only answered, how could my mother guess at such a thing. My countenance so betrayed me that I could not help owning it and the tears flowed out of my eyes. My father was then very sensible of my passion and told me the inconvenience of marrying so soon out of business, and besides said her fortune could not be anything considerable, a £1,000 or £1,500 would be the most could be expected. Besides her family was nothing, could bring me no acquaintance nor friends that could serve me in my business. That her father was nothing but a common ordinary tailor at first, but by great industry arrived at something considerable. He might perhaps be worth 5 or £6,000 but hardly more. As for Mrs Marshall, she was agreeable but nothing extraordinary. But he said if I was so deeply engaged in love as to interrupt me in my study or that I could not be easy without her, he could freely consent to my marrying of her, and would go himself to Mr Marshall and make up the match. Nothing can be more obliging and endearing than such a tender regard to me shown by my father. I desired my father not to mention anything of this to anybody, that I intended to stifle it as soon as possible within my own breast. He promised that he would not tell it to Brother or Sister or anybody but Mother who he said was very private and secret in anything entrusted to her. But desired he would not mention it to her because Aunt Billio is apt to inquire. He said he would not.

I think I find my mind much more easy now than it was and I am in hopes to be able to overcome my passion. When I told my father I was afraid that she herself would be against marrying me, he said then I should scorn to be in love with her. This has had some effect upon me. I wish I had that self-sufficiency as to be able to despise those that despise me.

[*Nothing came of Ryder's love for Sally Marshall. He did not marry until 1734, when he was forty-three and solicitor-general.*]

Matthews (ed.), *Diary of Dudley Ryder*, pp. 211–12, 230, 244–5, 249, 250, 326–7.

II

Married Life and Widowhood

Marriage in this period was expected to be an unequal partnership in which the husband's superior position was justified by his greater strength and wisdom. Harmony was supposed to prevail as a result of wifely obedience, the judicious exercise of husbandly authority, and mutual affection and forbearance. Yet marital disharmony is obvious in a number of the passages that follow, and the reasons for it evident in these cases are quite likely to have been common ones. In the first place, several husbands fell sadly short of the ideal of exemplary strength and wisdom. Drunkenness, improvidence, sullenness, bad temper, jealousy and overbearing insensitivity were the chief faults which undermined their authority and laid them open to reproach (16, 21, 24, 26, 28). Many wives for their part bore little resemblance to the solicitous yet submissive spouses of the prescriptive literature. Wifely criticism and complaint limited the freedom of action of such husbands as Adam Eyre and Edmund Harrold (18, 28). Mrs Eyre and Mrs Richards (27) seem from their husbands' accounts to have been wilful, irascible women of masterful temper who refused to accept husbandly reproof or control. In both sexes a tendency to bad temper was exacerbated by ailments (18,24). Yet it is remarkable how seldom the violent feelings present in some of these marriages found physical rather than verbal expression, even though some men gave vent to their rage in attacks on objects belonging to their wives (18, 21).

The most obvious sources of strain in these marriages apart from the characters of the partners themselves were problems of money and property. Some husbands were financially hard pressed (16, 18, 26). Various wives (Lady Anne Clifford, Elizabeth Freke and perhaps Lady Hoby too—16, 26, 15) would not accede to their husbands' wishes by giving up or transferring rights in land. Susannah Eyre apparently refused her husband financial help (18). All these instances illustrate the important fact that husbands' control over their wives' property was often limited. Lady Anne Clifford's diary affords an extreme example of the sorts of psychological pressure to which a woman might be subjected in an attempt to make her give up her rights, but also shows that, given sufficient resolution, such pressure might be resisted.

No marriage of this period is more fully and intimately documented than that of Samuel and Elizabeth Pepys (21). Elizabeth's boredom, due in large measure to her childlessness and comparatively limited responsibilities, was an important cause of tension. The extracts from Samuel's diary illustrate one of the marriage's phases, a chapter whose main theme was an attempt to alleviate Elizabeth's discontent. But the presence in the Pepys household early in 1663 of a lady's companion and the visits of a dancing-master ended by aggravating the malady they were intended to cure, creating new tensions and jealousies. Here the curtain comes down after the failure of these experiments.

One must not underline too heavily the negative aspects of matrimony revealed in these extracts. A number of them illustrate the reality of partnership and sharing in marriage. Lady Hoby's and Adam Eyre's diaries (15,18) show the importance of the wife's multifarious economic responsibilities in two very different types of household, and the ways in which couples might cooperate in work and management. Fleeting moments of shared leisure, which seldom leave their mark in any other sort of record, are captured here: games, visits, rides, walks, reading aloud, or simply talking in bed 'with great pleasure' (15, 16, 18, 21). The value of a spouse's 'comfortable', i.e. supportive, assistance, especially in ill health, is evident in some of these passages (15, 18, 24, 25, 28).

The diarists varied greatly in what they committed to paper on the subject of physical love. Most of the women, as we might expect, remained silent. Edmund Harrold was the most explicit of the men, though his entries are both terse and casual, and his references to the 'new fashion' adopted during his wife's pregnancy remain obscure (28). Pepys and Harrold clearly enjoyed this side of marriage; to the recently wed Isaac Archer it brought release from 'youthful desires' and 'extravagant thoughts' (21, 28, 23). Sexual relations were damaged by quarrels which on various occasions led husbands to sleep apart from their wives (16, 18, 27).

Death brought home to a number of diarists the full extent of their emotional and economic dependence upon their marriage partners. Some suffered devastating grief (20, 24, 25, 29). Apart from the touching description of his wife written by the newly married Isaac Archer (23), the eulogies printed here were devoted to spouses who were already dead (17, 19, 25). Husbands penned the most explicit descriptions of the qualities appreciated in spouses.[1] They included affection, respect and housewifely skill. Clergyman and gentleman alike paid eloquent and heartfelt tribute to the crucial importance of the wife's economic role (14, 17). Need of a wife's help in the household was one reason why some men remarried fairly speedily. Inability to remain celibate was probably another in Edmund Harrold's case (29).

Two diarists in the prime of life who willingly remained in their widowed state for some years after bereavement were Oliver Heywood and Katherine Austen (20, 22). (Heywood ultimately remarried; Mrs Austen never did so.) The prospects of remarriage were on the whole less good for women than they were for men. But Katherine Austen's willing acceptance of widowhood was inspired partly by loyalty to her husband's memory and partly by a desire to protect a child's interests, and these were probably the most widespread positive reasons for remaining single.

---

[1] But for a widow's eulogy of her husband in a biography, see Lucy Hutchinson, *Memoirs of the Life of Colonel Hutchinson*, ed. J. Sutherland (Oxford University Press, London, 1973). She specially mentioned his conjugal love and the 'prudence and affection' with which he 'manag'd the reines of government' (pp. 9–10).

14 RICHARD ROGERS PONDERS THE POSSIBLE LOSS OF HIS WIFE, 1588

[*1588*] ⟨January 12⟩ By occasion of the strange visitation of one of our neighbours, Mrs A., ⟨lying like one senseless, no cheer, nor words, which struck us that were present. Mrs Arg. died January 5[1]⟩, I seeing by much pain in wife and near childbirth many likelihoods of our separation, considered how many uncomfortablenesses the Lord had kept from me hitherto by those which I then saw must needs come if he should part us, that I might more thankfully use the benefit if it should be continued, and acquaint myself with thinking on some of them before, that they might not be altogether sudden; but alas this latter is hard.

> First, the fear of marrying again, dangerous as 2^2 marriages are.
> Want of it in the mean while.
> Forgoing so fit a companion for religion, housewifery, and other comforts.
> Loss and decay in substance.
> Care of household matters cast on me.
> Neglect of study.
> Care and looking after children.
> Forgoing our boarders.
> Fear of losing friendship among her kindred.

These are some: the Lord may cast me down with them also in sickness.

London, Dr Williams's Library, MS 61.13(17).

15 LADY MARGARET HOBY, 1599–1600

A week from the early part of the diary

[*1599, August*] ⟨The Lord's day 19:⟩ After I was ready I betook me to private prayer; [*MS torn*] then, because Mr Hoby was not

---

[1] These two marginal notes are separate.
[2] Unclear whether he meant 'two' or 'second'.

well, I kept him company till the sermon time, and did eat my breakfast; that done, I thank God who gave him will and ability, we went to church, where we received the sacraments. After I came home I prayed and so to dinner, at which, and after, both myself did talk and hear of more worldly matters than, by God's assistance, I will hereafter willingly do. Till 3 a clock I was with Mr Hoby, not so careful, the Lord forgive it me, as I ought, to meditate of what I heard, speaking and thinking of many idle matters; then we went to church and, after the sermon, I walked till 6 a clock, about which time I prayed and examined myself, craving pardon for these my infirmities. After, I went to supper, after which, till prayer time, I walked and, after repetition, went to bed.

⟨Monday 20:⟩ After I was ready I prayed privately; then I walked with Mr Hoby till 8 a clock, at which time I brake my fast, and so to work, and, at 11 of the clock, I took a lecture of Mr Rhodes,[1] and went to dinner. After dinner I wound yarn till 3, and then walked with Mr Hoby about the town to spy out the best places where cottages might be builded. After I came home I wrought till 6 and gave order for supper, and then I betook me to private prayer and examination, in which [*MS soiled*] I found myself a lacking in performing my duty I soon perceived, and therefore besought [*MS discoloured*] Lord for pardon. Then I went to supper, after which I walked a while, and because there [*was?—MS torn and soiled*] not Mr Rhodes to pray publicly, I prayed privately, and after I had helped Mr Hoby to look over some papers, I went to bed.

⟨Tuesday 21:⟩ After I was ready I prayed, and then I went a while about the house and so to breakfast, and then to work till Coueringe[2] came; then I went to private prayer but was interrupted. After I had dined I went to work till 6, and walked a little abroad, and then came to examination and prayer. After, I walked a little, and so to supper; after which I went to prayers, and not long after, according to my wonted use, to bed, save only I did not so diligently think of that I had heard, which I beseech the Lord to pardon for Christ sake. Amen. Amen.

---

[1] Richard Rhodes was possibly Lady Hoby's chaplain: see Meads (ed.), *Diary of Lady Margaret Hoby*, p. 243, n. 180. A lecture (here *Lector*) was a reading.
[2] Possibly a bailiff or steward: see Meads, *Diary*, pp. 244–5, nn. 186, 194.

⟨Wednesday 22:⟩ After I was ready I prayed, and after I had gone a little about the house, I writ[3] out notes in my Testament, and then brake my fast and walked abroad till dinner, before which I prayed, according to my wont; and after dinner I was busy despatching[4] one away to Linton[5] till 3 a clock. Then I writ notes out into my Bible, and after went a walking with Mr Hoby, and then returned into examination and prayer. After, I read of the Bible and walked alone, and then went into the kitchen, where Mr Rhodes and myself had some speech with the poor and ignorant of the some[6] principles of religion; and I had walked a little after in the court, Mr Hoby came, and so to supper and after to lecture and then to bed.

⟨Thursday 23⟩ In the morning I prayed; then I took order for things about the house till I went to breakfast, and soon after I took my coach and went to Linton, where, after I had saluted my mother, I prayed, and then, walking a little and reading of the Bible in my chamber, went to supper; after which I heard the lecture and soon after that went to bed.

⟨Friday 24:⟩ In the morning, being ready, I prayed, then [*MS torn*] brake my fast with Mr Hoby, and so rid[7] to church. After the sermon I presently went to dinner, after which I passed the time in talk with some friends, and then went to private prayer. That done I took the air in the coach with Mr Hoby, and so came in and walked in the garden, meditating of the points of the sermon and praying till hard before I went to supper; and after supper went to public prayer and thence to bed.

⟨Saturday 25⟩ In the morning I prayed and then I writ a letter to Doctor Brewer, and so to breakfast. After which I talked privately with Mr Hoby matters concerning conscience and our estates, which being concluded of between us, I took my coach and came home to Hackness, where, after I was well comed, I praise God, I went to prayer and meditation. Then I went about the house till supper time; after supper I talked with Mr Rhodes in the garden, and then to public[8] prayers, and soon after to bed.

---

[3] *wrett*; under 25 August *wreet.*
[4] *dispacting?*
[5] Where Lady Hoby's mother lived.
[6] *som.*
[7] *reed* or possibly *ried*; under 6 May 1600 *reed.*
[8] *publect*; under 20 July 1600 *bubleck.*

*A sample of further extracts from 1599–1600: some of Lady
Hoby's references to her husband and to her domestic activities*

[*1599, September*] ⟨Wednesday 5⟩ . . . having taken order for
dinner, I walked and kept Mr Hoby company almost till dinner
time. Then I read a little and prayed, and so to dinner; after
which I helped to read of the book for the placing of the people
in the church to Mr Hoby, and then we went to church. And
after we came home I talked with him and lay on my bed, not
being able well to go for my foot that was sore, till almost
supper time . . .

⟨Thursday 13⟩ In the morning, after private prayer, I writ
some things touching household matters; then I did eat my
breakfast and did order divers things in the granary. Soon after,
Mr Hoby came home, and I kept him company till he went
away again. After dinner I went to Birstall and see him who was
not well, and his apples tithed . . .

⟨October 1599. Friday the 5 day⟩ After private prayer I went
about the house, then I writ notes in my Testament; then Mr
Hoby came home, with whom I talked till dinner time. After
dinner I was busy about preserving quinces, and, a little before
supper time, I walked about the house . . .

⟨Tuesday the :9. day⟩ After private prayers I did eat my
breakfast with Mr Hoby; then I walked abroad and took a lecture.
After, I came in and prayed, and then went to dinner; then I
went about and delivered corn. Then I came into my chamber
and writ notes in my Testament, and after received rents and
walked awhile . . .

[*December*] ⟨Thursday the 13:⟩ . . . after dinner I was busy till
I walked abroad with Mr Hoby, then I went about among my
maids till almost supper time . . .

⟨Tuesday the :18:⟩ . . . almost all the afternoon I was busy
making ginger bread and other things . . .

⟨The Lord's day :30:⟩ . . . after dinner I, with Mr Hoby, talked
with some tenants that dined with us. After that we went to the
afternoon sermon and from thence came home and read of
Greenham,[9] and heard Meg Rhodes read. Then I walked and

---

[9] Richard Greenham, d. 1594, rector of Dry Drayton (Cambs.), a zealous puritan.

conferred with Mr Hoby, took order for supper, and then went to private examination and prayer . . .

[*1600, January*] ⟨The Lord's day :27:⟩ . . . after dinner talked with Mr Hoby till I went again to church; and after heard Mr Hoby read of Perkins[10] till almost 5 a clock . . .

⟨January, the 3 day of the week, 30: 1599 [1600]:⟩ After I had prayed privately I dressed a poor boy's leg that came to me, and then brake my fast with Mr Hoby. After, I dressed the hand of one of our servants that was very sore cut, and after I writ in my testament notes upon James. Then I went about the doing of some things in the house, paying of bills, and after I had talked with Mr Hoby I went to examination and prayer, after to supper, then to the lecture; after that I dressed one of the men's hands that was hurt, lastly prayed, and so to bed.

[*February*] ⟨The 3 day of the week 26[27]:⟩ After private prayer I did eat, then dressed my patients, read, talked with a neighbour, prayed, and then dined. After, I was busy weighing of wool till almost night and then, after talk with Mr Hoby and order for supper, I went to private exercises in my closet; then after I supped and after that prayed and so went to bed.

[*March*] ⟨The Lord's day 9:⟩ . . . upon the Lord's day I prayed privately and got Mr Hoby to read some of Perkins to me . . .

⟨The 5 day the :28:⟩ After private prayer I did eat, receive money of Steven Tubley, the last payment for his land, 60*li*; after, I read of the Bible, went about the house, prayed, and after dined. Then I took order for supper and rid abroad with Mr Hoby . . .

[*May*] ⟨The 2 day the :6:⟩ After private prayers I did eat some meat with Mr Hoby, and so took horse and rid to Harwood Dale to see our farm we bought of Thomas Calsone; then I came home and went to dinner . . .

⟨The 2 day :13:⟩ . . . After dinner, and all ceremonies ended, I came home and walked abroad, and after I had gone about the house I went to private meditation and prayer; after to supper, then to public prayers, and after I had talked a good time with Mr Hoby of husbandry and household matters, we went to bed.

---

[10] William Perkins (1558–1602), eminent puritan and immensely influential theological writer; fellow of Christ's College, Cambridge, 1584–95.

⟨19: of July 1600:⟩ After private prayer I writ an answer to a demand[11] Mr Hoby had given me overnight; after, I went about and then writ in my sermon book; after that I prayed and then I dined. The afternoon I wrought till almost 5 a clock, and then I went about the house. After, I returned unto my closet and altered that a little which before I had written, and then I examined myself and prayed. After, I went to supper, then to public prayers and lastly, after private, I went to bed.

⟨The 20 day the Lord's day⟩ . . . after the sermon, I prayed, then I dined; after, I talked with my neighbours of that we had heard, and read something to them. After, I prayed and went to the church again. After, I talked with my Cousin Isons, and when it was 5 a clock I went to private examination and prayer; after, I walked down and then went to supper. After, I heard the public exercise, and then praying, and giving Mr Hoby that that I had written, I went to bed.

⟨The 29:⟩ . . . after dinner I was busy in my chamber and about taking order for things almost all the afternoon, and then I wrought, walked about with Mr Hoby among workmen, and after, I went to private prayer and examination. After, I supped; then I talked with Mr Hoby of sundry things, and so, when I had prayed privately and read a chapter of the Testament, I went to bed.

British Library, MS Egerton 2614, ff. 3ʳ–4ʳ, 6ʳ, 7ᵛ, 10ᵛ, 11ʳ, 18ʳ⁻ᵛ, 20ʳ, 24ᵛ, 28ʳ⁻ᵛ, 31ʳ, 36ʳ, 37ʳ, 46ᵛ, 48ʳ.

16   MARITAL DISHARMONY: LADY ANNE CLIFFORD'S DESCRIPTION OF HER RELATIONS WITH HER HUSBAND, THE EARL OF DORSET, 1617

[*Anne's father, the third Earl of Cumberland, had left his lands in Westmorland and elsewhere to his brother and £15,000 to Anne. Her refusal to accept these provisions and insistence on maintaining her title*

---

[11] Possibly a demand that she make over her lands to him in her life-time: see Meads, *Diary*, p. 267, n. 357.

to the lands angered her husband, who was anxious to obtain the money
left by the third Earl.]

[*January 20*] . . . the King asked us all if we would submit to his
judgement in this case. My Uncle Cumberland, my Coz. Clifford
and my Lord answered they would, but I never would agree to
it without Westmorland, at which the King grew in a great chaff.
My Lord of Pembroke and the King's Solicitor speaking much
against me. At last when they saw there was no remedy, my
Lord, fearing the King would do me some public disgrace,
desired Sir John Digby would open the door, who went out
with me and persuaded me much to yield to the King. . . . Presently after my Lord came from the King when it was resolved
that if I would not come to an agreement there should be an
agreement made without me. . . . I may say I was led miraculously by God's providence, and next to that I trust all my good
to the worth and nobleness of my Lord's disposition, for neither
I nor anybody else thought I should have passed over this day
so well as I have done.

[*February 4*] . . . my Lord wrote me a letter by which I
perceived my Lord was clean out with me, and how much my
enemies have wrought against me. Upon the 19th[*14th?*] I sent
Mr Edward's man to London with a letter to my Lord to desire
him to come down hither. . . . [*Lady Anne was at Knole, her*
husband's house in Kent.]

Upon the 16th my Lord came hither from London before
dinner and told me how the whole state of my business went
and how things stood at the Court.

Upon the 17th about 8 o'clock in the morning my Lord
returned to London.

[*27*] . . . My Lord writ me word that the King had referred
the drawing and perfecting the business to the Solicitor.

My soul was much troubled and afflicted to see how things
go, but my trust is still in God, and compare things past with
things present and read over the Chronicles.

[*March*] Upon the 3d . . . I wrote a letter to my Lord to
beseech him that he would take Knole on his way as he goes to
London.

Upon the 12th I wrote to my Lord . . .

⟨The 14th being Friday my Uncle Cumberland and my Coz.

Clifford came to Dorset House where my Lord and they signed and sealed the writings and made a final conclusion of my business and did what they could to cut me off from my right, but I referred my cause to God.)

Upon the 15th my Lord came down to Buckhurst [*his house in Sussex*] and was so ill by the way that was fain to alight once or· twice and go into a house. . . . The 16th my Lord sent for John Cook to make broths for him and Josiah to wait in his chamber, by whom I wrote a letter to entreat him that if he were not well I might come down to Buckhurst to him. . . .

[*20*] . . . After supper I wrote a letter to my Lord to entreat him that he would come and see me and the child as soon as he could.

The 26th my Lord came here with Thomas Glemham from Buckhurst; he was troubled with a cough and was fain to lie in Leicester Chamber. The 27th my Lord told me . . . that the matter was not so fully finished but there was a place left for me to come in. My Lord found me reading with Mr Ran and told me it would hinder his study so as I must leave off reading the Old Testament till I can get somebody to read it with me. . . .

The 28th I walked abroad with my Lord in the Park and the garden, where he spake to me much of this business with my uncle. I wrought much within doors and strived to sit as merry a face as I could upon a discontented heart, for I might easily perceive that Matthew[1] and Lindsay had got a great hand of my Lord and were both against me. . . .

Upon the 29th my Lord went to London, I bringing him down to his coach. I found this time that he was nothing so much discontented with this agreement as I thought he would have been, and that he was more pleased and contented with the passages in London than I imagined he would have been.

[*April*] The 2nd my Lord came down from London with Tom Glemham with him . . .

The 5th my Lord went up to my closet and said how little money I had left, contrary to all they had told him. Sometimes

---

[1] 'Mr Matthew Caldicott, my Lord's favourite': see *A Catalogue of the Household and Family of the Right Honourable Richard Earl of Dorset . . . at Knole, In Kent*, in Sackville-West (ed.), *The Diary of the Lady Anne Clifford*, p. lvii.

I had fair words from him and sometimes foul, but I took all patiently, and did strive to give him as much content and assurance of my love as I could possibly, yet I told him that I would never part with Westmorland upon any condition whatever.

Upon the 6th after supper because my Lord was sullen and not willing to go into the nursery I made Mary bring the child to him into my chamber, which was the first time she stirred abroad since she was sick.

Upon the 7th my Lord lay in my chamber. Upon the 8th I set by my Lord and my Brother Sackville in the Drawing Chamber and heard much talk about many[2] businesses . . .

The 13th my Lord sat where the gentlemen used to sit. He dined abroad in the Great Chamber and supped privately with me in the Drawing Chamber and had much discourse of the manners of the folks at court.

The 16th my Lord and I had much talk about these businesses, he urging me still to go to London to sign and seal, but I told him that my promise was so far passed to my mother and to all the world that I would never do it, whatever became of me and mine.

Upon the 17th in the morning my Lord told me he was resolved never to move me more in these businesses, because he saw how fully I was bent.

[19] . . . The same night my Lord and I had much talk of and persuaded me to these businesses, but I would not, and yet I told him I was in perfect charity with all the world. . . .

The 20th being Easter Day my Lord and I and Tom Glemham and most of the folk received the Communion by Mr Ran, yet in the afternoon my Lord and I had had a great falling out, Matthew continuing still to do me all the ill offices he could with my Lord. . . .

The 22nd he came to dine abroad in the Great Chamber; this night we played at Burley Break[3] upon the Bowling Green.

The 23rd Lord Clanricarde came hither. After they were gone my Lord and I and Tom Glemham went to Mr Lane's house to see the fine flowers that is in the garden.

[2] Sackville-West read *my*.
[3] Or barley-break: a game in which three couples took part, one chasing the other two.

This night my Lord should have lain with me, but he and I fell out about Matthew.

The 24th my Lord went to Sevenoaks again. After supper we played at Burley Break upon the Green. This night my Lord came to lie in my chamber.

The 26th I spent the evening in working and going down to my Lord's closet where I sat and read much in the Turkish History and Chaucer.

[*May*] The 3d my Lord went from Buckhurst to London, and rid it in four hours, he riding very hard, a hunting all the while he was at Buckhurst, and had his health exceeding well.

The 8th I spent this day in working, the time being very tedious unto me as having neither comfort nor company, only the child.

[*12*] . . . I wrote not to my Lord because he wrote not to me since he went away. . . .

The 17th the steward came from London and told me my Lord was much discontented with me for not doing this business, because he must be fain to buy land for the payment of the money which will much encumber his estate.

Upon the 18th Mr Wolrich came hither to serve me, he bringing me news that all in Westmorland was surrendered to my Uncle Cumberland.

[*24*] . . . This time my Lord's mother did first of all sue out of her thirds[4] which was an increase of trouble and discontent to my Lord.

[*25*] . . . In the afternoon my Coz. Russell wrote me a letter to let me know how my Lord had cancelled my jointure he made upon me last June when I went into the North, and by these proceedings I may see how much my Lord is offended with me and that my enemies have the upper hand of me. I am resolved to take all patiently, casting all my care upon God. . . .

The 27th I wrote a letter to my Lord to let him know how ill I took his cancelling my jointure, but yet told him I was content to bear it with patience, whatsoever he thought fit.

Maidstone, Kent Archives Office, MS U269. F48/2.

---

[4] Her dower, one third of her late husband's estate, to which she was entitled as a widow.

17 SIR JOHN OGLANDER ON HIS WIFE FRANCES
(d. 1644)

[*The following words precede an account of Sir John's expenditure.*]

What moneys I have paid out [*of*] my estate since I came to it, which is wonderful; had I not God's great blessing and a careful, industrious wife who was no spender, nor ever wore a silk gown but for her credit when she went abroad in company I could never have done it. [*The account, totalling £7,350, is accompanied by the following comment.*] I could never have done it without a most careful, thriving wife, who was up before me every day, and oversaw all the outhouses, one that would not trust her maid with directions, she would wet her shoe to see [it?] all herself acted. . . .

London, National Register of Archives, no. 9841 (photocopy), account book begun in 1642, p. 61.

18 FINANCIAL PROBLEMS AND MATRIMONIAL DIFFICULTIES: ADAM AND SUSANNAH EYRE, 1647–8

[*April*] 26. – This morn my wife went to her mother . . . I sent by my wife to her father to see if he will give me 350*l*, and I will make Hazlehead to her for jointure and release all his land but Oliver's farm . . . [*The diarist mentioned his father-in-law Godfrey Mathewman fairly frequently thereafter, but his hopes of substantial help from him seem to have been disappointed.*]

[*May*] 20. – This morn I told my wife that if she would furnish me with 200*l* I would secure her all Hazlehead [*his estate*] for her life, and she should have the half of it for the present, if Edward Mitchell[1] would part with it; and she refused, unless I would release her land in Scholes, which I refused; and then I cast up my accounts since Christmas last . . .

---

[1] Eyre's tenant.

Sunday 23. – This day my wife, Edward Mitchell and I went to Holmfirth and heard Gamaliel Apleyard preach a very malicefull sermon, and dined at Godfrey Cuttill's; for which Godrey Mathewman paid for us 20*d*. And then we called on William Savile at Scholes Moor, and so came home; and after supper my wife and I walked into the Dickroyd.

Fast, 26. – . . . after dinner, I blooded my wife in her sore foot, which bled very well; then, after supper, at night, came two soldiers which had been quartered here, and Ed. Hawksworth, and kept a great stir about a bridle which was out of the way the last time they quartered here, and my wife was very extravagant in her old humorous way.

29. – This day I went with my wife to her mother, and by the way we laid our mare fast, and stayed there till 4 at clock, and then home again; here was nothing remarkable done this day. . . .

[*June*] 8. – This morn my wife began, after her old manner, to brawl and revile me for wishing her only to wear such apparel as was decent and comely, and accused me for treading on her sore foot, with curses and oaths; which to my knowledge I touched not. Nevertheless, she continued in that ecstasy till noon, and at dinner I told her I purposed never to come in bed with her till she took more notice of what I formerly had said to her, which I pray God give me grace to observe, that the folly of mine own corrupt nature deceive me not to mine own damnation. . . .

14. – This morn I rid to Edentree Head to borrow a pan for my wife to brew in; and so home again, six mile. . . .

23. – This morn I went to Bull House, and thence with Captain Rich to Bolsterstone, to bowls, where I lost 6*s* and spent 6*d*, and so came home again at night, eight miles. This night my wife was worse in words than ever.

[*July*] 10. – This morn I made my wife a place for chickens . . .

23. – . . . My wife sold twenty-one strokes of meal and gave me for it 3*l* 4*s* 2*d*.

29. – This day I stayed within till noon, and cast up my accompts since May Day, and find that my charges have been in these three months 10*l* 5*s* 6*d*, which is more than my allowance will extend to by half, and still I owe Woodcock for meat. . . .

30. – This day I stayed at home all day, by reason my wife was not willing to let me go to bowls to Bolsterstone . . .

[*August*] 6.– . . . This night my wife had a painful night of her foot, which troubled me so that sleep went from me. Whereupon sundry wicked worldly thoughts came in my head, and, namely, a question whether I should live with my wife or no, if she continued so wicked as she is; whereupon I ris and prayed to God to direct me aright. . . .

11. – This morn I went with Edward Mitchell to Barnsley, and called at Jo. Shirt's by the way, where I had my hair cut, and paid for nails 12*d*; to Woodcock, for meat, which we had three weeks ago, 6*s* 6*d*; for tobacco for my wife, 10*d*; for thread, 2*d*; and spent 1*s* 6*d*; and came by Coyts home with Jo. Ellisson. This morn I gave my wife 10*s*; who at night kept the yates shut, and said she would be master of the house for that night. . . .

Sunday 15. – I stayed at home all day, and my wife and I walked into the Raynow Stones in the afternon. This day I was very much perplexed with worldly cares, and laboured under a sore temptation all day.

17. – . . . I set up my wife a brewing tub . . .

[*September*] 24. – This last night my wife dreamed that she was overloadened with gold, and was therewith sore troubled; . . . in the afternoon I gave my wife 28*s*, to buy necessaries for the house.

[*October*] 2. – . . . This day was my wife very angry, and I stayed at home all day. . . .

5. – . . . when I came home, the yates were shut and they refused to open them, so that I was forced to break them. . . .

Sunday 10. – This day I rested at home all day . . . and in the afternoon I walked into the fields with my wife.

14. – . . . after I came home, toward night, my wife went with me, and we swam the skewbald in a pit in the Wayre Field. The last night she had a very painful night on her leg which swelled and was angry quite up to her body.

Sunday 17. – . . . I went with William Wordsworth of Softley onto the Bents, who promised to lend me 50*l* at or before the latter end of November, and more if it came in; so back to Bray's, and home; after which my wife was very angry all day, till night. . . .

[*November*] 20. – . . . at night my wife was exceeding angry and had much pain in her leg . . .

[*December*] Sunday 19. – This morn Isaac Beardsall called here, and I went with him to Peniston to church, on foot, and home again at noon, in all four mile. . . . after I came home my wife was very unquiet and uncharitable also. God forgive her!

22. – This day I rested at home all day, and cast up the accounts of my expenses for this year; and I find them to be near hand 100*l*, whereas I have not past 30*l* per annum to live on; wherefore I am resolved hereafter never to pay for anybody in the alehouse, nor never to entangle myself in company so much again as I have done; and I pray God give me grace that, slighting the things of this life, I may look up to him.

[*1648*] *January* 1. – . . . This morn I used some words of persuasion to my wife to forbear to tell me of what is past, and promised her to become a good husband to her for the time to come, and she promised me likewise she would do what I wished her in anything, save in setting her hand to papers; and I promised her never to wish her thereunto. Now I pray God that both she and I may leave off all our old and foolish contentions, and join together in his service without all fraud, malice or hypocrisy; and that he will for the same purpose illuminate our understandings with his Holy Spirit, which in the midst of worldly cares and cumbrances may be our guide and direction, and from all temptations and perils our perpetual protection, to the glory and praise of his great and glorious Name. Amen. . . .

[*February*] 18. – This day I went to Peniston to the burial of Roger Eyre, where I spent 6*d* and stayed till night, but came home in time; nevertheless my wife was far out of . . .,[2] whereat . . .[2] I broke her wheel and mended it again in the morning. . . .

26. – This day my wife was not well, and I rested at home all day . . . I paid Thomas Mill for mending a wheel for my wife and other work 2*s*, toto 3*s*.

[*March*] Sunday 5. – I rested at home all day, only my wife and I after dinner walked into the fields.

Sunday 12. – This day I rested at home all day, and my wife walked into the fields with me in the afternoon.

Sunday 26. – This day I went with my wife to Peniston to the church, and she received the Communion, and I spent (God

---

[2] These gaps are in Morehouse's edition.

forgive me) the afternoon in the alehouse, and spent in all *2s 6d*; and so we came home again, and I had abused myself in drinking. God have mercy on me. . . .

[*There is a gap between 4 April 1648, the eve of Eyre's departure on a journey to London, and 15 September, the day of his return.*]

[*October*] 10. – I rested at home all day, only in the morn I rid with my wife's father to Carlecotes and spoke to Francis Haigh concerning the sale of Hazlehead, but we differed much in the price . . .

11. – This day I rested at home all day and walked into the fields, and I told my wife sith she would not join with me in sale, she should keep the house as she would, neither would I meddle with her at all.

24. – This morn I went to Sheffield, met my brother and sister and took my wife's water to Dr Shirtcliffe, who promised to come hither on Thursday. . . .

Morehouse (ed.), 'A Dyurnall or Catalogue of all my Accions and Expences', pp. 29, 36–7, 39–40, 43–4, 46, 49–51, 52, 54–5, 63, 65–8, 75, 80–1, 84, 99–100, 102, 104, 111–13.

19 SIR ANTHONY ASHLEY COOPER ON HIS WIFE MARGARET, 1649

[*July*] 10th day. My wife, just as she was sitting down to supper, fell suddenly into an apoplectical convulsion fit. She recovered that fit after some time, and spake and kissed me, and complained only in her head, but fell again in a quarter of an hour, and then never came to speak again, but continued in fits and slumbers until next day.

11th day. At noon she died; she was with child the fourth time, and within six weeks of her time.

She was a lovely beautiful fair woman, a religious devout Christian; of admirable wit and wisdom beyond any I ever knew, yet the most sweet, affectionate and observant wife in the world. Chaste without suspicion of the most envious to the highest assurance of her husband; of a most noble and bountiful mind, yet very provident in the least things, exceeding all in anything she undertook, housewifery, preserving, works with the needle, cookery, so that her wit and judgement were expressed in all things; free from any pride or frowardness. She was in discourse and counsel far beyond any woman.

London, Public Record Office, Shaftesbury Papers, 30/24 8, pt 2 (written in *A New Almanacke* for 1649).

20   THE WIDOWHOOD AND REMARRIAGE OF OLIVER HEYWOOD, 1661–7

[*1661*] In the midst of these public fears and woeful disasters God called home to himself my dear and precious wife after she had lived with me to my exceeding comfort six years and about a month; it was the heaviest personal stroke that ever I experienced, yet the Lord hath abundantly satisfied my heart and supported my spirit under it, partly upon the consideration of her happy conditition, partly upon our grounded expectation of approaching judgements;[1] truth it is there are many things that may tend to aggravate, and on the other hand to moderate and extenuate the affliction, but that which I would study is what God's design is to me therein, and to look after the advantage thereof—for in all my losses the want of the fruit of an affliction is the greatest loss. She was as comfortable a daughter to her father and wife to her husband as ever lived, she grew up to a wonderful maturity far beyond her years; it may be much disputed whether her graces or parts were more pregnant and flourishing: certainly she excelled in both, but I say no more here, for I design an history of her life and death, which I am sure will be worth my labour. She died at Denton May 26 1661—yet this I may say, 'tis as apparent and afflictive a weakening of my strength in the way and in my work as ever I met with; to lose a wife, and such a wife, at such a time as this, seems to carry with it not only a grievous but [ominous?][2] breach; I want her at every turn, everywhere, and in every work.

---

[1] Probably a reference to the persecution of nonconformists.
[2] Horsfall Turner (ed.), *Rev.Oliver Heywood*, vol. I, p. 177, read 'anxious'. The word is very difficult to read.

Methinks I am but half myself without her. But why should I complain? She is at rest, God's will is done, I may shortly follow her; sure I am she cannot return, nor doth she desire it, and then I ought not. The affliction is more deep and cutting than any that ever I had, and the supporting, quickening and comforting grace beyond whatever I experienced before in all my life; my God supplies all my wants according to his riches in glory by Christ Jesus, only I am afraid of living and losing that frame of spirit begot by God's spirit under this dispensation: my encouragement is that to Paul: 'My grace is sufficient for thee.'

My present state for domestical affairs is this: July 28 1661 at the writing hereof, I keep house with one only maid and my two little sons, and I bless God we live sweetly together. I have had motions and tenders of another maid, but my friends judge it best to continue as I am, and, I bless God, I cannot be better furnished; she is my child as well as servant, one of my first and best converts to the faith, and that spiritual relation hath much endeared us; sober, solid, and of a tender conscience, though full of scruples yet fearing God above many, laborious, faithful, in whom the children take great delight, a great mercy to me in this solitary condition.

[*1667*] This day hath been a solemn and busy day with me; it is that which Almanacs call St Mark's Day, April 25 1667. I am sure 'tis a remarkable day with me, for upon this day twelve years ago was I married, and six years I enjoyed a comfortable wife, and now in May 26 I have been solitary other six years, and now at last I am thinking of changing my condition, and have been spending part of this day in solemn fasting and prayer to mourn for my sins and beg mercy . . .

June 25 I took a journey again into Lancashire upon a very solemn business which I had long thought of and prayed for, which was marriage, and accordingly upon Thursday June 27 I was married by Mr Hide at Salford Chapel by Manchester in a decent manner; we were under twenty persons of the nearest relations, and I am abundantly satisfied in my gracious yoke-fellow.

British Library, MS Add. 45964, f. 37^{r-v}; MS Add. 45965, ff. 34^v, 36^r.

21   SAMUEL PEPYS AND HIS WIFE ELIZABETH, 1663

[*January*] 1. Lay with my wife . . . till 10 a clock with great
pleasure talking; and then I rose. . . .

4. *Lord's day*. . . . At dinner my wife did propound my having
of my sister Pall at my house again to be her woman, since one
we must have—hoping that in that quality possibly she may
prove better than she did before.[1] Which I take very well of her,
and will consider of it . . .

9. . . . my wife begun to speak again of the necessity of her
keeping somebody to bear her company; for her familiarity with
her other servants is it that spoils them all, and other company
she hath none (which is too true); and called for Jane to reach
her out of her trunk, giving her the keys to that purpose, a
bundle of papers; and pulls out a paper, a copy of what, a pretty
while since, she had writ in a discontent to me, which I would
not read but burned. She now read it, and was so piquant, and
wrote in English and most of it true, of the retiredness of her
life and how unpleasant it was, that being writ in Enlish and so
in danger of being met with and read by others, I was vexed at
it and desired her and then commanded her to tear it—which
she desired to be excused it; I forced it from her and tore it, and
withal took her other bundle of papers from her and leapt out
of the bed and in my shirt clapped them into the pockets of my
breeches, that she might not get them from me; and having got
on my stockings and breeches and gown, I pulled them out one
by one and tore them all before her face, though it went against
my heart to do it, she crying and desiring me not to do it. But
such was my passion and trouble to see the letters of my love
to her, and my will, wherein I had given her all I have in the
world when I went to sea with my Lord Sandwich, to be joined
with a paper of so much disgrace to me and dishonour if it
should have been found by anybody. Having tore them all,
saving a bond of my Uncle Robert's, which she hath long had
in her hands, and our marriage licence and the first letter that
ever I sent her when I was her servant, I took up the pieces and
carried them into my chamber, and there, after many disputes

---

[1] She had served Samuel and Elizabeth as a maid from January to September 1661.

with myself whether I should burn them or no, and having picked up the pieces of the paper she read today and of my will which I tore, I burnt all the rest. And so went out to my office—troubled in mind. . . .

There coming a letter to me from Dr Pierce the surgeon, by my desire appointing his and Dr Clerke's coming to dine with me next Monday, I went to my wife and agreed upon matters; and at last, for my honour am forced to make her presently a new mohair[2] gown to be seen by Mrs Clerke; which troubles me to part with so much money, but however it sets my wife and I to friends again, though I and she never were so heartily angry in our lives as today almost, and I doubt the heart-burning will not soon over. And the truth is, I am sorry for the tearing of so many poor loving letters of mine from sea and elsewhere to her. . . .

31. . . . So to dinner, late and not very good; only a rabbit not half roasted, which made me angry with my wife. . . . In the evening examining my wife's letter intended to my Lady and another to Mademoiselle;[3] they were so false spelt that I was ashamed of them and took occasion to fall out about them with my wife, and so she writ none; at which, however, I was sorry, because it was in answer to a letter of Mademoiselle—about business. . . .

[*February*] 11. . . . at night my wife read *Sir Henry Vane's Trial* to me, which she begun last night, and I find it a very excellent thing, worth reading, and him to have been a very wise man. . . .

13. Lay very long with my wife in bed, talking with great pleasure—and then rise. . . .

15. *Lord's day.* . . . So home, and after prayers to bed—talking long with my wife and teaching her things in astronomy.

[*March*] 12. . . . Sat late; and having done, I went home; where I find Mary Ashwell[4] come to live with us, of whom I hope well and pray God she may please us—which though it cost me something, yet will give me much content. . . .

[*April*] 21. . . . and so home to supper—to play a game at cards with my wife, and so to bed. . . .

[2] *Moyre.*
[3] Lady Sandwich and Mlle Le Blanc, governess to her daughters.
[4] Daughter of Mr Ashwell of the Exchequer, an acquaintance of Pepys, come to be Mrs Pepys's companion.

25. . . . So in the evening home; and after supper . . . merrily practising to dance, which my wife hath begun to learn this day of Mr Pembleton;[5] but I fear will hardly do any great good at it, because she is conceited that she doth well already, though I think no such thing . . .

26. *Lord's day*. Lay pretty long in bed, talking with my wife . . . In the evening . . . my wife, Ashwell, and the boy[6] and I, and the dog, over the water and walked to Halfway House and beyond, into the fields gathering of cowslips; and so to Halfway House with some cold lamb we carried with us, and there supped; and had a most pleasant walk back again . . .

[*May*] 2. . . . So up and to my office (being come to some angry words with my wife about neglecting the keeping of the house clean, I calling her 'beggar' and she me 'prick-louse', which vexed me) and there all the morning; so to the Exchange and then home to dinner, and very merry and well pleased with my wife . . .

3. *Lord's day*. . . . And so a while to my office and then home to supper—and prayers, to bed—my wife and I having a little falling-out because I would not leave my discourse below with her and Ashwell to go up and talk with her alone upon something she hath to say. She reproached me that I had rather talk with anybody than her—by which I find I think she is jealous of my freedom with Ashwell—which I must avoid giving occasion of.

8. . . . Thence to my brother's, and there took up my wife and Ashwell to the Theatre Royal, being the second day of its being opened. . . . The play being done, we home by water, having been a little ashamed that my wife and woman were in such a pickle, all the ladies being finer and better dressed in the pit than they use I think to be. . . .

10. *Lord's day*. . . . And after a little while at my office, walked in the garden with my wife. And so home to supper and after prayers to bed. . . .

15. . . . and so . . . home—where I find it almost night and my wife and the dancing master alone above, not dancing but walking. Now, so deadly full of jealousy I am, that my heart

---

[5] Dancing-master.

[6] Wayneman, Pepy's footboy.

and head did so cast about and fret, that I could not do any business possibly, but went out to my office; and anon late home again, and ready to chide at everything; and then suddenly to bed and could hardly sleep, yet durst not say anything; but was forced to say that I had bad news from the Duke concerning Tom Hayter,[7] as an excuse to my wife—who by my folly hath too much opportunity given her with that man; who is a pretty neat black man, but married. But it is a deadly folly and plague that I bring upon myself to be so jealous; and by giving myself such an occasion, more than my wife desired, of giving her another month's dancing—which however shall be ended as soon as I can possibly. But I am ashamed to think what a course I did take by lying to see whether my wife did wear drawers today as she used to do,[8] and other things to raise my suspicion of her; but I found no true cause of doing it.

16. Up, with my mind disturbed, and with my last night's doubts upon me. For which I deserve to be beaten, if not really served as I am fearful of being; especially since, God knows, that I do not find honesty enough in my own mind but that upon a small temptation I could be false to her, and therefore ought not to expect more justice from her—but God pardon both my sin and my folly herein. . . .

21. . . . I home and danced with Pembleton and then the barber trimmed me; and so to dinner—my wife and I having high words about her dancing, to that degree that I did retire and make a vow to myself, not to oppose her or say anything to dispraise or correct her therein as long as her month lasts, in pain of 2s 6d for every time; which if God please, I will observe, for this roguish business hath brought us more disquiet than anything hath happened a great while.

After dinner to my office, where late, and then home; and Pembleton being there again, we fell to dance a country dance or two, and so to supper and bed. But being at supper, my wife did say something that caused me to oppose her in; she used the word 'Devil', which vexed me; and among other things, I said I would not have her to use that word, upon which she took

---

7 Clerk in the Navy Office.
8 Worn by French ladies since the mid-sixteenth century, but uncommon among Englishwomen: Latham and Matthews, *Diary*, vol. IV, p. 140, n. 1.

me up most scornfully; which before Ashwell and the rest of the world, I know not nowadays how to check as I would heretofore, for less than that would have made me strike her. So that I fear, without great discretion, I shall go near to lose too my command over her; and nothing doth it more than giving her this occasion of dancing and other pleasure, whereby her mind is taken up from her business and finds other sweets besides pleasing of me, and so makes her that she begins not at all to take pleasure in me or study to please me as heretofore. . . .

24. *Lord's day*. . . . my wife telling me that there was a pretty lady come to church with Peg Penn[9] today, I against my intention had a mind to go to church to see her, and did so—and she is pretty handsome. But over against our gallery I espied Pembleton and saw him leer upon my wife all the sermon, I taking no notice of him, and my wife upon him; and I observed she made a curtsey to him at coming out, without taking notice to me at all of it; which, with the consideration of her being desirous these two last Lord's days to go to church both forenoon and afternoon, doth really make me suspect something more than ordinary, though I am loath to think the worst; but yet it put and doth still keep me at a great loss in my mind, and makes me curse the time that I consented to her dancing, and more, my continuing it a second month, which was more than she desired, even after I had seen too much of her carriage with him. But I must have patience and get her into the country, or at least make an end of her learning to dance as soon as I can. . . .

[*June*] 7. ⟨Whitsunday.⟩ *Lord's day*. Lay long, talking with my wife, sometimes angry; and ended pleased and hope to bring our matters to a better posture in a little time, which God send. . . . my wife and I had an angry word or two upon discourse of our boy compared with Sir W. Penn's boy that he hath now, which I say is much prettier than ours and she the contrary. It troubles me to see that every small thing is enough nowadays to bring a difference between us. . . .

11. . . . And at night home and spent the evening with my wife, and she and I did jangle mightily about her cushions that she wrought with worsteds the last year, which are too little for

[9] Margaret, daughter of Sir William, commissioner of the navy.

any use; but were good friends by and by again. But one thing I must confess I do observe, which I did not before; which is, that I cannot blame my wife to be now in a worse humour than she used to be, for I am taken up in my talk with Ashwell, who is a very witty girl, that I am not so fond of her as I used and ought to be; which now I do perceive, I will remedy. . . .

14. [*Elizabeth was to go down on 15 June to stay with Samuel's parents at Brampton.*] . . . In the evening our discourse turned to great content and love, and I hope that after a little forgetting our late differences, and being a while absent one from another, we shall come to agree as well as ever. . . .

15. . . . My head aching with the healths I was forced to drink today, I sent for the barber; and he having done, I up to my wife's closet and there played on my violin a good while; and without supper, anon to bed—sad for want of my wife, whom I love with all my heart, though of late she hath given me some troubled thoughts.

29. . . . fell in talk with Mrs Lane[10] and after great talk that she never went abroad with any man as she used heretofore to do, I with one word got her to go with me and to meet me at the further Rhenish wine house—where I did give her a lobster and do so towse[11] her and feel her all over, making her believe how fair and good a skin she had; and indeed, she hath a very white thigh and leg, but monstrous fat. . . .

[*August*] 4. . . . This day I received a letter from my wife which troubles me mightily; wherein she tells me how Ashwell did give her the lie to her teeth. And that thereupon my wife giving her a box on the ear, the other struck her again, and a deal of stir; which troubles me. And that my Lady hath been told by my father or mother something of my wife's carriage; which altogether vexes me and I fear I shall find a trouble of my wife when she comes home, to get down her head again; but if Ashwell goes, I am resolved to have no more—but to live poorly and low again for a good while, and save money and keep my wife within bounds—if I can; or else I shall bid Adieu to all content in the world. . . .

---

[10] Betty Lane, a stall-holder in Westminster Hall.
[11] To dishevel, rumple.

12. . . . I hear my wife is come and gone home . . . where methinks I find my wife strange, not knowing, I believe, in what temper she could expect me to be in; but I fell to kind words and so we were very kind; only, she could not forbear telling me how she had been used by them and her maid Ashwell in the country; but I find it will be best not to examine it, for I doubt she's in fault too, and therefore I seek to put it off from my hearing; and so to bed and there enjoyed her with great content. And so to sleep.

13. . . . And before going to bed, Ashwell begun to make her complaint and by her I do perceive that she hath received most base usage from my wife; which my wife sillily denies, but it is impossible the wench could invent words and matter so particularly, against which my wife hath nothing to say but flatly to deny, which I am sorry to see, and blows to have passed and high words, even at Hinchingbrooke House among my Lady's people, of which I am mightily ashamed.

I said nothing to either of them, but let them talk—till she was gone and left us abed; and then I told my wife my mind with great sobriety and grief. And so to sleep.

14. Awake, and to chide my wife again; and I find that my wife hath got too great head to be brought down soon. Nor is it possible with any convenience to keep Ashwell longer, my wife is so set and concerned, as she was in Sarah,[12] to make her appear a liar in every small thing, that we shall have no peace while she stays. . . .

[*Ashwell finally left the Pepys household on 25 August.*]

Latham and Matthews (eds), *Diary of Samuel Pepys*, vol. IV, pp. 1, 3, 9–10, 29, 40–1, 43, 72, 107, 111–12, 121–2, 128, 131, 140, 149–50, 153–4, 176–7, 180, 183–4, 186, 203, 262, 273–4, 276.

[12] Maid with the Pepyses from November 1661 to December 1662.

22 KATHERINE AUSTEN'S REASONS FOR REMAINING A WIDOW, 1665

Surely when I consider the passages of my widow state, what a blessing I am to be thankful[*sic*] I made that resolution to continue seven years for the particular esteem to my Dear Friend, and that I have continued almost to that time. And certainly if my son's estate be taken away, I shall begin to take a new lease of seven years more, if God Almighty spare me so long, for the good of my son, for his welfare and resupportation. No, no fortune, no self interest I hope shall prevail on me for his prejudice. If his estate do hold, he would not much know my kindness; if it fail, my love, my affection, my zeal, my honour shall be expressed both to him, his dear father, and worthy grandfather, who have a deep obligation ever imprinted in my memory, respects and endeavours. Thus friends are not known till adversity; yet happy it is not to have adversity to try the generosity of friends. But to have no friends in the crosses of the world is a double calamity.

The Lord continue to this poor destitute family friends, and above all friends himself, the unfailing friend.

Let us still observe that which can never be too much observed, how divine providence never fails the innocent.

British Library, MS Add. 4454, f 68ᵛ.

23 ISAAC ARCHER'S REFLECTIONS SHORTLY AFTER MARRIAGE, 1668

February: 10. By marriage all my former youthful desires were cured, and extravagant thoughts ceased. I found it a remedy; but cares came on me, yet without distraction. I found my wife perfectly devoted to please me, and I blessed God for giving me one with a meek and quiet spirit, and well disposed, and apt to take in the best things. I found she was patient under her sickness, and willing to hear any instruction from me. The Lord confirm that which is good in her, and teach her more! And let us both draw in Christ's yoke till death. Amen.

Cambridge University Library, MS Add. 8499, f. 122.

24 THE COUNTESS OF WARWICK (MARY RICH) DESCRIBES HER HUSBAND'S LAST ILLNESS AND DEATH, 1673

[*June*] 21) . . . My Lord being this day very ill, I was taken up in my attendance upon him, but had some returns to God by short ejaculations. This evening my Lord without any occasion given him fell suddenly into a most violent passion with me, wherein he expressed himself more provokingly bitter {Jade} than I remember ever in my life to have heard him. I was much surprised at it, but found nothing of passion in myself, though I was much troubled at the unkindness of it. (O Lord from my soul I bless thee for keeping me from returning railing for railing, and for enabling me to obey thy inspired precept of overcoming evil with good.) Afterwards I committed my soul to God.

[*July*] 8) In the morning (as soon as Sir Walter and my Lady St Johns were gone) I retired and prayed, but was in a much more than usual manner backward to the duty and distracted in it. Afterwards, my Lord being ill, I was busy in attending him; and hearing him break out in swearing, I was much troubled to hear him to offend God so, and with much mildness desired him he would forbear offending God in that bold way. But for my doing so he fell in a much more passionate manner upon me than ordinary, and vented against me more passionate words than ever I heard him {whore} and forbid my giving him good counsel. I was by God's goodness to me kept from answering one word again, and I was enabled to go on in doing my duty to him, returning good for evil. (O Lord from my soul I bless thee for comforting me with bringing that place to my mind, that if ye do well and suffer for it and take it patiently, this is acceptable to God.)

14) In the morning read and prayed; I was dull and distracted in the duty. In the afternoon was employed in tending my sick Lord. Whilst I was so, without any manner of occasion given by me, he broke out into most violent passionate expressions {strawberries, hate sight},[1] wherein he was most provokingly

---

[1] The diaries are annotated, and some of the incidents recorded in them listed, in another hand (here distinguished as 'B'), probably that of William Woodrooffe, son of the earl's chaplain, Thomas Woodrooffe. See C.F. Smith, *Mary Rich, Countess of Warwick*

bitter. I was enabled to forbear giving him one passionate word, but endeavoured by soft answers to turn away wrath and returned good for evil; but whilst I was doing so, I found myself so overcome with grief that I wept exceedingly and found myself in an extraordinary manner cast down by my affliction. But I instantly retired, and with many tears begged of God support under, and a sanctified improvement of, my affliction. I found after I had done so some more composedness of mind. (O Lord I beseech thee humble me more for the great inward disturbance I found in myself though by thy goodness to me I was kept from breaking out.)

27) . . . was much to my trouble by my Lord's illness kept from having any retiring time. Whilst I was tending him, he falling into a sudden passion, and in it breaking out to the dishonour of God, after it was over I did with great respect beseech him to forbear offending God; upon which he then broke out of a sudden to speak like the piercing of a sword to me. I was enabled not only to bear it patiently, but returned good for his ill, and to strive to overcome him that way. (O Lord, from my soul I bless thee for enabling me to endeavour to overcome evil with good.)

[*August*] 2) . . . The afternoon I spent much of it in private converse with my brother Robin;[2] had much good and edifying discourse from him. . . .

6) In the morning (as soon as my Lord Ranelagh was gone) I retired into the wilderness[3] to meditate. I did so of my at this time sadly afflicted condition, being very much and almost sinkingly oppressed with the unkindness I met with. I did examine myself very strictly wherefore God did contend with me; and after I had done so, I went to pray. I was enabled to pour out my soul in prayer to God, and God was pleased to

---

(1625–1678): Her Family and Friends (Longmans, Green and Co., London, 1901), p. 168. A 'B' note on this cryptic interlineation, on f. 212ᵛ, reads 'Difference about strawberries & Lo. said he hated ye sight of her.' Yet the interlineation as it stands suggests that Warwick might equally well have said he hated the sight of strawberries.

[2] Robert Boyle (1627–91), the famous natural philosopher. The diary records the visits to Leighs, the Riches' home, of a steady stream of friends and relatives, many of whom do not appear in these extracts.

[3] This was a wooded hill to which Lady Warwick retired for meditation and prayer. See Smith, *Mary Rich, Countess of Warwick*, p. 107.

give me the sacrifice of a broken heart. I was this morning large in the confession of my sins, but those which in an especial manner I bemoaned was my undutifulness to my father in my youth and my having over-loved that endeared relation from which I now met with so much unkindness. . . .

12) . . . In the evening I retired and meditated upon my death, and prayed to be fitted for it. Whilst I was doing so, I was of a sudden sent for to come to my Lord. When I came to him, I was extraordinarily disordered and frighted, finding him not able to speak; nor did he know anybody. He was (as I was afterwards informed) of a sudden as he was drawn about in his chair in the garden heard to rattle in his throat; and when his servant Lawrence, {a footman} that drew him, looked upon him, they found he was fallen into a swoon.[4] Upon which, my Sister Ranelagh being called (who was near), and bringing some quick spirits and holding them to his nose, and pouring down some cordial waters, he was, just when I came, brought to life again. But after I came and that we had laid him into his bed, yet he continued for a long time not to know anybody, nor to be heard to speak that we could understand him, though he strove to do so. I was very much disordered at this grievous sight, and wept much, and with much earnestness besought the Lord to restore him to the use of his reason, and to spare his life, that he might recover strength before he goes from hence and shall be no more seen. Afterwards God was pleased to hear my prayer, and by giving him some rest to restore him to the use of his reason again, though his memory was not yet right. (O Lord from my soul I bless thee for it; Lord write a law of thankfulness in my heart for this great mercy.)[5]

13) . . . I poured out my soul to God for mercy for my poor afflicted husband's soul, which I begged with tears, following exceeding hard after God for repentance for him, and that he would spare his life to me. All this day I was attending of him, and after sent the expirations of my soul to God for my husband's salvation. This day God was pleased to bring him well to his senses and memory again. . . .

[4] *sond.*
[5] Two 'B' annotations on this day: 'I saw him ab[t] y[e] stables a little before this fit came upon him, he look'd like Death' and 'the 52[d] and last sickness'.

15) In the morning I prayed; the desires of my heart went out after God in prayer, and with much fervency did I beg repentance and remission of sins for my poor husband; who about noon, as Doctor Micklethwait[6] and I were sitting by his bed, in one moment without giving us the least warning fell into a sad fit again of convulsions, wherein his face was so [drawn?] that it was very terrible to me to behold it. He continued long in it, though all things the Doctor directed were done to bring him to life again, in which I assisted, but seeing him not come in so long time I was more frighted and troubled than I remember ever to have been in my life; but at last I retired, and in a short but fervent prayer poured out my heart to God to bring him out of that terrible fit, and to restore him to the use of his reason, that he might not die senseless, but be prepared for death before he was snatched away by it. I shed many tears in the duty, and it pleased God that at last he came again to himself pretty well. I was all day constant in my attendance upon him, and often as I could get an opportunity called upon him, and minded him of looking to make his peace with God, till he forbade my doing so (which was a trouble to me). But Doctor Walker[7] coming (which I had purposely sent for to assist him in his soul concernments) spake to him, giving him much good counsel which he could not neither with patience bear; the hearing that and him break out again with great violence by cursing and swearing did to a very high degree afflict me, and made me in an extraordinary awakened manner wrestle with God with many tears again for him. After supper I committed my soul to God.

20) . . . I got an opportunity to speak to my Lord about his soul concernment, and did with much plainness tell him of the great danger he had been in and how loud a call it was from God to prepare for death by making his peace with him, and did with much humility beseech him that he would repent, and never more offend God by swearing and cursing, who had been so gracious as to give him a new life. It pleased God, much to my comfort, to make him hear me patiently, which that he might do I had by prayer begged of God, and to make him

---

[6] So corrected by 'B': Lady Warwick wrote *Middellthwart* or (elsewhere) *Midellthaute*.
[7] Anthony Walker DD, Rector of Fyfield (Essex) 1662–92, formerly chaplain to the Earl of Warwick, d. 1692.

extremely affected with what I said, and startled to hear what sad fits he had had, which he did not at all remember anything of what had passed till I now informed him of it. In the afternoon was tending my Lord; after supper I committed my soul to God. This day my Lord said many kind things to me, and said he would make me amends for his unkindness formerly.

23) . . . of a sudden my poor Lord fell again into one of his sad fits of convulsions, at which I was in an extraordinary manner frighted, and sent away instantly for Doctor Micklethwait to London to join with Doctor Swallow, who was to my great comfort with him, coming in just as he fell into his fit. All that art could do was used to bring him again, but the fit had to so high a degree weakened his poor weak body, before wasted to a mere skeleton, that the Doctor and all of us about him thought he would instantly have died. I was at that sad spectacle so affected as I cannot express, and poured out many prayers to God with many tears for the yet saving his life (if it were agreeable with his will) and in an especial manner I begged his salvation, and the bringing him to the use of his reason again. At last it pleased God by those cordials that were given him to bring him to life again, but yet he continued much disturbed in his head. I sat up that night with him, in which, though he slept, yet he did not come to the perfect use of his reason, which was great grief to me.

Bartholomew Day, August the 24) Sunday morning as soon as up I retired, and finding my poor Lord still extraordinary weak, and in a dangerous condition, was in an extraordinary manner sad and troubled. I retired then and prayed. I was enabled to pour out my soul in prayer to God for his salvation, which I begged with many tears. . . . Towards [evening?] my Lord grew much worse, and when Doctor Micklethwait came that night from London, he judged him in a very dangerous condition, which did in an extraordinary manner afflict me. I did mightily cry to God for mercy for his soul, and got Mr Woodrooffe[8] and many more good people to join with me to beg mercy for his soul; and I did too mightily wrestle with God to bring him to the perfect use of his reason again, and to show him (if it were

[8] Or Woodruffe (spelt by Lady Warwick *Woodrooffe, Wodrof, Woodroofe*), Thomas, chaplain to the Earl of Warwick, 1660–73, d. 1689.

his blessed will) some token for good before he took him from hence; and when I saw him come at any time to himself did earnestly beseech him that though he could not speak without difficulty he would lift up his heart to God for mercy; and once when I did so, he answered me in a very serious and [a?]wakened frame, 'So I do, so I do,' and called upon me to pray for him, which was a great comfort to me. After the Doctor came, he and Doctor Swallow used a great many unsuccessful remedies, for my poor husband still continued weak, and being so very weak as he was[9] found himself unable to bring up the phlegm that did even choke him. Thus he continued till about ten or 11 o'clock at night, and then was taken with another violent convulsion fit, out of which, though all possible remedies were by both the doctors tried, he never came well out, but with that and the phlegm {together} died about 12 o'clock that night. I was not in the room when he did so, having by God's mercy to me a sudden motion put into mind to go out of the room, which I did afterwards, being kept by my Sister Ranelagh's care from going in when he was a dying. This sad news was first told me by Doctor Micklethwait. I received it with unexpressable grief, and found myself more sadly afflicted than ever in all my life I was, but did sincerely strive with my passion, and endeavoured to submit to God's will now it was determined, and mightily prayed to him to enable me to do so; but this night with grief I found myself very ill. (O Lord, make up this loss to me by being all in all unto me.)

25) This morning having not slept I found myself very ill and in a very sadly afflicted condition, but yet found much inward comfort that I had done my duty to him and had neglected nothing for either his soul or body. This day I was forced, in order to his funeral, to hear my dear husband's will read, which whilst I was hearing did in an extraordinary manner afflict me; though by hearing it I was informed he had for my life given me all his estate, yet the loss of his person was to me so very grievous that all was as nothing to me now he was gone. I spent this whole day in a very stunned[10] and astonished condition, not being yet enough recollected to do any spiritual duty as I ought

[9] *was* apparently deleted here.
[10] *stoned.*

to do, or as formerly I use to do. I had many good and Christian friends that came to visit me and did endeavour by good counsel to comfort me, and some of the ministers [pr?]ayed with me.

26) In the morning I found myself much bodily discomposed, having never been able to take any rest or to eat, my stomach being with my extraordinary grief quite gone, and I finding such terrible tremblings of heart that I was much discomposed; but did still strive to bear with Christian patience what God had laid upon me. I continued all this day in my bed much discomposed and stunned, but got Mr Warren to pray with me. The desires of my heart went out to God in that prayer, and after supper I committed my soul to God.

27) In the morning found myself still much bodily discomposed, having not yet been able to sleep; and finding still that great discomposure in my head, I prayed, but was dull in all I did; got Mr Woodrooffe to pray with me, but still continued, much to my trouble, in that dead and stupid frame.

29) This morning it pleased God that I waked something better, having by God's mercy to me got some rest. . . .

[*September*] 9) In the morning found myself in an extraordinary manner grieved and oppressed with melancholy, this being the day my dear husband's body was to be buried at Felsted. I wept exceedingly, and found it very hard to bear up this day, being often passionately affected to think he was gone to his cold bed of dust. But at last I was able with some tolerable composure of mind to think upon my own death, and then retired to God, and prayed with some fervency, that now he had brought death into my own bed, and taken by it from me my dear husband, I might more than ever think upon and prepare for my own end; but finding still after doing so my mind too passionately affected, I did meditate upon eternal glory, and I found the consideration that my afflictions were but momentary, and my happiness hereafter would be eternal, did in some weak measure revive my weak body and made me to rejoice in hopes of future glory, even upon {one of the}[11] saddest days that I ever yet saw, in which I buried my husband decently and honourably, and gave very considerably to the poor of the two parishes[12] in which

---

[11] *one of the* replaces *this*.

[12] 'B': 'viz. Felsted & Little-Leighs'.

Leighs stands. (O Lord, though thou hast now separated me from my dear husband with whom I lived more than thirty-two years, yet I beseech thee make up this dear relation and all I have before parted with in thyself, by being unto me all in all, infinitely above all, and better than all.)

British Library, MS Add. 27353, ff. 186[r–v], 192[r–v], 194[r–v], 198[r], 200[r], 202[r], 205[v]–206[r], 207[r–v], 210[r], 211[r]–212[r], 214[r]–216[v], 221[r]–222[r].

25   THOMAS JOLLY'S FOURTH WIFE'S DEATH, 1675

. . . Though my dear wife did much suspect it would cost her life if ever a fever took her, and the fever was rife in the neighbouring village, yet the importunity of her sister in a fever prevailed with us that I let her go to and attend upon her sister for some time. The fever soon after seized on my wife, and the scurvy withal, which she was subject to. Seven days she was gently handled, and we had hopeful signs of her recovery. On the eighth day it altered with her as to her body, more as to her spirit; that evening and the morning after she expressed her good hope concerning her spiritual condition upon the manifold experience she had of God's fatherly care ever since she had taken him to be her father, withal bewailing her manifold failings, especially her inconstancy[1] in secret duties and in walking amidst her house as she ought, yet comforting herself in this, that she had not wickedly departed from her God. She spake to all about her and about her dissolution without any distraction, though she was not without temptation. The grace of God was wonderful in this thing, for her ordinary frame in health was doubling[2] and she had a dread of death beforetime above ordinary; but especially his grace was wonderful in that he was pleased to overlook her infirmity and afford his good presence to her much more than in her former sickness. On the Lord's day following she was much endeavouring to get above her affliction and not to heed her vile body, that she might get into the spirit of the day and keep a Sabbath to the Lord, acknowledging his great love to her,

---

[1] *inconsistancy* in edition, presumably a mistake.
[2] Perhaps a mistake for 'doubting'.

desiring to be refreshed therewith. She very much had her desire granted, for she said it was the best Sabbath she ever enjoyed, and she did much honour God in it. On the eleventh day she had a lightening in the morning as to her body, so that she had thoughts of a recovery and a desire thereof upon my account; this might be the occasion of her spirits not being carried on in the same strain, and indeed she was not now altogether so sensible. On the twelfth day after a weary night she told me she was sorry she could give me no better account as to her outward condition, yet was she so sensible as to mind me of a promise I had made to visit a sick person that day. About 8 a clock upon the eighth of fourth month she quietly slept in the Lord, having finished the forty-second year of her age (I think to a very day). She was eminent in denying herself for the Gospel's sake to the leaving of all her relations, from whom she had many temptations, and to the doing of service on that account. She lost not by it, for God did signally own and honour her. She took delight in doing good to all, which made her generally and greatly beloved and bewailed. She was a most loving wife and tender nurse to me; if she at any time offended me, she could not be quiet until she had acknowledged her offence and was reconciled. She was cordially loving and very faithful to my children which I had by my former wife. She had a dear love for all the Lord's people, more especially for this people, whom she desired to live and die with. She had a most hospitable spirit towards those who visited us, especially towards good people, more especially towards ministers. She had a most ardent affection towards her relations, especially as to their eternal estate, begging a blessing to them (at her departure) and desiring her death might be life at least to some of them. When anything pressed her sore, her way was to get alone and pour out her soul to God; indeed she had notable experience of God helping her in ordinary, but she took more special notice of his signal owning of her in some secret days, or some extraordinary occasions. She had her infirmities which at times appeared and which she was very sensible of; it's probable she might have met with temptations too hard for her, yea she might have been a temptation to me if she had longer continued with me. The day following I was torn in pieces with temptation, my head was so sore and sinking as was unexpressible and intolerable if it had continued, whether it was through the inordinacy[3] of my affection or my natural infirmity, through[4] weakness of grace or strength of temptation. On the evening of the day after I had some staying of my sinking, some binding up of my broken spirit, a little support, the tempter a little rebuked, was of no little account in that season; I thought my soul should never forget that distress I was then in and that relief I had from above thereupon. At the interring of my dead I felt suitableness of the thirty-ninth psalm to my case, and verses 7, 8, were more especially spoken to me. At a fast day under my roof upon this sad occasion my business was to get help in judging myself before the Lord that I might take just measures and feel the due weight of my affliction and sin, to humble myself before his judgement seat, which also is a mercy seat; that I might indeed repent and find grace in his sight. The Lord took away my wife formerly before the turn of the times, and those troubles ensued; when he took away my son he raised up comfort in my last wife and gave in public liberty.[5] That God would please now to raise up comfort to me in my children, bless the dispensation to her surviving relations, but especially that I might be comforted in Jerusalem. Her text she left to be preached upon was Psalm 73, 24, was of special use to my soul in this trial; another friend leaving this as her funeral text for me to preach upon, the Lord did keep me that I was not borne down with the violence of the temptation nor did carry unbecomingly in any respect.

Fishwick (ed.), *Note Book of Rev. Thomas Jolly*, pp. 21–4.

26 EPISODES IN THE UNHAPPY MARRIED LIFE OF MRS ELIZABETH FREKE, 1682–5

[*1682*] ⟨July 7⟩[1] So soon as I came to my dear father he made me promise him that I would not leave him whilst I lived, which

---

[3] *inordinary*, in edition, preumably a mistake.

[4] *though* in edition, presumably a mistake.

[5] His third wife died in 1656; 'public liberty' perhaps refers to the 1672 Declaration of Indulgence. His first son, Thomas, died in 1671. I have moved the semi-colon which Fishwick placed after 'son'.

---

[1] The previous paragraph says that she arrived on 24 May.

I readily and gladly did. And then he bid me take no care, for
I should want for nothing in[2] his life, who made [h]is words
good with the greatest kindness to me and my son. A great
alteration it was to what I found in Ireland from a husband; and
on my looking a little melancholy on some past reflections, he
fancied it was my want of money, and my dear father without
saying a word to me went up into his closet ⟨August 15⟩ a[nd]
brought me down presently in two bags two hundred pounds,
which (200*ll*) he charged me to keep private from my husband's
knowledge and buy needles and pins with it.

This was very kind in my father, and which the very next
post I informed Mr Freke[3] of, who presently found a use for it.
But I, that had not had two and twenty shillings from my
husband in the last two and twenty months I were in Ireland
with my son, kept it for my own use; which, with more my
father had given me and the interest, all which made up eight
hundred pounds,[4] took from me the year after my son married,
and so left me at Bilney a beggar again.

⟨1682/3 February 18⟩ About the middle of February Mr Freke
came to my father's to Hannington, unknown to me, and to
fetch me and my son over for Ireland; but, on the ill usage I had
there suffered from them,[5] I positively refused ever more going
with him, alleging my promise to my dear father and their
unkindness to me whenever I were in their power of command,[5]
besides his last parting wish at Kinsale, which was[6] etc. This
stuck deep in my stomach, though to this day (1702)[7] I never
let my father know the least of difference between us, or any
unkind usage from the family I have received in that kingdom
or elsewhere, for fear of grieving of him.

⟨1683 July 24:⟩ But prepared to go for Ireland with Mr Freke
again, when, I taking my last leave of my dearest father, he gave

---

[2] *his his* in MS.

[3] Usually *Frek* in MS.

[4] Supply 'which Mr Freke' or similar phrase to make sense of this passage.

[5] *them*, *their* and *their* in this sentence were altered from *him*, *his* and *his*. Between 1702
and 1712, Mrs Freke apparently added some phrases to this section of her manuscript
and also made some deletions and alterations. Many of the latter, perhaps made after
his death in 1706, removed harsh remarks about her husband's behaviour.

[6] *that he might never see my face more* deleted.

[7] The date, repeated at the top of the next page, was there altered to 1712.

me up the bond Mr Freke was bound for to him of a thousand pounds he borrowed on the purchase of Rathbarry, for which he had only my thanks—for that and all his other blessings to me since I married.

Thus having stayed about thirteen months with my dearest father and the last time I ever saw him I went Thursday 25 of July to Bristol with Mr Freke . . .

⟨1683/4 January 1⟩ My dear father sent me into Ireland a hundred pounds for a New Year's gift, it being my unhappy birthday, and ordered me that if Mr Freke meddled with it, it should be lost, or he to answer it with the Irish interest to my son. But Mr Freke took it from me, and I were fain to make it good to my son with the full Irish interest the day after he was of age, when I gave him two hundred pounds and five pound for a purse to put it in, Eliz. Freke [paid?] (1696).

About the 24 of February, and the dreadful hard winter, my dear father sent to me to come to him to Hannington with my husband and family, where I should meet my two sisters the Lady Norton and my Sister Austin, a[nd] be merry there together a little before he died; and that he would pay the charge of my journey, and give me his last blessing. . . .

But oh, the saddest of fates that ever attended mortal was mine, for on the 24 of April my God took to himself by death my dear dearest father, to my great loss, grief and unspeakable sorrow, before I could get a ship to see him and receive his last blessing, which of all things in this world I desired. But my God knew what was best for me, for in the eighty-ninth year of his age he joyfully gave up his soul into the hand of his God, and his body to be privately interred in the chancel of Hannington. . . .

Being Monday, and the 7 of July, Mr Freke and I took shipping at Kinsale in a man of war with Captain Clemont, and came round to England by long sea; that night we were most grievously stormed, but by God's great mercy (after we were like to be lost on the Goodwin Sands near Dover) we were all safe landed at Billingsgate in London the Saturday following,⟨12⟩ for which great mercy I humbly thank my great and good God.

⟨August 4⟩ Mr Freke went into Norfolk,[8] and returned to

---

[8] To visit the West Bilney estate.

London again the seventeenth of August, leaving me a lodger in Brownlow Street in the house with my Cousin Clayton, where I lay about ten weeks and never had his company at dinner with me ten times, which I cannot forget, it was so grievous to me.

⟨September 17⟩ Mr Freke went again for Ireland with the Lord Inchiquin, unknown to me till the night before he went. And left me with my son and a man and maid at lodgings at Mrs Murry's in Brownlow Street to shift for myself and family, declaring the morning he left me, before his nephew Barnard and my Cousin Clayton and the three Gookins, with several others, that his estate in Norfolk would not find him in bread and cheese, besides the charges of it, which estate is now let for four hundred and fifty pounds a year (1712)[9] and bought by my dear father for the yearly rent of 526 pound a year. . . .[10]

⟨September 28⟩ Being thus left by my husband to shift for myself and family, and but fifteen pounds in the world . . . I were forced to try my fortune amongst my friends, and hearing my dear Sister Austin was very ill, and brought to bed of a dead child, I went down to Tenterden to my dear sister and brother about the 15 of October, making a virtue of necessity by being thrown off,[11] but with my dear sister I stayed, with all the kindness imaginable, till the 15 of June following . . .

[*Frustrated in her efforts to go to West Bilney first by Monmouth's rebellion and then by her son Ralph's smallpox, Mrs Freke spent the summer of 1685 with her sister Lady Norton.*]

Thus left by Mr Freke I attempted again to seek my fortune to Bilney to seek my bread, where on the 29 of September I came with my son and three servants to Lynn, where I boarded in private lodgings till the eight of February following.

⟨December 24⟩ Mr Freke came over by Dublin from Ireland, I having hardly heard of him or from him in three quarters of a year. As he came unlooked for by me, so he was very angry with me for being on this side of the country, though in all his times of his being from me, he never took care for a penny for my subsistence or his son's, for which God forgive him.

---

[9] Altered from *1702*.
[10] A little later appears the added note '& in 1710 is lett for: 400*li*'.
[11] *by my unkind husband, who never in his life took any care for me, or what I did* deleted.

My husband's errand for England was to join with him in the sale of West Bilney to Sir Standish Harts Tongue, for the like in Ireland; but I being left the only trustee for myself and my son, God gave me the courage to keep what I had, rather than part with it and be kept by the charity of my friends, or trust to his or any one's kindness; so in a great anger Mr Freke left me alone again and went for Ireland, where he stayed from me almost two years.

British Library, MS Add. 45718, ff. 50ᵛ–52ʳ, 53ʳ.

27 SOME INCIDENTS FROM THE TURBULENT MARRIED LIFE OF JOHN AND ALICE RICHARDS OF WARMWELL, 1699–1701

[*The following passages are written for the most part in rather bad Italian. Translated portions are in italic here, with words supplied by the editor in roman within brackets.*]

Tuesday the 12th ditto [September 1699]. *This evening A.*[1] *was mad as usual about M.,*[2] *telling me that I loved her more than herself, and that because of the ill-treatment in this house, [she] had often [thought] of killing herself.*

Friday the 15th December 1699. *This morning ecla*[1] *was mad to the greatest degree, telling me that I had got into such a bad humour that in a short while nobody would serve me, and many other insolent, insupportable speeches which shall cost her dear.*

Wednesday the 3d ditto [January 1700]. *This evening I beat Jack for his bad behaviour in play, and upon that ecl.*[1] *showed herself so insolent that I put her out of the room etc.*

Wednesday the 14 ditto [February]. *At table I had words with elca*[1] *about my son John, who*[3] *in the end became extravagant, and the next day after dinner [downstairs?*[4]*] she went back to renewing the quarrel in a blustering fashion.*

---

[1] His wife Alice or Alce.
[2] Mary Lillington?
[3] *che*, presumably referring to Alice.
[4] [*in basso?*]

Friday the 23th. *Having kept my distance for two days [with?] Ecla, she said to me this morning* [that] *if I* did not mend my manners *before long she declared*[5] *etc. Upon which insolence, losing all patience, I burnt my will before her eyes.*

Sunday morning the 21th ditto [July]. *Thomas shat*[6] *in bed, and Alce made herself mad because of that mishap. Tonight I slept in* cellar chamber *to be at rest from ecla.*

Thursday the 3d October. . . . *this night I made my* [own] *bed, being angry with ecla.*

Monday the 21th Ditto. . . . This afternoon *Ecla was mad to the greatest degree,* and roared all the while till night, when [*I locked her?*[7]] in dining-room.

Monday the 9th ditto [December 1700] Mr Traheron's late servant maid came to me at the coffee house in Dorchester to ask if I wanted a servant. That evening relating it to my Alce, she began to suspect something extraordinary in it, and showing her old humour, grew extravagant etc. *as usual. . . .*

Monday the 19th [May 1701] *Today ecla became mad again to the greatest degree and treated me like a slave for nothing.*

Monday the 26 ditto Mary Lillington came hither.

Sunday the 29th ditto [June] [*I kissed Mary Lillington for the first time?*[8]]

Dorchester, Dorset Record Office, MS D. 884, ff. 112, 130,132, 137–8, 154, 161–2, 166, 180, 181, 185.

28   EDMUND AND SARAH HARROLD, 1712

[*Mrs Harrold was to give birth to their daughter Sarah on 23 November.*]

[*June*] 4 Finished one of Mr Chadwick's wigs, and begun of another. I've been taken up with a review of my life past since 1709, in which I find things a many to humble me, as well as raise me up. I pray God it may have this effect[1] on me, to mend

[5] *se dichiarava.*
[6] *cacava.*
[7] *Lei seravassi.*
[8] *Besai M: L: pr[i]me vez.*

---

[1] *affect.*

what I have in my power to mend for the time to come. Amen. This day Tim Runigar and Mr Jones fought. I would fain had gone to Mr Jones house, but my wife would not hear on't, so I stayed within.

8th This being White Sunday, I had thought to had stayed sacrament, and had but for this reason: my wife would have said that I was over presumptuous and would wonder how I durst receive weekly. Indeed I know it's my duty as oft as the Church provides to come and it was not for any irregularity in living this week or disorder of mind, but for fear of giving offence to my weak wife that I absented myself, so I sinned for peace. . . .

10 Remarkable for Peter Nedom's being drowned, and Peter Downes being married to Grace Hulme. My wife and I was very merry there at night. On the 9th at night I did wife two times couch and bed in an hour an[d] half time.

16 . . . I swapped one wig with Robert Parley of Whitehaven for one wig and two boxes, long ones of wood. . . . came in almost one a clock.[2] Swapped and unswapped with Robert Parley to please wife. . . .

17 . . . My mother is very ill and my wife carries well to her. . . .

18 Wife was busy; I went [to] see Mother . . . Wife over-tired and ill this night.

19 . . . I smoked one pipe at Aunt's, came home, and about eleven I enjoy wife etc. . . .

20 . . . Both scolded and did wife two times got [?] we was merry at last.

25 . . . I observe that it's best to keep good decorum and to please wife; it makes everything pleasant and easy . . .

[*July*] 7 This morn I had my old melancholy pain seized on me, with a longing desire for drink . . . I spent 2*d* with Hall etc., then 4*d* with Mr Allen, 'torney; then fought with S.B. at Jane Win's about chat; then had a [hurry?] with wife on [bed?] etc.; then went into the ditch a ramble—Key, Dragon, and Castle, and Lion, till near 12 [*o*']clock, till I was ill drunken; cost me 4*d*½ from 6 till 12. I made myself a great fool, etc.

---

[2] He had been drinking.

8 This day I lay in bed till almost 11 clock . . . I've drawn my wig but cannot weave. I've drunk no ale today, yet on 6 at night I'm vexed about my ramble last night. I've missed pub[lic?] priv[ate?] prayer two times. It's a very great trouble to me that I thus expose myself, hurt my body, offend against God, set bad example, torment my mind and break my rules, make myself a laughing-stock to men, grieve the Holy Spirit, disorder my family, fret my wife (now quick), which is all against my own mind when sober, besides loss of my credit and reputation in the world. What must I do? What can I do? Use the creatures and I abuse them, be sure, before I done. Use them not, and I'm like nobody else. I'm resolved what to do—not to drink any in a morning in the alehouse {a very good rule if followed} upon no occasion whatever for the time [*to*] come, which that [*I*] may do I beg on God his gracious assistance to withstand temptations with courage. There [*is*] nothing too hard for willing mind and virtuous inclinations, knowing how pleasant it is to conquer one's self and passions. Grant O God that I may overcome my vices and for the time to come attain the contrary virtues and this I beg for Jesus Christ his sake. Amen. I'll go to prayers now.

14 . . . I writ two letters to Warrington to Unsworth and Bonnor, then I read them to wife; she's well pleased thus far. A[*t*] last sent the two letters . . .

16 . . . [*on his return home*] wife was in bed; she's been ill two or three days and nights but I hope she's better.

23 . . . came home, read some in Sherlock[3] and did wife new fashion . . .

25 . . . I came home, went to bed, did wife new fashion, fell asleep . . .

26 . . . About quarter past ten my wife was kneading and she had teemed the berm off o'th two buled pot,[4] a new one, which she set down in the tub quickly. It gave a crack. 'What[*'s*] that?,' said she, 'is that the pot?' Says Sarah Sharples, 'Ay, and it's a

---

[3] Almost certainly William Sherlock (1641–1707), master of the Temple, dean of St Paul's, and author of discourses concerning death and judgement.

[4] *tem'd*: poured; *berm*: barm, the froth from the top of fermenting malt liquors, used for leavening bread; *buled*: handled.

sign of death,' says she. So as the[y] was talking it gave two
cracks more. At last my wife took up the pot and rung it and
it is as sound as can be. I have told several people. Some are of
one opinion and some another. Some says it's ominous, others
not; but I have noted it down in order to observe the event
concerning theirs or our families to come. . . . did her old
fashion.

[27] . . . came home, read some of Sherlock, went to bed and
did wife new fashion: 'tis most convenient at this time. Fell
asleep.

30 . . . came at ten, went to bed, did wife old fashion, then
fell asleep.

31st . . . ruffled with wife['s] clamour about my last drunken
bout at So's, and likewise about starch and gagers[5] . . .

[*August*] 5 . . . My wife was ill indeed; the lads, with a false
alarum, raised the street about thieves. . . .

6 . . . Spent 4*d*, came home at quarter past ten, went to bed,
did wife old fashion. . . . [*Several more entries of the same sort,
including references to both 'new' and 'old' fashions, are scattered through
August.*]

September the 1st in morning I was full of pain and dull and
melancholy. The very first thing that wife said was about dunning
T.C. and Robert Bradshaw, which I did; but T.C. I thought
must be a drinking bout with Robert Morton, which was so;
for after dinner wife saw Robert Morton go to T.C.'s, who[6]
then never rested till I had seen them, who ordered me to Golden
Key, Blomily's, where we had a sad tug for't; but a[t] last passion
ceased, and we brought T.C. to do fair things and order a note
of particulars to be drawn, and he would pay in time by 12*d* a
time. . . .

6 . . . did wife after a scolding bout:[2] now we are friends.

8 . . . did wife and talk a long time; we was pleasant.

11 . . . remarkable for my wife and I make a bargain; she's to
refrain washing clothes,[7] and I'm to refrain drinking to excess,

---

[5] *gageers* (?).
[6] Mrs Harrold.
[7] Presumably Harrold's drinking had made it necessary for her to take in washing.

till January the 1st, and we have shaked hands and kissed as a ratification of the same. . . .

14 My wife was very ill; I stayed from church both ends to attend on her. . . .

Manchester, Chetham's Library, MS Mun.A.2.137 (unfoliated). The entries for each day run on in continuous text in manuscript.

29   EDMUND HARROLD ON BEREAVEMENT AND WIDOWHOOD, 1712–13

[*1712, December*] 17 My wife lay a dying from 11 this day till 9 a clock on the 18 in the morn; then she died in my arms, on pillows. Relations most by. She went suddenly, and was sensible till quarter of an hour before she died. I have given her work day clothes to Mother Boardman[1] and Betty Cook, our servant now. Relations thinks best to bury her at meetin[g]-place in Plungeon Field, so I will. According to her mind,[2] I'm making me a black suit[3] on her black mantue[4] and petticoat I bought her on Edwards, and if God gives life and health I will wear them for her sake. I beseech[5] God Almighty who has taken my dear assistant from me to assist me with grace and wisdom to live religiously and virtuously and to eye his providence in this dispensation and to weigh and consider before I act anything, and the Lord direct me to the best. Amen.

19 This day, at about half hour past four at night, my wife Sarah was carried to the meet[ing]-place in Plungeon Field to be buried, and Parson Birch preached on this etc.—'Be ye also ready, for ye know not at what hour the Son of Man cometh.' . . . Then we came home and had all the wakers and her acquaintance that I could get to supper and treated them handsomely, but was very ill myself; children wept sore, and my condition is very melancholy. I gave her bible to Sister

---

[1] Mother of his just deceased wife Sarah.
[2] *according to her mind:* it is not clear how this sentence should be punctuated, and the phrase may refer to the burial place rather than the black suit.
[3] *shute.*
[4] *mantue:* mantua or manteau, a loose upper garment, mantle or cloak.
[5] *besweech.*

Martha and her white gloves to Mary, her mother and Betty her worst clothes, and I have done and will do, if I live, all her mind.

20 I had a very midering day.

21st. Sunday. Very ill in forenoon; I went to church in afternoon; heard Mr Copley on 'Rejoice in the Lord always, and again I say rejoice,' but in my circumstances it did not relish very well to nature then, though I own it my duty so to do and will do so to my power at all times and in all conditions.

22 Ill out of order. Abram promised to get me a housekeeper of A[*nn*] Moore, so I went with him to Salford, and him and I and Coz. J. [Parin?] was three hours at side of chapel, but at last she came. The first sight we was very merry; cost 2*s* on five or six persons.

23 Very busy; paid Mr Birch 10*s* for preaching wife's funeral.

24 Christmas Eve. Paid Mrs Smiths for my mourning clothes 11*s* in full.

25 Had my Sarah and nurse to dinner, and Mother Boardman; gave Mary Ashton and Nurse Cather one pair of gloves of wife's for memorial. . . . Heard no sermon today for business and trouble. Then I dressed at noon; then I saw Coz. J. [Parin?] with discouragement about Ann. Then I went to prayers Old Church at night. Then to Father Bancroft's[6] to supper one hour and half. Then who should come but Ann. She spent 2*d* with me. Then I sent for the Jolly Hart, could not find him, but he came at last. We was merry four hours. Agreed for her to come to be my housekeeper.[7] Much eased in mind.

26 . . . I was in drink and ramble, yet came staunch[8] home . . .

31 For going at quarter past seven to Calf's Head Club, and ended the old year with drunkenness and quarrelling with Father and Brother Bancroft . . . talk on Anna's[9] education and bringing up and portion. I very ill.

January 1st 1712 [*1713*] I entered on this year with bad health, a troubled mind and scant of money . . . [*References to sickness,*

---

[6] Joseph, father of his first wife, Alice Bancroft.
[7] This arrangement fell through.
[8] *stanch*.
[9] Harrold entrusted Anna, presumably his daughter by his first wife, to the care of Father Bancroft on the following 24 June.

depression and drunkenness are common in the entries of the following weeks.]

6 . . . nobody at home but self; children and Betty at Gorton. . . .

14 Ill this morning . . . no servant yet but Betty. I'm upon new measures. . . .

19 Went about a housekeeper to Mee's and Crowder's and Coz. Throp's; there I had a lecture for my debauches the month past, and instead of counsel, discouragement in my condition. . . .

23 Betty Cook went; Alice Hardman came. . . .

30 Went none to church, but drank all day 31 and thus I ended the month of January with loss, grief, shame and pain.

[*March*] 5 . . . Shaved three heads, dressed nine wigs, and worked close. All persuades me not to meddle with widow and children, but a bachelor with some money, etc. . . .

8 . . . I'm now beginning to be uneasy with myself, and begin to think of women again. I pray God direct me to do wisely and send me a good one or none; if it be his will, I must have one. . . .

13 . . . I've seen Ellen at Coll[ege?] tonight, kept her Lent company one hour 1/2; then saw another soft soul, as I think, in Salford; and thus I ramble on about matters, but cannot settle. I pray God direct me for the best; he knows best etc.

[*Nothing came of Harrold's interest in Ellen. He was married to his third wife, Ann Horrocks, on the following 22 August, apparently after less than three months' courtship.*]

Manchester, Chetham's Library, MS Mun.A.2.137.

III

Pregnancy, Childbirth and Infancy

Many of the fullest and most vivid descriptions in these diaries are those devoted to childbirth and the events which preceded and followed it. In them, writers gave particularly strong and spontaneous expression to feelings of anxiety, grief, relief and gratitude.

Some diarists made careful note of early signs of pregnancy and of life in the foetus (the 'quickening') (34, 35), though John Dee (30) seems to have been unusual in the assiduity with which he recorded his wife's menstruation. Predictions of the sex of children were sometimes made (34, 36); their basis is unknown, and they were not always accurate. Expectant mothers often suffered from sickness or anxiety during pregnancy (28, 30, 34, 35). Second only to worries on the pregnant woman's own account were those surrounding the child (34, 36). Miscarriage was a feared and fairly common experience (35, 39).[1]

The help of other women during childbirth was considered essential, and a number were usually present. The services of a reliable midwife were naturally thought to be very important, and secured in advance if possible (31, 34, 36). Among midwives there were some differences of technique, for example in the choice of the best position for delivery (36).[2] Their skill was

---

[1] Macfarlane, *Family Life of Josselin*, p. 200, tabulates five miscarriages suffered by Mrs Josselin.

[2] See A. Eccles, *Obstetrics and Gynaecology in Tudor and Stuart England* (Croom Helm, London and Canberra, 1982), p. 91.

often insufficient to deal with the complications confronting them. Because he lived in London, Nehemiah Wallington, by no means a wealthy man, was able to call on the services of the famous man-midwife Peter Chamberlen during the difficult birth of his daughter Sarah in 1627 (32). The length of labour and the sharpness of the pain were mentioned by various writers (32, 33, 34, 35, 36, 39).

The danger of maternal death due to complications during birth or sepsis or puerperal fever afterwards was far higher than it is today. The most hazardous hours of life were those of birth and the ones immediately following it. The father, the man most closely concerned in the birth, was probably prevented by custom from assisting at the delivery in most cases. Confined to a neighbouring room where the news of the birth would be brought to him, he could suffer acute anxiety, somewhat assuaged, perhaps, by energetic prayer. This is most graphically conveyed in Samuel Woodforde's account, apparently written during the very time of labour (36; cf. 38, 39). Safe delivery was a cause for joy and relief, and perhaps some convivial celebration on the part of those who had attended the birth (34). The hour was often recorded; this was considered particularly important by parents who, like John Dee (30), were keen students of astral influences. Early facial comparisons might be made. After birth the mother might remain confined to her bed for several weeks, though during this period visits from neighbours and kinsfolk were customary (31). The rite of churching or thanksgiving was supposed to mark her return to the world (30, 33).

Diary testimony underlines the differences of attitude and practice in respect of baptism which existed in this period. The length of time between birth and baptism depended partly on the infant's prospects of survival, partly on the strength and nature of parents' and clergy's religious beliefs. Some children who looked as though they might shortly die, and the offspring of Alice Thornton, a staunchly loyal member of the Church of England (35), were baptized within a day or two of birth. The puritan minister Ralph Josselin, and John Greene, a man of more secular cast of mind, usually allowed many more days to elapse (33, 34). According to Protestant doctrine, baptism was not essential to salvation. As Isaac Archer put it, God 'is a God of the faithful, and their seed'; the happiness of the children of believing parents was assured. Nevertheless, it was the latter's duty to ensure the celebration of the rite, and Archer's acute unease about the death of his fifth child, still unbaptized eighteen days after birth, is evident in his diary (37). Whenever it took place, the christening might be accompanied by a feast or party (33, 36).

Diaries are also a useful source of information about godparenthood. Conservative or conformist diarists recorded godparents' names with some care (33, 35), while puritans tended to refer to them only incidentally or not at all. Strict puritans rejected godparenthood altogether and insisted on the paramount responsibility of parents for the Christian upbringing of their children. The moderate puritan Ralph Josselin noted that his daughter Mary's godmother acted in Mrs Josselin's place (34). A number of these passages illustrate the traditional courtesy of allowing one of the godparents to bestow a name upon the child: Josselin accepted this in Mary's case. The variety of terms applied to godparents in this period is apparent in these extracts. 'Gossip' was ancient, popular and confessionally neutral, 'godparent' more formal. 'Witness' reflected a relatively restricted view of the godparents' role, often associated with puritanism. Alice Thornton changed the terms she used between the 1650s and 1660s, probably in response to the developing religious situation.[3]

A very important decision—whether the child should be suckled by its mother or by a paid wet-nurse—had to be made soon after birth. Social convention among the upper classes dictated the latter course. Medical opinion, though divided, was predominantly in favour of the former, which Christian teaching also tended to support. There were some other particular reasons for using wet-nurses. The 'blessing of the breast' was by no means to be taken for granted by those mothers who wanted to feed their own children (35, 37). Country nursing might be thought advisable for children born in the disease-ridden metropolis, especially if they were sickly. Children entrusted to

---

[3] These changes underline the fact that Alice Thornton's 'autobiographical' writings consist in large part of memorials and occasional meditations composed soon after the events which gave rise to them.

careless or unhealthy nurses certainly incurred increased hazards, but some parents who chose their wet-nurses judiciously and maintained adequate contact or supervision achieved good results (30, 33). During the period of breastfeeding, the arrival of the early teeth was sometimes noted down: teething, widely considered dangerous to the child, was a source of parental anxiety (33, 34, 37). The length of the period of breastfeeding varied greatly between families and sometimes even within the same family.

These passages leave a sombre impression of the extreme fragility of infant life and the terribly high wastage suffered by some families. There was, it is true, a considerable variety of experience. Known infant mortality (deaths in the first year of life) ranged from nil among John Dee's children to over fifty per cent in Isaac Archer's family. The anguish of loss was poignantly expressed by many of these diarists. A recently born infant may have been easier to part with than an older child, but attachment soon began to grow. The absorbing interest for parents of the early development of infants' faculties and personalities is evident in some of the following testimony (34, 35, 37).

Only religion could place events apparently so cruel and devoid of meaning within the grand frame of God's purpose, while also offering the consolation of assured happiness in another life. God meant to bring both child and parents to himself, or so the pious believed: the child directly, the parents by recalling them with the rod of correction from earthly affections, favourite sins and the neglect of duties. Under its strokes, men and women sought reasons for gratitude, and counted their blessings (31, 34, 35, 39).

30   THE BIRTH AND NURSING OF JOHN DEE'S
FIRST THREE CHILDREN, 1579–83

[*These extracts cover the period up to Dee's departure for a long sojourn on the continent in 1583. Translations from Latin are in italic.*]

[*1579, May 4?*] [*By chance the foetus in the womb had been damaged as a result of very great movement and work?*][1]

[*May 11–12*] *The infant in the womb turned in the opposite direction.*[2]

[*June 17*] Nurse Wells came.

[*July 13*] *Arthur Dee born, a boy, at nearly thirty minutes past four in the morning, or rather twenty-five minutes, at the moment of sunrise, as I think.*

16. Arthur was christened at 3 of the clock after noon; Mr Dyer and Mr Doctor Lewys, judge of the Admiralty, were his godfathers, and Mistress Blanche Parry of the Privy Chamber his godmother. But Mr John Herbert[3] of East Sheen was deputy for Dr Lewys, and Mistress Aubrey was deputy for my cousin Mistress Blanche Parry.

[*August 9*] Jane Dee churched.

[*15*] Nurse Wells went home.

[*October 24*] Jane had them early in the morning before day.[4]

[*November*] 28. 29. Jane had a small show.

[*December*] 9. This night my wife dreamed that one came to her and told her saying 'Mistress Dee, you are conceived of child, whose name must be Zacharias. Be of good cheer: he shall do well as this doth.'

[*29, 30*] Jane had them abundant.

[*1580, January 16*] Arthur fell sick, stuffed with cold phlegm; could not sleep, had no stomach to eat or drink as he had done before.

[*29*] Jane had them a little.

---

[1] *forte in vtero conceptus Iesus erat ex summo motu et labore.*
[2] *Infans in vtero vertebat se in oppositas partes.*
[3] *Harbert.*
[4] This entry, like many others about Jane's menstruation, is written in Greek characters. So too is the entry of 9 December.

[*March*] 9. This night following Jane had them abundantly.

[*April 8*] Jane had them.

[*June 1*] Jane had them.

[*July 3*] Jane had them plentifully *and at almost 7 p.m. miscarried of a conception of eight days; but where [are] the [separate?] limbs etc?*[5]

[*30*] Jane had them.

[*August*] 27: Arthur was weaned this night first.

30 Nurse Darant was discharged and had 10*s* given her, which was the whole quarter's wages due at a fortnight after Michaelmas.

[*1581, June 7*] *At half past seven in the morning, Katharine Dee was born.*

[*10*] *Katharine baptized at half past five in the afternoon.* Mr Packington of the court, my Lady Katharine Crofts, wife to Sir James Crofts, Mr Controller of the Queen's house[hold?], Mistress Mary Skidmore of the Privy Chamber an[d] cousin to the Queen by their deputies christened Katharine Dee.

[*July*] 5 My wife churched.

[*17*] Jane had them.

[*August 4*] Katharine was sent home from Nurse Maspely of Barnes for fear of [*illegible word*] her maid's sickness, and Goodwife Benet gave her suck.

[*11*] Katharine Dee was shifted to Nurse Garret at Petersham . . . my wife went on foot with her, and Ellen Cole my maid, George and Benjamin, in very great [showers?] of rain.

[*20*] From this night till Sunday night following Jane had them abundantly.

[*29*] Jane had them [abundantly?] again.

[*September*] 29. Jane had them.

[*November 21*] Jane had them suddenly *at half past seven after noon* and so in the night following.

[*December*] 1. Katharine Dee her nurse was paid 6*s*, so nothing is owing to her.

[*December 25*] Jane had them abundantly this night etc.

[*1582 January 23*] Jane had them. 23. My wife went to Nurse Garret and paid her for this month ending the 26 day. Mistress Herbert went with her.

---

[5] *et hora 7. fere a mer[idie?] abortiebatur ex concept[i]one 8 dier[um] sed vbi [distincta?] membra etc.*

[*February 21*] Jane had them this morning.

25. Paid Nurse Garret for Katharine till Friday the 23 day vis then reckoning due to Nurse for four pound of candle and four pound of soap.

[*26*] Katharine my daughter became very sick.

[*March 23*] Jane had them this Friday and the night following plentifully.

[*April*] 16. Nurse Garret had her 6s for her month ending on the 20 day next.

[*20*] Jane had them.

[*June*] 22. Nurse Garret had 6s for a month ending the 18 day of May. She is to have for a month wages ending the 15 day of this June. 22. My wife went this Friday thither with Benjamin.

[*July 16?*] Jane my wife went to Nurse Garret's to pay her 12s for her wages due till Friday last, which was Saint Margaret's Day, and to give her xiid for candles. She went by water; Mistress Lee went with her, in Robin Jacke's boat.

[*16*] Jane this Sunday night very sore troubled with a colic and cramp in her belly. She vomited this Monday morning very much green stuff and by the stool likewise.

[*August 8*] Kate was sickly.

[*20?*] Katharine still seemed to be diseased.

25. Katharine was taken home from Nurse Garret of Petersham and weaned.

[*October 21*] Jane my wife swooned[6] in the church.

[*1583 January 28*] *Rowland Dee was born at fifty or forty minutes past one*[7] *in the afternoon.*

[*February 2*] *Rowland Dee baptized.*

[*11*] Rowland went with his nurse to her house to East Sheen.

[*24*] Jane churched.

[*March*] 8. Nurse Lydgatt at East Sheen was paid for 6 pound candle, 6 pound soap and her wages due from Rowland his birth till [*sic*].

[*April*] Nurse was paid for Rowland all her wages till Monday the 22 of this month, 16 pence a week. She had all her candle

---

[6] *sownded.*

[7] 2 deleted and replaced by *1*[a].

and soap before. [*Further payments were made in the three following months.*]

[*April 12?*] Jane had them plentifully.

[*The Dees left home for the continent on 21 September.*]

Oxford, Bodleian Library, MS Ashmole 487 (entered in a copy of Ioannes Stadius, *Ephemerides Novae . . . secvndvm Antverpiae Longitvdinem Ab Anno 1554 vsque ad Annum 1600* (1570).

31   BIRTH AND DEATH OF A CHILD OF NICHOLAS ASSHETON'S, 1618

February 16. My wife in labour of childbirth. Her delivery was with such violence as the child died within half an hour, and, but for God's wonderful mercy, more than human reason could expect, she had died; but he spared her a while longer to me, and took the child to his mercy; for which, as for one of his great mercies bestowed on me, I render all submissive, hearty thanks and praise to the only good and gracious God of Israel. Divers met, and went with us to Downham; and there the child was buried by Sir James Whalley in our own pew, and the company such as of a sudden could be provided at Michael Browne's. A few days after I gave to the poor of Twiston, Downham, Worston, Chadburn and Clitheroe, according as their several needs required. My mother with me laid the child in the grave.

February 20. . . . Some wives of Clitheroe here this day.[1] . . .

February 24. The midwife went from my wife to Coz.[2] Braddyll's wife. She had given by my wife xx*s* and by me v*s*.

March 4. . . . My Coz. Assheton's wife came a presenting, very merry.

March 8. Sunday. Downham wives and Worston wives presented my wife.

Raines (ed.), *Journal of Nicholas Assheton*, pp. 81–4.

---

[1] In order to visit Mrs Assheton.
[2] *Cooz.*

32 SOME OF NEHEMIAH WALLINGTON'S ACCOUNTS OF HIS WIFE GRACE'S SAFE DELIVERANCES IN CHILDBED, 1622–7

On the 13 day of October being Saturday 1622 my wife was in great pain of childbearing, and so continued in great and sharp labour till 5 a clock on the next day at night; and then it pleased the Lord of his great mercy to give her safe deliverance of a daughter, but there was but small hope of the child's life. But the Lord of his mercy restored the child to us again: his Name be praised forever. Amen. Although this mercy of childbearing is a common mercy of God, yet it is none of the least, and therefore we ought to take notice of it and to be thankful unto God not only for a month but for ever: to live thankfully.

[*1625*] . . . And on the first day of December about six a clock in the morning my wife was safely delivered of a man child, contrary to our expectation: the Lord's Name be praised for it. For she was delivered before the midwife could come, having then but two or three women with her. {His name was Nehemiah.}

One or two weeks before my wife fell sick, I did hear of three score women with child and in childbed that died in one week in Shoreditch parish, and scarce two of a hundred that was sick with child that escaped death. And the thing that here I take notice of is the great mercy of God is in the restoring of my wife to health and giving her safe deliverance in childbed, having so small means as she had, and she and the child being both well. The Lord's Name be praised now and for evermore. Amen. Amen.

On the xxiiii day of December {1627} my wife was in great pain of travail day and night, and the midwife was with her; and on the next day at three a clock in the morning we were driven to send for Master Chamberlin[1] to deliver her, and my wife was

---

[1] *The Dictionary of National Biography* lists Peter Chamberlen Jr (1572–1626), Peter Chamberlen Sr (d. 1631) and Peter son of Peter Chamberlen Jr (1601–83), all of whom used the forceps which was the family's special contribution to English obstetrics.

in exceeding great pain and in no hope of life when she did see him come; and others thought that the mother or the child would have miscarried if not both. But God of his great goodness and mercy heard our prayers and gave safe deliverance unto both: his Name be praised for ever and ever. Amen. The child was christened on Christtide[2] Day and her name was called Sarah.

London, Guildhall Library, MS 204, ff. 401, 410, 419.

33   THE BIRTH AND INFANCY OF JOHN GREENE'S FIRST FOUR CHILDREN, 1644–8

[*1644*] On the 8th of March, about ten minutes after sunset, being a little after 6 of the clock, my wife was delivered of my eldest son (her first child). She had been in labour all that day and all the night before, the midwife being sent for at 12 of the clock on Thursday night . . . The child was baptized on Friday the 15th the same month by my uncle, Doctor Jermyn, in the house. He used the Common Prayer Book, but signed it not with the cross. My own father and my Father Jermyn and my Grandmother Blanchard were gossips. My Father Jermyn would have had it named John Alexander, but my father had no great mind to it, so it was named only John. I had a great banquet; stood me in about £4. I had not much company. Goodwife Aylett should have nursed him, but she came to town and fell sick, so we sent her down, and she commended one Goodwife Smith, whom we used, and gave 15/- a month . . . My nurse went away with my boy on Tuesday the 26th of March. She had 15/- for a month's wages when she went. On the last of this month my wife came downstairs to dinner . . .

(April) 3rd. My wife at lecture and churched . . .

[*1645*] Upon Friday the last of January my nurse came to town with my child; he had but two teeth. . . .

(February) Nota: my wife was delivered of her 2 child, being a daughter, on the Saturday the 15th of February about 2 of the

[2] *Christed:* Christmas.

clock afternoon . . . My Aunt Beresford came in and told me it had a face as big as my boy, and that it was a worthy babe. It was baptized upon Monday the 24 of February, being Matthias Day, privately at home by Mr Burdale the minister of our parish. The witnesses were my own father and my wife's grandmother, my Lady Cooke, who being ill my Aunt Ogles stood deputy for her. The other godmother was my Lady Martin. It was named Mary, being my wife's own name and my Lady Martin's also. My Lady Cooke and my Lady Martin were both heretofore my wife's godmothers also. The next day, being Tuesday, the children went both down in Hill's coach. . . .

(March) On Wednesday the 12th my wife at lecture, it being also Thanksgiving Day. She was then churched. . . .

[*1646*] (February) The 9th of this month my son Alexander born.

(July) On the 4th of this month I take home my daughter Mary from nurse, she having eight teeth and having been weaned three quarters of a year before . . .

[*1648*] (January) . . . On the 14th, being Friday, my wife was delivered of her third son and her fourth child about half an hour past 12 of the clock at noon . . . The child was upon Tuesday the 25th of the same month baptized by the name of Thomas. My Brother Chambrelan, Brother Bysshe and my Sister Penrice witnesses. We had about twenty-five guests at the christenings and Mr Henshaw our lecturer baptized it in the chamber . . . Nota: my boy Alexander, being almost two year old, cannot go yet alone, but by holding he can go about the house. He hath twenty teeth, as his nurse saith and I do a little fear that his right shoulder grows a little bigger than the other, which we observed last Michaelmas.

Symonds (ed.), 'Diary of John Greene', *English Historical Review*, 43 (1928), pp. 599, 603; 44 (1929), pp. 107, 109.

34 PREGNANCY, CHILDBIRTH AND INFANCY AS DESCRIBED BY RALPH JOSSELIN, 1645–58

Jane Josselin, born 25 November 1645

[*1645*] ⟨Apri⟩l: 3: My wife divers days very ill; this day she began to persuade herself she was breeding; if it be so, God in mercy give her a contented, thankful spirit, preserve her and her fruit, and make it his own and provide every way for it.

⟨4:⟩ My wife was now even confident she was breeding, and supposed it a daughter: the Lord give us thankful contented spirits . . .

⟨Octo⟩ber. 26: . . . my wife [*troubled*] with the illness of her condition, being big . . .

[*November*] ⟨24:⟩ I had sought to God for my wife (that was oppressed with fears that she should not do well on this child), that God would order all providences so as we might rejoice in his salvation; I had prayed with confidence of good success to her. About midnight on Monday I rose, called up some neighbours; the night was very light, Goodman Potter willing to go for the midwife, and up when I went; the horse out of the pasture, but presently found; the midwife up at Bures, expecting it had been nearer day; the weather indifferent dry; midwife came, all things even gotten ready towards day. I called in the women by daylight, almost all came; and about 11 or 12 of the clock my wife was with very sharp pains delivered November 25 of her daughter intended for a Jane; she was then twenty-five years of age herself. We had made a good pasty for this hour, and that also was kept well. Wife and child both well, praise be my good and merciful Father.

⟨November:⟩ 30: God good and gracious to us in my wife's and babe's health, enabling her to nurse, in many favours both for soul and body; good in his word: to him be the praise.

⟨December:⟩ 4: My dearest very ill, as if she would have even died; she uttered as formerly these words: 'Thou and I must part;' but my God continue us together to praise him.

⟨Dece⟩mber: 7. . . . the Lord good in his word on the Sabbath, in the baptizing of my daughter: he in mercy accept me.

⟨Dece⟩mber. 14: My wife weakly and faint, yet cheerly when not troubled with toothache; my babe troubled with a cold . . .

⟨Dece⟩mber: 21: . . . my daughter Jane a cold; nurse went home from us.

[*1646, April*] 26: Mrs Mary Church[1] gave her little Jane a coat; is it not the Lord who puts this love into her towards us? Lord, requite it a thousand fold into her bosom.

[*May*] ⟨25:⟩ My daughter Jane had a tooth cut; this day she was just six months old.

⟨August⟩: 23: This week . . . God was good in my wi[*fe's health*] and the little babe, whereby we enjoyed our rest well in the night, and her nu[*rsing*] help . . .

⟨November⟩: 15. . . . my little daughter Jane began to go alone . . .

⟨Dece⟩mber. 20: . . . my little Jane was ill two or three days with teeth . . .

[*1647*] ⟨May⟩: 9. . . . this week my wife weaned her daughter Jane; she took it very contentedly; God hath given me much comfort in my wife and children, and in their quietness . . .

Ralph Josselin, born and died 1648

[*1647*] ⟨Aug⟩ust: 22: . . . my wife quickened this week: the Lord in mercy carry her safely through . . .

⟨August⟩: 29: . . . my wife exercised with qualms and weakness incident to her condition . . .

⟨Sept⟩ember: 5: . . . my dear wife ill of this child: the Lord in mercy sanctify his dealing, and give her strength, and cheerfulness of spirit, and an happy deliverance . . .

⟨Nov⟩ember: 28: The Lord good in the continuance of our health, only my wife very ill many times with this child: the Lord in mercy blow over those fits . . .

⟨Dece⟩mber: 5: . . . my dear wife under great fears she shall

---

[1] Mary Church, evidently Jane's godmother, a close friend of Josselin's, was the spinster daughter of Robert Church DD (d. 1617); see A. Macfarlane, *The Family Life of Ralph Josselin, a Seventeenth-Century Clergyman: An Essay in Historical Anthropology* (Cambridge University Press, 1970), p. 151, n. 2.

not do well of this child; ill in her head and back, one night ill as if she should have died: the Lord in mercy revive her spirits, and give her comforts, and lengthen her days. . . .

⟨Dece⟩mber: 12: . . . the Lord in mercy remember my dear wife, who lieth under many sad fears by reason of her approaching travail: teach her to trust in thee, and do thou command deliverance for her . . .

[*1648*] ⟨January:⟩ 30. The Lord good and merciful to me and all mine in our outward enjoyments; my wife still holding up her head, and going to church with me: the Lord in mercy preserve her and give her a comfortable lying down, and rising up . . .

[*February*] ⟨11.⟩ On Friday morning one hour and half before day my wife was delivered of her second son, the midwife not with her, only four women and Mrs Mary; her speed was great, and I think the easiest and speediest labour that ever she had, and she was under great fears: oh, how is the Lord to be noted and observed in this mercy. . . .

⟨17:⟩ My child was ill, full of phlegm. We sent for the physician. He gave it syrup of roses; it wrought well. My wife persuaded herself that it would die; it was a very sick child indeed. I took my leave of it at night, not much expecting to see it alive, but God continued it to morning, and it seemed to me not hopeless. Lord, it's thine, I leave it to thy disposing: only I pray thee give me and my wife a submitting heart.

In this week died in this town one woman in childbed and two children, or before her time she travailed and died; two young children more, and one young woman. The Lord make me sensible of my mercy. Mrs Mary would not go home, but stayed all night with our babe. Hitherto my wife preserved from fevers, and upwards: the Lord perfect her recovery; and if thou Lord break in with death into my family, oh, make me more careful to live unto my God, and wait until my change cometh.

⟨18:⟩ . . . Mr Harlakenden[2] came in to me; we had some discourse about baptizing my infant, and in that time came in Mr Thompson, who was ready to perform that act for me. The Lord wash my Ralph and sanctify him and accept him, and give

---

[2] Richard Harlakenden, impropriator of the living of Earl's Colne, was Josselin's patron and steadfast friend; see ibid., index entry on p. 237.

him this life together with a better if it be his will. My son finely revived, but the night was unto it a very sick night, but God preserved the life in it.

⟨19:⟩ . . . Presently the child was as if it had fallen asleep; the sickness was very strong, and that cannot but move bowels; but thou shalt go my infant into the land of rest, where there is no sickness nor childhood, but all perfection. Everyone expected its death, but it revived again, blessed be my God, and gave us hope of its recovery. . . .

⟨20:⟩ This night again my son very ill. He did not cry so much as the night before; whether the cause was want of strength I know not. He had a little froth in his mouth continually; in the morning there came some red mattery stuff out of his mouth, which made us apprehend his throat might be sore. Lord, thy will be done. He cheered up very sweetly at night, and in the night was very still. What God will do I know not, but it becometh me to submit to his will.

⟨February:⟩ 20: This week . . . my wife getting upwards, as well if not better than ever. All my family in health except my little Ralph; he is not so tedious to us, because he doth not shriek nor cry in his fits, but lieth quietly. We gave him breast milk at last, and little else. . . .

⟨21:⟩ This day my dear babe Ralph quietly fell asleep, and is at rest with the Lord. The Lord in mercy sanctify his hand unto me and do me good by it, and teach me how to walk more closely with him: I bless God for any measure of patience and submission to his will. Oh Lord, spare the rest of us that are living for thy Name sake we entreat thee. This correction, though sad, was seasoned with present goodness. For first, the Lord had given it us until both myself and wife had gotten strength, and so more fit to bear it than if in the depth of our sickness.[3] The Lord gave us time to bury it in our thoughts; we looked on it as a dying child three or four days. 3, it died quietly without shrieks or sobs or sad groans; it breathed out the soul with nine gasps and died. It was the youngest, and our affections not so wonted unto it. The Lord, ever the Lord, learn me wisdom and to know his mind in this chastisement.

---

[3] Josselin had just recovered from an attack of ague.

⟨22:⟩ These two days were such as I never knew before; the former for the death, and this for the burial of my dear son, whom I laid in the chancel on the north side of the great tomb. There thy bones rest out of my sight, but thy soul liveth in thy and my God's sight, and soul and body shall assuredly arise to enjoy God, and these eyes of mine shall see it: yea, and my God shall make me see this dealing of his to be for the best.

This little boy of ten days old when he died was buried with the tears and sorrow not only of the parents and Mrs Mary Church, but with the tears and sorrow of many of my neighbours. Mrs King and Mrs Church, two doctor of divinity's widows, the gravest matrons in our town, laid his tomb into the earth, which I esteem not only a testimony of their love to me, but of their respect to my babe. Mrs King and Mr Harlakenden of the Priory closed up each of them one of his eyes when it died; it died upwards, first in the feet and then in the head, and yet wonderful sweetly and quietly.

⟨February:⟩ 23: As oftentimes before, so on this day did I especially desire of God to discover and hint to my soul what is the aim of the God of heaven more especially in this correction of his upon me; and when I had seriously considered my heart and ways, and compared them with the affliction, and sought unto God, my thoughts often fixed on these particulars:

whereas I have given my mind to unseasonable playing at chess, now it run in my thoughts in my illness as if I had been at chess; I shall be very sparing in the use of that recreation, and that at more convenient seasons;

whereas I have walked with much vanity in my thoughts and resolved against it, and had served divers lusts too much in thought and in actions, whereas both body and soul should be the Lord's who hath called me to holiness, God hath taken away a son;

I hope the Lord will keep my feet in uprightness, that I may walk always with him, and I trust it shall be my endeavour more than ever;

and also that I should be more careful of my family to instruct them in the theory of God, that they may live in his sight and be serviceable to his glory. . . .

Mary Josselin, born January 1658

[*1657, May*] . . . 16° in the morning on Saturday my wife guessed that she was with child and about three weeks gone: the Lord show us mercy therein . . .

⟨May⟩. 24: God good in many mercies to us; my wife only very ill, but concludes it is childing, and a girl: the Lord be our portion and its in mercy . . .

⟨31:⟩ . . . my poor wife concludes herself with child and of a son; she is very sick in her stomach, but I trust in a short time she shall do well: the Lord for Christ sake be good to her and carry her on comfortably in the work . . .

[*June*] ⟨23.⟩ This morning my wife quickened; she concludeth a son. God bless her and it. The women met with her in prayer . . .

[*December*] ⟨19.⟩ . . . When I came home I found my wife had gotten sprats, which though a small thing was a great mercy, she much longing to eat of them before she lay down, and that she daily looked for . . .

[*1658, January*] ⟨12.⟩ Baptized my neighbour Burton's son; at night the midwife with us, my wife thinking she might use her, but being sent for, my wife let her go, that another that was in present need might be holpen, and it was a mercy to us so to dispose my wife's heart, her going tending to save a poor woman's life. But within half an hour, as soon as I had done family prayer, my wife had so sure a sign of her labour and speedy that put us all to a plunge; I sent two messengers after her, and it was at least four hours before she came. Mr Richard Harlakenden['s] man fetched her, but she came time enough for us, God be praised; my wife was wonderfully afraid and amazed but help was speedily with her, and in particular young Mrs Harlakenden, who put forth herself to the utmost to help her, and her presence was much to my wife.

⟨13.⟩ Her pains ceased; the labour very strange to her, which set her heart, but her eye was towards him who is the helper; my faith was up for her. She judged at the labour it would be a daughter, contrary to all her former experience and thought. Prayer was for her; we commended her to God and her warm bed early, and all to their rests, none watching this night as formerly. Her sleep was a comfort to her mixed with pain, fear, which made her quake and tremble.

⟨14.⟩ And so increased on her by two of the clock in this morning that I called up the midwife and nurse, got fires and all ready, and then her labour came on so strongly and speedily that the child was born. Only two or three women more got in to her, but God supplied all; young Mrs Harlakenden got up to us very speedily, and some others; my wife's labour was different from all former, exceeding sharp; she judged her midwife did not do her part, but God did all, and hath given us new experience of his goodness. The child was dead when born; I bless God who recovered it to life. We baptized it this day by the name of Mary, young Mrs Harlakenden holding it in my wife's place. God hath evened my number and made up the three which he took from me; my heart was very lightsome and joyful in the God of my mercies.

⟨15. 1⟩6. My wife very well. A tedious cold time. Our child was born with a sore, my wife thinketh done with lying near one of her short ribs.

⟨January.⟩ 24. The Lord good to me and mine [*in*] outward mercies. My wife upwards; as she rests in the night, so commonly she is in the day; so he giveth his beloved sleep; do it Lord for her, my God accept my praise for his mercy. . . .

[*December*] ⟨11:⟩ Mrs Harlakenden the younger bestowed a silver candlestand and porringer cover on my daughter Mary, whom she named. The Lord return all their love into their bosom. . . .

Macfarlane (ed.), *Diary of Ralph Josselin*, pp. 37, 48, 50–1, 59, 61, 67, 75, 80, 93, 101–2, 108, 110–5, 399–403, 413, 415–16, 435.

35 SOME OF MRS ALICE THORNTON'S
DESCRIPTIONS OF PREGNANCY, CHILDBIRTH AND
INFANCY, 1654–67[1]

*Upon the birth of my second child and daughter, born at Hipswell on
the 3rd of January in the year 1654.*

Alice Thornton, my second child, was born at Hipswell near
Richmond in Yorkshire the 3rd day of January 1654, baptized
the 5th of the same. Witnesses, my mother the Lady Wandesford,
my uncle Mr Major Norton, and my Cousin York his daughter,
at Hipswell, by Mr Michael Siddall, minister then of Catterick.

It was the pleasure of God to give me but a weak time after
my daughter Alice her birth, and she had many preservations
from death in the first year, being one night delivered from being
overlaid by her nurse, who laid in my dear mother's chamber a
good while. One night my mother was writing pretty late, and
she heard my dear child make a groaning troublesomely, and
stepping immediately to Nurse's bedside she saw the nurse fallen
asleep with her breast in the child's mouth, and lying over the
child; at which she, being affrighted, pulled the nurse suddenly
off from her, and so preserved my dear child from being
smothered. . . .

*[Her third child, Elizabeth, was born at Hipswell on 14 February
1655.]*

It pleased God to take from me my dear child Betty, which had
been long in the rickets and consumption, gotten at first by an
ague, and much gone in the rickets, which I conceive was caused
by ill milk at two nurses. And notwithstanding all the means I
used, and had her with Naly at St Mungno's Well[2] for it, she
grew weaker, and at the last, in a most desperate cough that
destroyed her lungs, she died.

---

[1] The prayers and meditations which accompanied these descriptions have been almost
entirely omitted from the following extracts.
[2] St Mungo's Well, at Copgrove near Knaresborough, was a spring famous for curing
rickets in children: see *Autobiography of Mrs Alice Thornton*, p. 94 n.

That dear, sweet angel grew worse, and endured it with infinite patience; and when Mr Thornton and I came to pray for her, she held up those sweet eyes and hands to her dear Father in heaven, looked up, and cried in her language, 'Dad, dad, dad' with such vehemency as if inspired by her holy Father in heaven to deliver her sweet soul into her heavenly Father's hands, and at which time we also did with great zeal deliver up my dear infant's soul into the hand of my heavenly Father, and then she sweetly fell asleep and went out of this miserable world like a lamb.

Elizabeth Thornton, my third child, died the 5th of September 1656 betwixt the hours of five and six in the morning. Her age was one year, six months and twenty-one days. Was buried the same day at Catterick by Mr Siddall.

[*On 14 September 1657, just under three months before the birth of her fifth child, Mrs Thornton suffered a dangerous fall.*]
It pleased God in much mercy to restore me to strength to go to my full time, my labour beginning three days; but upon the Wednesday, the ninth of December, I fell into exceeding sharp travail in great extremity, so that the midwife did believe I should be delivered soon. But lo! it fell out contrary, for the child stayed in the birth, and came cross with his feet first, and in this condition continued till Thursday morning between two and three a clock, at which time I was upon the rack in bearing my child with such exquisite torment, as if each limb were divided from other, for the space of two hours, when at length, being speechless and breathless, I was by the infinite providence of God in great mercy delivered. But I having had such sore travail in danger of my life so long, and the child coming into the world with his feet first, caused the child to be almost strangled in the birth, only living about half an hour, so died before we could get a minister to baptize him, although he was sent for.

I was delivered of my first son and fifth child on the 10th of December 1657. He was buried in Catterick Church the same day by Mr Siddall. This sweet goodly son was turned wrong by the fall I got in September before, nor had the midwife skill to turn him right, which was the cause of the loss of his life and the hazard of my own. . . .

My dream, 1660.

Upon my removal to St Nicholas,[3] and Mr Thornton was gone to London about the suits of my brother Sir Christopher Wandesford, I, being great with child, dreamed one night that I was laid in childbed, had the white sheet spread, and all over it was sprinkled with small drops of pure blood, as if it had been dashed with one's hand, which so frighted me that I told my aunt of it in the morning; but she put it off as well as she could, and said dreams was not to be regarded; but I kept it in my mind till my child died.

My delivery of my son William, my sixth child, and of his death, April the 17th, 1660, at St Nicholas

It was the good pleasure of God to continue me in the land of the living, and to bring forth my sixth child at St Nicholas. I was delivered of a very goodly son, having Mrs Hickeringgill with me, after hard labour and hazardous, yet, through great mercy, I had my life spared, and was blessed with a happy child abut 3 or 4 a clock in the morning upon Tuesday the 17th of April 1660. That day also was my child baptized by Mr Kirton of Richmond, called William after his father. His sureties were my cousin John Yorke, my cousin William Norton, and my cousin James Darcy['s] lady of Richmond. Thus was I blessed with the life and comfort of my dear child's baptism, with its enjoyment of that holy seal of regeneration; and my pretty babe was in good health, sucking his poor mother, to whom my good God had given the blessing of the breast as well as the womb, of that child, to whom it was no little satisfaction, while I enjoyed his life; and the joy of it maked me recruit faster, for his sake, that I might do my duty to him as a mother. But it so pleased God to shorten this joy, lest I should be too much transported, that I was visited with another trial; for on the Friday sennight after, he began to be very angry and froward after his dressing in the morning, so that I perceived him not to be well; upon which I gave him Gascoyne powder and cordial, lest it should be the red gum, in children usual at that time, to

[3] Near Richmond, the home of Mrs Thornton's paternal aunt, Anne Norton, where she stayed for a time after her mother's death.

strike it out of his heart at morning after his dressing. And having had three hours' sleep, his face when he awaked was full of red round spots like the smallpox, being of the compass of a halfpenny, and all whealed white over, these continuing in his face till night; and being in a slumber in my arms on my knee he would sweetly lift up his eyes to heaven and smile, as if the old saying was true in this sweet infant, that he saw angels in heaven. But then, whether through cold upon his dressing then, or what else was the cause, the Lord knoweth, the spots struck in, and grew very sick all night, and about nine a clock on Saturday morning he sweetly departed this life, to the great discomfort of his weak mother, whose only comfort is that the Lord, I hope, has received him to that place of rest in heaven where little children beholds the face of their heavenly Father, to his God and my God; whom I humble crave to pardon all things in me which he sees amiss, and clean away my sins by the blood of my dearest Saviour and Redeemer. . . .

My son William Thornton was buried at Easby in the same grave with his eldest sister, which died before baptized, by Mr Kirton, he being scarce fourteen days old, near my Lady Wharton's grave at Easby, April 29th 1660; his father being much troubled at his loss, whom the child was exceedingly like in person, and also his eldest sister. . . .

Upon my deliverance of my son Robert Thornton, my seventh child, born at East Newton, the first child that was born in the new house, September 19, 1662.
Almighty God, the wise disposer of all good things both in heaven and earth, who seest what and how much of the comforts of this mortal life is conveniently fit for us to enjoy in this earth, hath at length had pity on my afflictions, and gave me such a mercy and dear enjoyment to myself and husband, after all his and mine several troubles and losses of sons, as I could not hope for or expect; making me a joyful mother of a sweet son, born at full time, after five great trials and hazards of miscarriage when I was with him . . . I was delivered, after great danger and peril of my life in travail of my son Robert Thornton upon Friday the 19th of September 1662. He was born at East Newton betwixt the hours of eight and nine o'clock at night, having been

since the night before in strong labour of him till that time. [*Soon after her son was born, Mrs Thornton suffered a serious 'flux' or haemorrhage, which looked for a time as though it might be fatal.*] . . . The Lord God had great pity upon my distress, and gave me after this a competency[4] of health and strength to be able to give my child suck, which, by his blessing, I did till Robin was above two years old, he continuing very healthful and strong.

My son Robert was baptized on Saturday the 20th of September 1662 by Mr Luckock, at our house in East Newton, in my own chamber, where the Lord gave me opportunity to see his admittance into the church militant by holy sacrament of baptism, when I hope the Lord did enter into covenant with him to be his God, and he to be his faithful servant to his life's end. The Lord give him also the grace of his means as well as the means by which he gives his grace unto us. Amen. His godfathers and godmothers were Mr Thornton for my Nephew Best, Dr Wittie, my Lady Cholmeley. . . .

The birth of my son Christopher Thornton, my ninth child, November 11, 1667 and of his death, December 1, 1667.
Of my ninth child it was the pleasure of God to give me a weak and sickly time in breeding, from the February till the 10th of May following, I not having fully recruited my last September weakness;[5] and if it had been good in the eyes of my God I should much rather (because of that) not to have been in this condition. But it is not a Christian's part to choose anything of this nature, but what shall be the will of our heavenly Father, be it never so contrary to our own desires. . . . I had not my health till about the 10th of May, when I perceived myself with quick child. Afterwards, during the time of being with child, till within a month of my delivery, very well as of any other, walking a mile to the church each Sabbath day. . . . The birth of my ninth child was very perilous to me, and I hardly escaped

[4] *competency.*
[5] Mrs Thornton had fallen into a 'very sad and desperate condition' in August 1666, when she was about eight weeks pregnant, as the result of a ride to York followed by 'grief' caused by the discovery that a settlement for her children had been altered without her knowledge: *Autobiography of Mrs Alice Thornton*, pp. 152–3.

with my life, falling into pangs of labour about the 4th of November, being ill, continuing that week; and on Monday the 11th of November 1667 I fell in travail, being delivered betwixt the hours of ten and eleven a clock at night. . . . Christopher Thornton, my ninth child, was born at Newton on Monday the 11th November '67, baptized the 12th at Newton. His godfathers and godmother were my Brother Denton, my Brother Portington, and Mrs Anne Danby.

After this comfort of my child I recovered something of my weakness, better recovering my breasts and milk, and giving suck, when he thrived very well and grew strong, being a lovely babe. But, lest I should too much set my heart in the satisfaction of any blessing under heaven, it seemed good to the most infinite wise God to take him from me, giving me some apprehensions thereof before any did see it as a change in him. And therefore with a full resignation to his providence I endeavoured to submit patiently and willingly to part with my sweet child to our dear and loving Father, who see what was better for me than I could, begging that his will might be mine, either in life or death. When he was about fourteen days old, my pretty babe broke into red spots like the smallpox; and through cold, gotten by thinner clothing than either my own experience or practice did accustom to all my children, they following the precept of M.D.[?], it presently, though then unknown to me, upon this accident, with the extreme cold weather, fell into great looseness, and, notwithstanding all the means I could use, it continued four days, having endured it patiently; then fell into some little struggling, and at length it pleased his Saviour and mine, after the fifth sick night and day, to deliver him out of this miserable world. He sweetly fell asleep on Sunday at night, being then the 1st of December 1667, who was at that time three weeks old on the next day, the 2nd, when he was buried at Stonegrave by Mr Comber, who preached a funeral sermon December 2nd 1667.

After my dear child's death I fell into a great and long continued weakness by the swelling of my milk, he having sucked last, in his pain, of the left breast, had hurt the nipple, causing it to gangrene, and extreme pained with torment of it made me fall into a fever . . .

Jackson (ed.), *Autobiography of Mrs Alice Thornton*, pp. 91, 94–6, 123–5, 139–43, 164–6.

36 SAMUEL WOODFORDE'S DESCRIPTION OF THE
BIRTH OF HIS SON HEIGHES, 1664

[*1663, 28 October*] . . . Bless my poor wife I beseech thee. I
continually pray for her and the fruit in her womb that it may
have right form and shape, that it be the servant of the Almighty
and an heir of glory, a member of his Church militant here and
of his Church triumphant hereafter; and that he would order all
things as seemeth best to him for my poor wife's lying in and
direct us to do that which may be most for his glory and our
good, himself providing midwife, nurse and what he sees we
stand in need of in such a time. . . .

[*30 November*] . . . The Lord rem[ember?] this day next month
and appear for his poor servant; bless my poor wife who grows
very big and the fruit in her womb, and my poor child who is
weaned, her nurse being with child, and all my family, and dwell
in the midst of us by thy especial presence.

[*3 December*] . . . I have now been at prayer in private and
begged for a blessing upon my poor wife who grows exceeding
big and draws near her time; the good Lord stand by her in that
hour and let his strength and power be seen in the weakness of
a poor creature. I prayed for right form and shape for the fruit
in her womb: and oh let not the sins of the parents cause thy
wrath and displeasure against the little one . . .

December 4. 63 Will Kitchener was here and seemed to doubt
as if Mrs Legg could not be as good as her word to come to
my wife about the 14th of January next, whereupon Alice wrote
to her. The Lord order all things for the best, and let her midwife
be ready when she shall have occasion, but especially my God
do thou stand by her in her greatest extremity, a present help in
the time of her trouble. . . .

[*28 December*] . . . My aunt told me this day she thought it
might be a boy . . .

January 9th 1663 [*1664*] Before we went to bed last night my
poor dear had some kind of grumbling pain which she could not
tell well what to think of, and about 10 at night or a little after
we went to bed. I slept a while, but, poor chicken, she lay by
me all the while in pain till about 1 [when?] that I awaked and

called up the maids and sent for old Goodwife Tailer and Mrs Norton's family. And now my dear God it is almost 3 a clock in the morning and my poor wife is in travail and her midwife Mrs Legg that she spoke to is [not?] here, a great many miles off so that we cannot send to her by any means, and we have only a poor old woman that hath the palsy very much, one that hath been a good midwife in her time, [yet who?] my wife was always afraid of. Oh my God it is all one with thee to help with small and inconsiderable means as the best in the world; thou art not confined to them, though we must make use of them. Oh my God stand by thy poor weak handmaid and put under thine everlasting arms; thou hast brought to the birth, oh give strength [only?] to bring [forth?]; command the loins to give up and the womb not to forbear. Oh Lord bless these small and weak means that we have and show thyself more eminently in behalf of thy poor handmaid: oh my God answer the prayers that I have at any time put up unto thee for her; keep up her spirit, deliver her from all fainting and swooning fits, put under thy everlasting arms and give her easy and speedy deliverance if it be thy good will . . .

Almost 4: they have got my wife out of her bed according to the country fashion; what they will do with her my God I cannot tell . . . Here is now in the house old Goodwife Tailer the midwife, Mrs Norton, Mrs Katherine and Mrs Ann, Goodwife Smith and Goodwife Missingham and my cousin Joan Smith. The Lord make them helpful to thy poor handmaid.

A little after six, blessed be my dear God, my wife is delivered of a boy. Oh my God what cause have I to pray to thee [and?] magnify thy holy name . . . Oh Lord perfect what thou hast begun and now take care both of my wife and my child for Christ Jesus sake. Now indeed thou hast been seen and I will for ever acknowledge it with thankgiving unto thee: vouchsafe to bless the house of thy servant and cause thy favour to be our protection for evermore, oh my God. Amen, even for Christ's Jesus sake. Mrs Ann Norton brought me the news.

My aunt came in the afternoon to see my wife and the child and seems to be very well pleased. I asked her to be gossip but she would not; however will be there and would have us christen the child tomorrow in the evening and would have it named

Heighes; is exceeding careful about the welfare of my poor family; blessed be our God who hath made her to be such a friend to us of so great an enemy as she was. I can only say it is the Lord's doing and it is wonderful in our eyes. Oh sanctify the infant from the womb and now that thou hast made it my child, make it thine own by grace and adoption, and impress thy image upon it for Christ's Jesus sake. Blessed be my God for providing a midwife and a nurse and all conveniences, I beg my dear Father to look now upon my wife; give her this night rest and sleep and [refresh?] her poor wearied body. Praised be thy Name that her heart is so cheery; it is thou alone that dost sustain; even so let it continually be for Christ sake. Amen. . . .

Sabbath 10 January 63[4] Sabbath. This day after evening prayer my poor child was baptized and at my aunt's desire named Heighes; the Lord be pleased to sanctify the ordinance of baptism unto it and grant that his soul may be washed in the laver of regeneration and that all his sins may be purged away by the blood of his and my dear Saviour the Lord Jesus. Mr Brookes baptized it in our chamber where my wife lies in and I got Mr Norton to stand as godfather and Mrs Norton as godmother if my Aunt Heighes will not take it off from her. Whatever they have undertaken I know it my duty to bring him up in the fear of thy Name and here my God I promise before thee that if thou givest me life I will to the very utmost of my endeavour: and now the good Lord bless my poor family and build us up for Christ Jesus sake. I made as little clutter as could be had; only Mr Norton [*word illegible*] family and about six more who were present and with a cup of beer and a small piece of cake; being out of all put ourselves to no further trouble. Wherein I have failed this day, my God I beseech thee to pardon and forgive me for my Saviour's sake, Amen. . . .

[*Alice Woodforde fell ill, and died on 14 January.*]

Oxford, Bodleian Library, MS Eng. misc. f. 381, ff. 14ᵛ–15ʳ, 25ᵛ, 26ᵛ–27ʳ, 28ʳ⁻ᵛ, 39ᵛ, 47ʳ–51ʳ.

37   THREE OF ISAAC ARCHER'S INFANT
CHILDREN, 1670–5

Death of his first-born, Mary, 1670 (born 3 April 1669)

March 31. On Maundy[1] Thursday my child died at 10 of the clock in the forenoon, in its mother's lap. It never outgrew its sickness in November, when two teeth came; it looked fresh, and fat in the face, but it wasted in the body exceedingly. The continual cheerliness made us think 'twould recover, but sure it had a consumption in the lungs (as my Father Peachy said) of which, with hard breeding teeth, it died. A fortnight before, 'twas taken with vomiting fits, which would make it ready to die; and that was our beginning of sorrow. Oh what grief was it to me to hear it groan, to see its sprightly eyes turn to me for help in vain! 'Twas as pretty and as knowing a child as they had ever seen that came to see it! But its [beauty][2] is laid in the dust (in the north aisle of Isleham church, at the end of its grandmother's seat). I have resigned to God, I think, willingly, though I would have given anything for its life. Our grief was great, but I was more able to bear it than my dear wife; I hope this loss hath done us good! God saw we were unsettled, and so took our babe to settle with himself! He saw we loved it too well, and took it away; God knew how much time it stole from me, which I ought better to have spent, and so hath warned me of my duty. I think of my untimely marriage, and fear my wife's relics of the ague laid the foundation of that fatal consumption! The Lord pardon former iniquities for Christ's sake and send me a child who may be Jedidiah! And send me strong consolation! His comforts I hope will possess and delight my soul! Amen!

In the morning I prayed for the pardon of its original sin with many tears, and begged its life, if God pleased, or that God would rid it out of its pain, and so he did, blessed be his Name!

1 *Maunday.*
2 Possibly *body.*

Mrs Archer's difficulties in feeding Anne (born 27 November 1670)

December 10. We had tried all means to make my child (who had been baptized December 8 and named Anne) suck of my wife. She would suck greedily of others, but could not lay hold by reason of the short nipples, and the tongue not so long as in some; we had a child older and that would not fasten; we got a puppy, and could not make it lay hold, in so much that we despaired of what I had so desired of God, the blessing of the breast as well as that of the womb, and my wife was resolving to try no more. When she thought not of it, the child took the breast, and so continueth, which we look on as a remarkable providence of our God! And shall not I [live?] more to that God who doth so much for me?

The death of an unbaptized child (born 7 August 1675).

[*The baptism of this recently born child had been put off because of the sickness of Archer's three-year-old son Will. On Archer's list of his children, this and two others are labelled 'Anonymus' or 'Anonyma', showing that they died unbaptized.*]

. . . August 25 in the night the little one died, which was the same day my father died five years since. I had taken a nurse into the house to suckle it because my wife was not able, as having suckled the last too long. The woman knew of its illness, and yet told us not of it, so that it died whilst she slept, and unbaptized, which I could not in the least help, as knowing nothing of its illness. I know God is a God of the faithful, and their seed, and baptism is a sign of it; and I no more question that child's happiness (whatever St Austin thought) than that of the Jewish children who died before the eighth day. I take God to witness I do not, did not despise that sacrament, but now 'tis fallen out so, not through the fault of the infant, or our wilful neglect, but through an unavoidable necessity, because of God's hand in Will's sickness, and my not knowing 'twas ill. I comfort myself with hopes that God, who is not tied to means, hath washed its soul in Christ's blood!

My wife was not as she used to be eight weeks before, and that morning she cried out; the child was small, and came to its favour too soon, so that many said it would not live, though it sucked heartily. Some said it could not be but my wife or the child should die; which comforts me somewhat, because God might have taken wife, or the other son, or all of them, and hath taken the poor babe only. He is pleased thus to make a breach upon me; the Lord grant me patience and faith to trust in him, though he slay me! I laid it in Freckenham chancel near my seat, and I expect to meet it at the resurrection of the just. Amen!

Cambridge University Library, MS Add. 8499, ff. 127–8, 143, 174–5.

38   OLIVER HEYWOOD RECALLS HIS SON JOHN'S BIRTH, 1683

It came into my thoughts this morning, July 25 1683, when I was at prayer in my study, that when my son John was born, as my wife was travailing of him twenty-seven years ago, I withdrew myself into this chamber into this very corner where now my study is made and there sought God for my wife, and J.L. brought me notice of a son born, and I returned to this window, praised God, but oh how many pangs and throes[1] have I had in the very same place within this eight years since my study was made there for that child none but God knows, and I have also had occasion and a heart sometimes to be thankful . . .

Horsfall Turner (ed.), *Oliver Heywood's Autobiography, Diaries, Anecdote and Event Books*, vol. II, p. 222.

---

1 *throws.*

39 ELIAS PLEDGER'S DESCRIPTIONS OF HIS WIFE'S EXPERIENCES OF CHILDBIRTH AND MISCARRIAGE, 1691–4

. . . On the 9th day of September 1691, half an hour past 7 in the morning, my wife was brought to bed of a daughter after a tedious labour of two nights and a day, so that it was a wonderful providence that the child was born alive. I was extremely affected and put up frequent prayers and ejaculation when her pangs were upon her, and I hope her safe delivery was an answer of prayer. She was baptized Elizabeth on the 9 of September [by?] Mr T Cruso.

On the 28 day of November 1692, about 1/4 past x at night on Monday, my wife was brought abed of [a] son after a tedious and dangerous labour, two days and almost two nights. I was much enlarged in prayer on her behalf, and I hope her delivery was an answer of prayer. I desire that we may never forget such an extraordinary appearance of providence. Her case was hazardous and difficult before, but a great deal worse now.
. . . I have many engagements upon me, many deliverances wrought [out?] for me: that of my wife and child and that so very lately, who were both almost given up by the standers by, but yet God seasonably stepped in, and when heart and strength both were ready to fail, then God made good that promise which [David?] experienced of being the strength of her heart and her portion for ever. My son was baptized by Mr Cruso on the 6 day of December and named Elias.

About . . . the beginning of August 1694 my wife miscarried at Bethnal[1] Green (she went there with the child for change of air in order to remove her ague); it was God's great mercy she did not receive great prejudice, it being at a time and in a place where no help could be had for her. If there had happened any frightful symptoms (and there was much cause to believe there

---

1 *Bednal.*

would at the beginning of her illness) no place were about her that could assist her, and she herself was under sad apprehensions of being lost for want of it. But in the [mount?] God was seen, and afforded his help when others' could not be had, for which I hope we shall ever adore his goodness.

London, Dr Williams's Library, MS 28.4, ff. 49ᵛ, 53ʳ⁻ᵛ, 65.

IV

Childhood

The world of early modern childhood is now largely impenetrable save through the personal testimony contained in diaries and autobiographies. But very few children's diaries have survived; the one kept by Thomas Isham between 1671 and 1673 is an outstanding exception (52). We are in the main dependent upon autobiographies for our perception of the child's point of view. Diaries, however, throw much light on parental feelings and attitudes, and they possess the added advantage of having been composed within a shorter time after the events they describe.

Milestones of the passage from infancy to maturity noted in some diaries include the first unaided walk, beginning to read, and (in the case of boys) the donning of the first breeches, which marked the transition from earlier to later childhood (41, 43, 44, 45). The age at which formal instruction commenced, and whether this took place predominantly in the household, or in a school, depended upon the family's circumstances and the perceived needs and aptitudes of the child. Schools were more numerous and accessible in the towns, and there formal schooling tended to start relatively early (45). For girls, social and domestic accomplishments were considered of paramount importance, though they might receive some academic education from a tutor or in a girl's school, and it was not unknown for them to attend the same school as their brothers, at least when they started (40).

Unfortunately we learn little from diaries about the inculcation of 'good manners' and other social skills, but we see children in the company both of adults and of their contemporaries, making visits, receiving guests, having a ball, and enjoying a great range of games and pastimes, from the 'show of childish marriage' mentioned by John Dee, to the bandy-ball recalled in a superbly Proustian reminiscence of Henry Newcome's (40, 41, 48–50, 52–5).

It was especially while at play that children ran the risk of near fatal accidents from such hazards as high stairs, deep water, fire, animals and sharp objects. Deliverances from accidental death bulk large in many pious journals as instances of God's mercy (40, 42, 44, 46, 48, 49, 54). Far more important causes of child mortality were various diseases, including ague, plague, measles, and, especially in the second half of the period, the dreaded smallpox (42, 47–9, 51). The anxieties parents suffered in the face of the dangers to their children and the difficulties they encountered in coming to terms with children's deaths are evident in a number of these passages, but nowhere more poignantly expressed than in Nehemiah Wallington's event book (42). Belief that God had called their children home to himself was the key, for the pious, to acceptance of their loss, but such acceptance was hard to achieve. Mrs Wallington used the vivid simile of a wet-nurse called upon to return a child to its parents to bring home to her husband the Christian's duty willingly to yield up the child entrusted to him by God.

The divine trust was felt by pious parents, whether nonconformists or loyal members of the Church of England, to convey a heavy responsibility. This is especially evident in Henry Newcome's diary entries (49). Newcome worried about his own bearing towards his sons and daughters, and the example he set them. Patience with children was, he realized, essential, but so, he believed, was correction in season, much though he disliked it. Religious instruction was the most important of all parental duties in the eyes of the godly. Newcome's diary refers to various forms of it. Among the consequences of early and thorough exposure to religious teaching and imagery were dreams of Jesus (44), consciousness of sin, a vivid belief in the after-life (48) and a precocious ability to die a 'good' death. In much of this material twentieth-century readers may think they see something morbid. That will be above all because they no longer fully share these writers' beliefs about the nature of God, the reality of sin, of judgement and of resurrection to an eternity of bliss or pain.

Christian doctrines provided powerful comforts in face of the terrible waste of young life experienced by the people of Stuart England, but these comforts had their price.

The experience of childhood in the households of the pious was not necessarily a dreary one, however; nor were all their children amenable to the inculcation of parental beliefs. Boisterous games and mischievous pranks were described by a number of diarists. Henry Newcome seems to have been quite unable to curb his son Daniel's inborn propensity for risking his life in dangerous sports. He approached the task of correction with the heavier heart because the scapegrace Daniel was his favourite son. Objective assessment in the light of his guiding beliefs might tell him that his dutiful and studious son Henry was his 'best child', but there is no mistaking the affectionate pride with which he described Daniel as his 'finest boy' (49). The pious were capable of wholehearted natural enjoyment of their children despite their paramount concern with their duty to God. Among the delights of Nehemiah Wallington's often sombre life was the pretty 'prattling' of his little daughter Sarah (42).

An excellent study of colonial America[1] has convincingly demonstrated that there existed during this period different patterns of upbringing, to which parental beliefs, temperament and social circumstances all contributed. The godly examined themselves and their actions more thoroughly than did other diarists, and their views of parental duties were the most coherent and explicit. It is more difficult to do justice to other modes of upbringing in a selection of this kind. Yet some of these diaries betray a much more secular temper in family life. Sir Henry Slingsby seems to have believed that only an apparently mortal danger during a Humber crossing aroused in his son Thomas a genuine impulse to pray, despite the instruction he had received from his mother (43). In Thomas Isham's chronicle of country sports, social life and estate management there are few signs of spiritual concerns (52). Betty Morris was encouraged by her indulgent father to appreciate worldly pleasures (55).

---

[1] P. Greven, *The Protestant Temperament: Patterns of Child-rearing, Religious Experience, and the Self in Early America* (Alfred A. Knopf, New York, 1977).

Diaries show that the bond between parents and children, in an age sometimes portrayed as one of distance and deference, was often close. The last recorded words the little Elizabeth Wallington spoke to her parents are full of affectionate spontaneity rather than enforced respect (42). All the puritan ministers among these diarists participated personally in their children's education; the fact that two of them sometimes found their offspring trying is a pointer to the genuineness of their effort. Among the upper classes parents could if they wished delegate to servants much of the work of upbringing. This might make for a more distant relationship, but it was no barrier to the interest of an affectionate or conscientious parent. Only children perhaps enjoyed an exceptional share of their parents' attention, and Lady Anne Clifford's attachment to her daughter Margaret was enhanced by the fact that she looked to 'the child' as a source of the affection denied her by her estranged husband (41). Fathers often took a close personal interest in their eldest sons' preparation for their future responsibilities as head of the family: Sir Justinian Isham is an excellent example (52). But other diaries show that only or eldest children were not the only ones to enjoy their parents' affection and frequent contact with them. The Countess of Bridgewater delighted in her little daughter Katy (47). Sir Richard Newdigate could try to play the patriarch in a rather tiresome fashion, but we catch charming glimpses of him picking fruit for his girls and teaching one of them how to count money (53). Newdigate left the indelible imprint of his strong if somewhat eccentric personality on the exiguous surviving scraps of his journal. But even the dullest diary has a unique pattern, and the abiding impression left by these passages is one of great variety in the quality of relationships between parents and children.

40   JOHN DEE'S CHILDREN, 1582–96: GAMES,
ACCIDENTS AND EDUCATION

[A selection from Dee's notes about his children, which also mention during this period various of their illnesses, and (very briefly) Michael's death in July 1594. The Dees were on the continent between September 1583 and December 1589.]

[1582, January] 22/23 Arthur Dee and Mary Herbert, [*illegible word*] being but three year old the eldest, did make as it were a show of childish marriage, of calling each other husband and wife. . . .

[July] 3. *At a quarter past twelve*, Arthur Dee fell from the top of the Watergate Stairs down to the foot from the top, and cut his forehead on the right eyebrow.

[1587, September] 1. Tuesday mornïng, covenanted with John Bassett to teach the children the Latin tongue, and I to give him seven ducats by the quarter, and the term to begin this day; and so I gave him presently seven ducats Hungary in gold before my wife. God speed his work.

[1588, January] 1. On New Year's Day, about nine of the clock after noon, Michael, going childishly with a sharp stick of eight inches long and a little wax candle light on the top ot it, did fall upon the plain boards in Mary's chamber, and the sharp point of the stick entered through the lid of his left eye towards the corner next the nose, and so pierced through, insomuch that great abundance of blood came out under the lid, in the very corner of the said eye; the hole on the outside is not bigger than a pin's head; it was anointed with St John's oil. The boy slept well: God speed the rest of the cure. . . . The next day after it appeared that the first touch of the stick's point was at the very middle of the apple of [his?] eye, and so (by God's mercy and favour) glanced to the place where it entered with the weight of his head and the force of his fall. Thus I may make some show of it.[1] To the praise of God for his mercies and protection.

---

[1] A sketch illustrates the accident at this point.

[*August*]·5· After dinner the little boy, son to the Captain of Rhaudnitz,[2] hurt Arthur's nose with a razor, not in anger, but by chance wantonly.

[*1589, May 21*] Katharine by a blow on th'ear given by her mother did bleed at the nose very much, which did stay for an hour and more; afterward she did walk [in?]to the town[3] with Nurse and [after?] her coming home an hour, she bled again, very sore, by gushes and [pulses?], very fresh good blood, whereupon I perceived it to be the blood of the artery . . .

[*1590, March 25*][4] My children at this Lady Day in Lent began to go to school at Mortlake with the schoolmaster Mr Lee; I gave him his house rent and forty shillings yearly for my three sons and my daughter.

[*May*] 21.31 . . . Katharine my daughter was put to Mistress Bracye at Brentford;[5] her mother, Arthur etc. went with her af[ter?] dinner.

[*July 29*] Theodore had a sore fall on his mouth at midday.

[*August 5*] Rowland fell into the Thames over head and ears about noon or somewhat after.

[*1591 June*] 27. Arthur wounded on his head by his own wanton throwing of a brickbat upright, and not well avoiding the fall of it again, at Mr Herbert's, about sunsetting. The half brick weighed 21lib½.

[*September 22*] Madinia fell from the bed and hurt her forehead about one of the clock afternoon.

[*1592 May*] 3. Wednesday, at 10 of the clock, Arthur was put to Westminster School under Mr Grant and Mr Camden.

[*1593 August 17*] I and my wife and Katharine our daughter dined with the Lord Keeper at Kew.

[*September*] Remember that the last day of this month Elizabeth Kyrton, who had served me twelve years, . . . was paid her full payment now remaining due; . . .and I gave her moreover an half angel [noble?] in gold, and my wife another; Arthur half-a-

---

[2] Roudnice (Czechoslovakia).
[3] Bremen.
[4] Dates in MS 488 are new style, but for the incidents recorded in England, old-style equivalents are given here.
[5] *Braynf[o?]rd*. There is a pointing hand beside this entry.

crown for him and his brethren;[6] Katharine half-a-crown for her and her sister. . . .

[*1596 September*] 1. Mary Goodwyn came to my service to govern and teach Madinia and Margaret, my young daughters.

Oxford, Bodleian Library, MSS Ashmole 487 and 488 (written in A. Maginus, *Ephemerides Coelestivm motvvm . . . ad annos XL . . .* (1582); 1588–90 entries come from this).

41 LADY ANNE CLIFFORD AND HER DAUGHTER MARGARET (B. 2 JULY 1614), 1616–19

[*1616, December 23*] . . . About 5 o'clock in the evening my Lord and I and the child went in the great coach to Northampton House, where my Lord Treasurer and all the company commended her; and she went down into my Lady Walden's chamber, where my Coz. Clifford saw her and kissed her, but I stayed with my Lady Suffolk.

[*1617, January*] Upon the 22d the child had her sixth fit of the ague in the morning. Mr Smith went up in the coach to London to my Lord, to whom I wrote a letter to let him know in what case the child was . . . The same day my Lord came down to Knole to see the child.

[*23*] . . . The same day the child put on her red baize[1] coats.

Upon the 25th I spent most of my time in working and in going up and down to see the child. About 5 or 6 o'clock the fit took her, which lasted six or seven hours.

[*February*] Upon the 4th should have been the child's fit, but she missed it. . . . Upon the 6th the child had a grudging of her ague again at night. . . .

Upon the 12th the child had a bitter fit of her ague again, insomuch I was fearful of her that I could hardly sleep all night, so I beseeched God Almighty to be merciful to me and spare her life. . . .

---

[6] brethern.

---

[1] Bays.

After supper the child's nose bled, which I think was the chief cause she was rid of her ague.

Upon the 21st the child had an extreme fit of the ague and the doctor set by her all the afternoon and gave her a salt powder to put in her beer.

[*March*] The 11th we perceived the child had two great teeth come out so that in all she had now eighteen. . . .

[*April*] The 28th was the first time the child put on a pair of whalebone bodice.

[*May*] Upon the 1st I cut the child's strings off from her coats and made her use to go² alone, so as she had two or three falls at first but had no hurt with them.

The 2d the child put on her first coats that was laced with lace, being of red baize.

. . . The 14th the child came to lie with me, which was the first time that ever she lay all night in a bed with me since she was born.

The 15th the child put on her white coats and left off many things from her head, the weather growing extreme hot.

[*August 3*] . . . This night the child lay all night with my Lord and me, this being the first night she did so.

[*October*] The 25th, being Saturday, my Lady Lisle, my Lady [*blank in MS*], my Coz. Barbara Sidney and I walked with them [*sic*] all the Wilderness over and had much talk with her of my Coz. Clifford and other matters. They saw the child and much commended her. . . .

The 30th fell the child to be something ill and out of temper like a grudging of an ague, which continued with him [*sic*] about a month or six weeks after.

[*No entries for 1618 survive.*]

[*1619, January 1*] . . . This day the child did put on her crimson velvet coat laced with silver lace, which was the first velvet coat she ever had. . . .

[*June 4*] . . . This night was the first that Lady Margaret lay alone, Marie having a bed made hard by.

---

² Sackville-West read *togs*.

[*July 2*] . . . This night my Lady Margaret was five years old so as my Lord caused her health to be drank throughout the house.

22d My Lady Margaret began to sit to Mrs [*sic*] Vansommer for her picture.

Maidstone, Kent Archives Office, MS U269. F48/2,3.

42 NEHEMIAH WALLINGTON'S CHILDREN: DEATHS AND DELIVERANCES, 1625–32

That in the year of our Lord 1625, it pleased God to send among us in this city and the suburbs such a plague (for our sins and abominations) that there died in one week in August 5205, and from the 6 of January to the twenty-seven of October, fifty-three thousand two hundred sixty and five. I and my wife and my children continuing still in this doleful city, hearing of bells tolling and ringing out continually, could not but make us wonder at the hand of God to be so hot round about us, and yet we should escape; and hearing of the death of so many of our acquaintance, and seeing of coffins[1] going by almost every day, and hearing how God swept away whole families, and taking away fifteen or sixteen out of some houses, leaving one or two in the house; and we did hear that one woman laid eight pair of sheets in Mary Whitechapel churchyard. And we did hear of three score children died out of one alley and thirty out of another alley, and many more out of other places, made us wonder that the Lord should spare us and ours, we being as great sinners as they: and thus would I say to my family, 'Although we escape now, yet when there dieth but two or three in a week, one of us may be one of them; and therefore not to be secure, but every one of us to prepare for death.' . . .

And thus would I meditate with myself alone: 'What if the sickness should come into this house: who would I willing spare?' Then would I say: 'The maid. Who next? My son John. Who

[1] *coffings.*

next? My daughter Elizabeth. Who next? Myself. But what if God should strike thy wife or thy father, or thy Brother John? How would I take it then?' I did think to take it patiently, and to comfort myself in the Lord, considering the sorrows and troubles they were gone out of, and the pleasure and joy that they are gone into. For ⟨Psalm xvi 11⟩ 'In thy presence is the fullness of joy, and at thy right hand there are pleasures for evermore.' Many tears I did shed with these thoughts; and I desired the Lord if it might stand with his glory and my soul's good that I might die first and never see that day. . . .

And on [*Saturday, 8 October 1625*] . . . in the afternoon, Ruth[2] told my wife that she had a pricking in her neck, which words put us all in fear, and toward night she went to bed. And about eight a clock at night my wife was in the kitchen[3] washing of dishes; my daughter Elizabeth, then being merry, went unto her mother and said unto her, 'What do you here, my wife?' And at night when we were abed says she to me, 'Father, I go abroad tomorrow and buy you a plum pie.' These were the last words that I did hear my sweet child speak. For the very pangs of death seized upon her on the Sabbath day morning, and so she continued in great agonies (which was very grievous unto us the beholders) till Tuesday morning, and then my sweet child died at four a clock in the morning, being the eleventh day of October, and was buried that day at night. The grief for this child was so great that I forgot myself so much that I did offend God in it; for I broke all my purposes, promises and covenants with my God, for I was much distracted in my mind, and could not be comforted, although my friends spake so comfortably unto me. And my wife said unto me, 'Husband, I am persuaded you offend God in grieving for this child so much. Do but consider what a deal of grief and care we are rid of, and what a deal of trouble and sorrow she is gone out of; and what abundance of joy she is gone into. And do but consider it is your daughter's wedding day, and will you grieve to see your daughter go home to her husband Christ Jesus, where she shall never want, but

---

[2] a servant of Wallington's.
[3] *cheaching*.

have the fullness of joy for evermore? Consider how willingly Abraham went to offer up his only son Isaac, although he were to be his own executioner.' Then said I unto my wife, 'Do you not grieve for this child?' 'No, truly, Husband, if you will believe me, I do as freely give it again unto God as I did receive[4] it of him.' . . .

On the xxv day of March 1626 it pleased the Lord to afflict my son John so that he was very sick and ate nothing for one whole week, but only took some cold beer. The night before he died he lay crying all that night, 'Mame, O John's hand! O John's foot!', for he was struck cold all one side of his body; and about three a clock in the morning Mistress Trotter that watch with him wakened my wife and I and told us he was a departing now. And my wife started up and looked upon him; he then being aware of his mother, he said, 'Mame, John fall down, opaday. Mame, John fall down, opaday.' And the next day he had two or three fits that we thought he would have died at that time, and at eleven a clock at night he said unto the maid, 'Jane, some beer', and she gave him some beer. Then he said, 'Opaday!' These are the last words that my sweet son John spake; and so ended this miserable life on Tuesday the fifth day of April 1626.

My daughter Sarah began to be sick in September 1628, and she continued six weeks very sick that we all thought she would have died; but, God be thanked, she recovered: his Name be praised. And before she was quite well it pleased the Lord to visit my sweet son Nehemiah with sickness; and he continued four[5] weeks very sick, and three weeks he ate nothing to speak of but drunk cold drink, and one week he lay speechless. We used all the means we could both outward and inward, and made many bills and sent them to the churches and had the prayers of many of the children of God both public[6] and private; but the Lord would not hear us, but took from us our sweet son Nehemiah the seventh day of November 1628 for causes best known to himself. A bitter portion indeed it was to part from

---

[4] *reseued.*
[5] *fore.*
[6] *puplike.*

an only son; yet it was wholesome. For no affliction seemeth for the present joys,[7] but grievous, but afterward it bringeth forth the pleasant fruits of righteousness. So this affliction brought to our minds many heavenly meditations. My wife's meditation to me is this: 'Husband, say we should put our child forth to nurse; and when we see time fit we send for our child, and if Nurse should deny us our child and should think much at us that we fetch it home again, we should then be very angry with her. Even so stands the case with us, for God gave us this child to nurse for him for a while, and now he requires it of us again; therefore let us give it to him willingly.' I told her 'It is true indeed; for it is said (in Matthew xx 15) "Is it not lawful for me to do as I will with my own?".' I did meditate on the II Samuel xii chapter and the 19 20 to the 24 verse and on the first of Job 18, 19, 21, 22 verse and on the second Corinthians the first chapter and the 3, 4, 5, 7, 8, 9, 10 verse. And I did say unto my wife, 'God doth intend us more good than we are aware of, for where a man's treasure is, there is his heart: now that our child is gone to heaven, our heart will be there.' Many more meditations we had which would be too tedious[8] for me to write of.

[*27 November 1630 was notable as a day on which three potentially fatal accidents involving members of Wallington's family were by God's mercy narrowly averted. The following was the third.*]

Again that day at night I and my wife sitting by a good fire and my daughter Sarah was blowing the fire with a small pair of bellows, and she had fell flat into the fire had not the Lord kept her, for as she was falling, my wife gave a sudden start and shoved her at one side so that she had none hurt, blessed and praised be the Lord for it. Amen. My sweet child being very merry all that day and prattling to me prettily the next day, it could not but make me call to mind God's great love and mercy in preserving and delivering us and it. For I thought within myself: 'Whereas now I am delighting to see my child merry, I might have been heavy and weeping over it, to hear the doleful

---

[7] *Ioyes.* Did he mean 'joyous'?
[8] *dedious.*

scrikes[9] and of it [*sic*]; but God hath kept it and us: his Name be praised for evermore. Amen.'

A while after I did hear of a child in Barbinder Lane that did fall into the fire and was burnt to death; it made me call to mind this God's great mercy unto me to deliver me and mine: his name be magnified for ever and ever. Amen.

Another mercy of God toward me in my poor child Sarah is this: that on the xiii day of August {1631} being Saturday at night at five or six a clock my child Sarah went forth with another little child to play, as we had thought; but it seems my daughter Sarah left the other child and went herself as far as the further Tower Hill [*sic*], and as she was going into East Smithfield she fell down and hit herself a sore blow on the forehead. Then she began to cry, then a woman spake unto her, but she could not answer her. Then the woman took her up and began to carry her into Wapping, thinking she had dwelt there; but a porter, seeing her, asked the woman where she carried that child, and she said 'Into Wapping.' Then the porter told her that she dwelt in East Cheap. So the woman brought her home again to us, thanks be given unto God. Now I had been to look for her, but could not find her, and when I came home I was told all this as is aforesaid. Then I began to think of God's great mercy unto me and unto my wife, for it might have been that we should have seen it no more, or if we had it might have been a great while after; and then what strange distractful thoughts should we have had, and how could we eat or have slept that night with thinking 'What is become of our poor child?', thinking 'It may be it is drowned at the water side, or some other mischief hath befallen it'; and how should we have gone to church the next day, being the Sabbath, being full of grief and such distractful thoughts as we should have had? But oh, oh, the goodness of my God in sending this my child in safety home again: his Name for evermore have the praise and glory of it. Amen. Amen.

By reason that my son Samuel did not thrive but consumed and wasted after that he had the fits of the convulsion, we were

---

[9] Shrill cries or screeches.

counselled to put him forth to nurse into the country, and so we did send him to Peckham in January {1632}. And on the 6 of October 1632 we heard our son Samuel was well, and I and my wife went to see him the Tuesday following, being the 9 day of October. And on the next Thursday at night word was brought that my son was very sick, and I went to see him the next morning betimes and one met me by the way and told me my son was dead. Then I returned back again with this heavy news, and we went to the burial of our sweet son Samuel on the 13 day o[f] October being Saturday, which was a very wet day; and we went[10] a mile and half from their house to his grave, and we were wet to the very skin, for it was a very wet and doleful day.

London, Guildhall Library, MS 204, pp. 407–9, 417, 421–2, 434–6, 432.

43   SIR HENRY SLINGSBY, LADY SLINGSBY, AND THEIR SON THOMAS, 1640–1

A rough Humber crossing, 1640

The 28 of August [*September*] we went from Hull to Barton in a passage boat, and having the wind to cross upon us made us sail with more difficulty and danger; and as every present evil seems the most unsupportable, so the fear that my wife sought to avoid seems now less than that she was in by reason of the roughness of the water. And that which made my wife the more apprehensive of danger, was the trouble we had in getting out of the harbour, among the boats that lay there; and being clear of them, we unfortunately fell foul upon another ship that was coming in, which bore us under her, and broke a little of the forepart of our boat, which set my wife and her sister my Lady Vavasour into such a fright as they ceased not weeping and praying till we came ashore at Barton. And my son Thomas was

---

[10] *wend.*

so affrighted with the waters that he gave not over crying, and cried so vehemently as if he would have burst himself, and prayed as heartily. His mother had taught him to say his prayers, but I dare say he never prayed to God before. . . .

Thomas Slingsby's first breeches, 1641

In 1641 I sent from London against Easter a suit of clothes for my son Thomas, being the first breeches and doublet that he ever had, and made by my tailor Mr Miller; it was too soon for him to wear them, being but five years old, but that his mother had a desire to see him in them, how proper a man he would be . . .

Parsons (ed.), *Diary of Sir Henry Slingsby*, pp. 58–9, 71–2.

44 RALPH JOSSELIN AND HIS YOUNG CHILDREN, 1644–57

Deliverances from mishaps

[*1644*] ⟨October:⟩ 7: . . . When I came home . . . I found God had graciously kept my daughter Mary, who was struck with a horse, her apron rent off with his nails, and her handkerchief rent, and yet she had no hurt; many thought she had been spoiled. The Lord he appoints his angels to keep his from hurt. Lord keep her for thine and let us never forget the same . . .

[*November*] ⟨11:⟩ . . . Mary my daughter was preserved from hurt by the fall of a wainscot door at the Priory: thy name Lord be praised . . .

[*December*] ⟨28:⟩ . . . my son was held out of the fire by his little sister, who held and cried until I came to him. . . .

[*1645, February*] ⟨4:⟩ This day God was good to me . . . in a deliverance from a desperate fall with my daughter in my arms; mercies are multiplied: Lord make me thankful.

[*December, or 1646, January*] ⟨30:⟩ This day I received a merciful providence from God in my son, who fell most dangerously off a chair; his mother feared his skull had been broken; also before in freeing him and his sister from scalding, of which they were in very great danger.

[*1646, March*] ⟨11:⟩ . . . God good in the preservation of my son in a very dangerous fall from a horse-block.

⟨19.⟩ God good to me in preserving my house from fire, the children having made a fire in the room under my study, which might have been a more than ordinary damage in respect of my books. My wife spied it and quenched it, so that it took hold of nothing in the room: to God be the praise. . . .

⟨Apri⟩l: 1: . . . my daughter Mary was a means to save her brother out of the pond; he being on the stairs, his sister called out to the maids: this was thy mercy, oh Lord.

[*1647, October*] ⟨30:⟩ My little Jane fell down the stairs; I was going up and so catched her and saved her falling down half of them; the mercy of God was great that she should fall and have no hurt, and I also there so opportunely to save her: blessed be the Lord for all his goodness herein.

[*1648*] ⟨February:⟩ 20: . . . On the Lord's day Jane fell into the fire, and afterwards dagged a pair of scissors in Thom[*as's*] eyebrow; but God preserved both from any great hurt, blessed be his Name . . .

[*1650, March*] ⟨5:⟩ . . . my son Thomas escaped a great danger from a great mastiff bitch who run mad and snapped at him, and a little grated his flesh, his stocken being down. . . .

The children's progress, development and attainments

[*1644, December*] ⟨6:⟩ . . . my son Thomas now would walk up and down the house of his own accord; he wants above three weeks of a year old.

[*1645, February*] ⟨7:⟩ . . . my son Thomas, now thirteen months old, would easily shut the parlour door, the first time I observed it.

[*1646*] ⟨November⟩: 15. . . . the Lord was . . . good in the towardly disposition of my daughter [*Mary*], giving her an aptness to her book: the Lord make me wise to train her in his fear. . . .

[*1648*] ⟨Octo⟩ber. 1: This week past was a very comfortable and cheerful season, a summer time indeed; therein God was good to me and mine in our peace, health, plenty, in my little ones, who answer their mother's pains and learn comfortably with her . . .

[*1649, July*] ⟨12.⟩[1] . . . My son Thomas went to school with Mr Harrington. God in mercy bless him and fit him for education and make him a comfort.

⟨November⟩: 1: My boy is now lively, somewhat fuller of spirit, of a good memory, a good speller, apt to learn and attain the hardest words in his Bible or accidence in which he reads; he was almost moped in his disposition, that he would not by any means be drawn to speak; I fear his master's severity was the cause of it. I bless God for his goodness towards him, and his sister Mary, and Jane, who are hopeful and promising buds. . . .

⟨25:⟩ Both these weeks God was good to me and mine in our health . . . Mary was out at Mrs Elliston's, where she learned to sew; God was good to me in my son Thomas, who learned well, and I wish if ever he be a man he would remember I undertook the teaching the school at this time chiefly for his sake among the boys, though my highest aim was to do good while I live . . .

[*1657, June*] ⟨17.⟩ . . . the follies of my young children awakened me to see the sad effects of our fall in Adam, how operative corruption is tainting of us, which I hope shall put me to exercise faith in the blood of Christ, and to receive daily grace to live and walk more exactly.

[*October*] ⟨3.⟩ John put in breeches; I never saw two sons so clad before. Lord let thy Christ hide their and all our nakedness I entreat thee. . . .

Tom recounts a dream, December 1654

⟨8.⟩ . . . this morning my son Tom told me his wonderful dream. Jesus Christ in a white robe came into my pulpit while

---

[1] He possibly went on 13 July.

preaching and hugged me, and I him. Then he came to him and put his inkhorn in his pocket, and carried him into the churchyard, and asked him what he would have. Tom said 'A blessing'. Jesus Christ bade him follow him, and mounted up to heaven, and he after them next Jesus Christ. They ascended in [shoals?];[2] none could go so fast as he; divers would have gone and Jesus Christ bade them go back and not follow him. When in heaven, they were singing melodiously and praying all in white. Jesus Christ and the company passed through over a mountain and over the sea, and then on the land we fell a praying and could not see Jesus Christ. The devil came and made a burring, but presently Jesus Christ came and drave him away and bid him 'get him behind his back, Satan.' Then Christ returned the same way with his into heaven, all returning to earth but he, and his sister Mary[3] would not let him come away; then Jesus Christ told him he must, and he saw him sit at the Father's right hand, which was wonderful. Then, while in heaven, he thought there was terrible thunder, but he was not afraid; and there was, he knew, an earthquake below. I turned him to some texts like these passages: the Lord do my child good by such things.

Macfarlane (ed.), *Diary of Ralph Josselin*, pp. 23–4, 27, 29–30, 33, 53, 56, 57, 75, 107, 113, 139, 172, 183–4, 192, 335, 402, 407.

45   THE PROGRESS OF JOHN GREENE'S ELDEST SON JACK, 1648–52

[*1648*] (April) On the 17th my boy John went first to school in Ironmonger Lane. . . .

[*1649*] . . . This Christmas Day my boy John in breeches, being almost six year old. He could read a chapter pretty well and spell pretty well, having learnt to St Luke in his Testament.

[*1652*] (April) The last day of this month I carried my eldest son John to school to Mr Atkinson's house in Hadleigh parish. I pay £24 per annum, and carried sheets and six napkins and a piece of plate, but no bedding . . .

---

[2] *schoules.*
[3] Mary had died 27 May 1650.

[*December*] My son Jack came home this Christmas; is much improved in learning, can decline any part of speech readily, knows what is Latin for many things, and can make a shift to construe two or three words of very easy Latin, but hath as yet made no Latin at school.

Symonds, 'The Diary of John Greene', *English Historical Review*, 44 (1929), pp. 110, 112–13.

46 RICHARD EVELYN SAVED BY HIS PARENTS, 1654

[*December*] 31 By God's special providence we went not to church, my wife being now so very near her time: for my little son Richard, now about two years old, as he was fed with broth in the morning, a square but broad and pointed bone of some part of a ract[1] of mutton stuck so fast in the child's throat and cross his weasand[2] that had certainly choked him, had not my wife and I been at home; for his maid, being alone with him above in the nursery, was fallen down in a swoon, when we below (going to prayers) heard an unusual groaning over our head, upon which we went up, and saw them both gasping on the floor; nor had the wench any power to say what the child ailed, or call for any help. At last she said she believed a crust of bread had choked her little master, and so it almost had, for the eyes and face were swollen and closed, the mouth full of froth and gore, the face black – no chirurgeon near: what should we do? We called for drink, pour it down, it returns again, the poor babe now near expiring I hold its head down, incite it to vomit, it had no strength. In this despair, and my wife almost as dead as the child, and near despair that so unknown and sad an accident should take from us so pretty a child, it pleased God that on the sudden effort, and as it were struggling his last for life, he cast forth a bone of this shape and form.[3] I gave the child

[1] 'Probably a slip for, but perhaps an unusual form of, rack, the neck, especially used of mutton or veal', De Beer, *Diary*, p. 145 n.4.
[2] Gullet, windpipe or throat.
[3] Diagram sketched in text.

some Lucotellus balsam[4] for his throat was much excoriated. O my gracious God, out of what a tender fear and sad heart into what joy did thy goodness now revive us! Blessed be God for this mercy: wherefore begging pardon for my sins, and returning thanks for this grace, I implored his providential care for the following year.

De Beer (ed.)., *Diary of John Evelyn*, vol. III, pp. 145–6.

47 THE COUNTESS OF BRIDGEWATER, ELIZABETH EGERTON, ON THE DEATH OF HER DAUGHTER KATE[1] *c.* 1660

When I lost my dear girl Kate

My sorrow is great, I confess, I am much grieved for the loss of my dear girl Katy,[2] who was as fine a child as could be. She was but a year and ten months old when, by the fatal disease of the smallpox, it was God's pleasure to take her from me, who spoke anything one bid her, and would call for anything at dinner, and make her mind known at any time, and was kind to all, even to strangers, and had no anger in her. All thought she loved them; her brothers and sister loved her with a fond love. She was so good she never slept nor played at sermon nor prayers. She had received the sacrament of baptism, which washed her from her original sin, and she lived holily. She took delight in nothing but me, if she had seen me; if absent, ever had me in her words, desiring to come to me: never was there so fond a child of a mother. But she now is not in this world, which grieves my heart, even my soul, but I must submit, and give God my thanks, that he once was pleased to bestow so great a blessing as that sweet child upon me.

British Library, MS Egerton 607, ff. 232–6.

[4] Medicine invented by Luigi Loccatelli, d. 1637; see De Beer, *Dairy*, p. 146 n. 1.

[1] Date uncertain, but most probably written between early 1659 and spring 1661.
[2] *Keatty*.

48 MRS ALICE THORNTON'S CHILDREN, 1659–68

Alice Thornton's preservation, 1659[1]

I must not forget to glorify my gracious Lord God, who did deliver my dear Naly from falling into the fire in my chamber at Hipswell, when I was sitting in the chair; then did the child stumble on the hearth and fell into the fire on the range with one of her hands, and burned her right hand three fingers of it, and by God's help I did pull her out of the fire by her clothes. I catched her out of it before she was exceedingly burned; only three of her fingers sore burned to the bone, which I, being but three weeks laid in of Betty, could not dress, but was cured by my dear mother's help, for which eminent deliverance I humbly bless and praise the Holy One of Israel. Amen. . . .

Alice consoles her mother, 1660

. . . After the death of my dear Willy Thornton I took the cross very sadly, that he died so soon, and had many sad thoughts of God's afflicting hand on me, and one day was weeping much about it. My dear Naly came to me, then being about four years old, and looked very seriously on me, said, 'My dear Mother, why do you mourn and weep so much for my Brother Willy? Do you not think he is gone to heaven?' I said, 'Yes, dear heart, I believe he is gone to heaven, but your father is so afflicted for his loss, and being a son he takes it more heavily, because I have not a son to live.' She said again, 'Mother, would you or my father have my brother to live with you, when as God has taken him to himself to heaven, where he has no sickness, but lives in happiness? Would you have him out of heaven again, where he is in joy and happiness? Dear Mother, be patient, and God can give you another son to live with you and my father, for my

[1] Italicized headings have been taken from Jackson, *Autobiography of Mrs Alice Thornton*; others are my own.

brother is in happiness with God in heaven.' At which the child's speech I did much condemn myself, being instructed by the mouth of one of my own children, and begged that the Lord would give me patience and satisfaction in his gracious goodness, which had put such words into the mouth of so young a child to reprove my immoderate sorrow for him, and begged her life might be spared to me in mercy.

Kate hurts Alice in a boisterous game, 1661

My two children was playing at Oswaldkirk[2] in the parlour window, and Kate being very full of sport and play did climb into the window, and leaping down fell upon her sister Alice and thrust her upon the corner of the same with a great force and strength she had, and her sister cried out with pain and soreness which had grievously hurt the inner rind of her belly so sore till I was afraid she had broken it. But it continued a long time; though I put a cerecloth[3] on it, yet doth it now very often hurt and pain her, so that I have cause to bless and praise the name of my God for ever that she was not wounded so as to break her bowels, it being in so dangerous [a] place and hazard in her bearing of children. O praise the Lord for this his great mercy to my poor child and make her thy servant.

My daughter Katherine Thornton's preservation in the smallpox, the 29th of September, 1666

Upon the 29th of September, when I was yet very weak, began my daughter Kate with a violent and extreme pain in the back and head, with such scrikes[4] and torments that she was deprived of reason, wanting sleep, nor could she eat anything. For three days she continued, to my great affliction, not knowing what this distemper would be. At last the smallpox appeared, breaking out abundantly all over; but in her unguidableness struck[5] in

---

[2] Village close to the Thorntons' home at East Newton, where they stayed with Mr Thornton's brother-in-law while their own house was being finished.
[3] Waxed cloth used as a waterproof covering or winding sheet.
[4] Shrill cries or screeches.
[5] *stroke.*

again, so that my brother Portington used many cordials to save her life, after which they appeared, and then we had more hopes, but was in great danger of losing her sight. She was all over her face in one scurf, they running into each other. But lo, by the goodness of God, for which I humbly bless and praise his holy Name, she passed the danger of death, beginning to heal. Her extremity being so great, crying night and day, that I was forced to be removed, though very weak, as before, into the Scarlet Chamber, for want of rest. Blessed be our gracious God, through his infinite mercy directing to good helps and prospering the means, she was preserved and healed again. Hanna Ableson and Mary Cotes was her keepers. About November she went abroad in the house; only lost by this sickness her fair hair on her head, and that beautiful complexion God had given. The Lord supply her soul with the comeliness of his grace and spirit in her heart, making her lovely in his sight. And praised be the Lord my God which was entreated for my child's life. The Lord give me a thankful heart, and that she may live to his glory, for Christ's sake. Amen.

Robert survives a fall, 1668. Early signs of his religious inclinations

It pleased God to give my sweet Robin Thornton a very great deliverance upon the 25th of July. In his play with his sister Kate and cousin Willy Denton, standing in the window in the hay lathe[6] at Newton, which is above four yards from the earth, he fell down into the lane near a great stone, which, if he had light on, might have killed him, falling so high; so that the danger was very great, and his deliverance also, and ought to be had in remembrance with gratitude and hearty thanks to the God of heaven, which sent his angel to preserve my poor child from death or any harm, save a tumble on his face. The glorious name of Jehovah be praised and magnified for his life, and the preservations thereof from all casualties, dangers, sicknesses, dislocations and evils, and giving him a competent share of understanding, wit, memory, a loving and affable nature, with

---

6 *laith:* barn.

several other good gifts tending to the accomplishment of his person with natural endowments. But I do adore the Lord's Name and mercy, which hath begun upon dawning hopes of his grace in his heart, appearing in his being affected with good instructions in the knowledge and fear of God, and his desire to be informed of all things concerning God; with notions of fear in hearing his judgements, with several pathetical expressions of God and his ways. One day, being about four years old, he told me of his own accord that God was a pure, holy, wise and merciful spirit; but the devil was a wicked, lying, malicious spirit. Was it not better to believe the holy good God and serve him than that wicked evil spirit, which would destroy us? I must therefore with humble gratitude take notice with comfort in his mercy, which did not despise the prayers of his handmaid, but given me a gracious answer to my humble supplications when I wanted a son; for this blessing I begged of the Lord as Hanna did Samuel, and has dedicated him to his service, even all his days, further craving the continuance of his favour and grace of his spirit upon my son . . .

Jackson (ed.) *Autobiography of Mrs Alice Thornton*, pp. 122–3, 126–7, 133–4, 157, 170–1.

49   HENRY NEWCOME AND HIS CHILDREN, 1657–65

[*1657*] July. 21. (Tuesday) Daniel, in fishing, fell dangerously into the water at the Ware,[1] and escaped drowning very narrowly.

[*1658*] January 27, (Wednesday) About this time, by the carelessness of a servant, my little boy Peter had a dangerous fall off the dresser; fell upon his head. He might well have been slain thereby. . . .

August 8 (Lord's day) . . . I left Dan very ill when I went. When I came home the next morning I found him well, and Harry very sick. I even thought it must be which child the Lord pleaseth. I thought when I feared Daniel that I should then have

[1] Probably meaning weir.

lost my finest boy; and now Harry is sick, I think I should lose my best child. The one then seemed to have better parts some way, the other a better disposition. It may be that which is to go is usually, with us, the best, which we can worst part with. But I desire to put it to the Lord. The child raved this night, and was sadly out of order; and it pleased God the next morning his distemper was gone. So that *heaviness endured for a night, but joy came in the morning.* Psalm 30.5.

. . . November 23. Rose being got up before day, and sat dressing her by the fire in the dining room, and a brickbat fell down the chimney, by occasion of the chimney-sweeper sweeping in another chimney, and yet it was wonderfully diverted, so as not to hurt her or touch her. Blessed be God!

. . . December 8. (Wednesday) my son Daniel was in the College Court, and was about, in his play, to throw a snowball, and a dog of Mr Greene's came upon him, and pulled him down, and got hold of his leg. He frighted the child sadly. It was black with his teeth, and yet he had no hurt by it. Not long after, he fell in the school yard, and might have fallen down the rock to his utter spoiling, if the Lord had not prevented. Thus this child hath been saved by the Lord.

[*1659*] . . . May 14., being Saturday, I was abroad, and, as I find it recorded, was in a lazy frame; and behold, when I came home, my son Daniel had fallen off the mill-dam as he had been a fishing. If he had fallen on the fall side, he had in all likelihood been drowned; and falling on the other side, he hardly escaped, nobody being with him but his brother, and they both little ones. But the Lord helped him out. I came home, and found him just put in bed. I was much amazed at the danger; thought how the Lord might have exchanged the thoughts of my heart for me. O what a sad thing had this been! And what a mercy hath the Lord afforded me this night! I consider the sad things that befall parents about children. May not one beg of God, that if it be his will, he will save us from such afflictions, and if he sees it good, (1) That my children may be kept in health, or from sad and grievous distempers; (2) However not to die immaturely, if God see it good, especially not untimely deaths; (3) That they may not die while they live; nor be a cross and exercise to us, by rebellious untowardliness . . .

[*The following entries from the years 1661–3 come from Newcome's one surviving original diary instead of from the later abstract.*]

[*1661*] ⟨Sabbath October 6. Children.⟩ . . . I read in Mr White his manual for parents and children,[2] and I was hugely I thought concerned in several passages in it. . . .

When I came in I found my little boy[3] had been ill ever since I went. An affliction I should be thankful to God for, and pray for the removal and mitigation of it. . . .

⟨Wednesday October 23.⟩ I got up about 7, after a weary night with my poor lad. . . . the Lord gave my child some reviving. It may be the Lord will be entreated for the child.

⟨Thursday October 24.⟩ The Lord was very kind to us in the child's reasonable rest this night. . . .

⟨Saturday November 2.⟩ . . . [*On one of his customary Saturday lists of reflections and resolutions*] . . . 7, [*To be*] careful of my children and wise to know how to carry to them. . . .

The Lord hath restored my child. But my great security hath moved the Lord to lay my wife somewhat low this day by distemper and great pain upon her. The good Lord awaken me and relieve her.

⟨Wednesday November 6.⟩ . . . ⟨Patience.⟩ What a deal of patience is requisite to bear any converse with our little children. How peevish and foolish are they! And what fits doth our heavenly Father bear with us in!

⟨Saturday December 1.⟩ . . . I catechized and instructed my children after supper, and we had family duty, and went to bed, and the Lord heard prayer and we had comfort and ease before we slept. Blessed be the Lord.

⟨Sabbath December 22.⟩ . . . I had conference with my children at night, and very comfortable repetition and prayer.

[*1662*] ⟨Tuesday February 4.⟩ . . . After supper I sat with the children till after 8. . . .

⟨Friday February 7.⟩ I rose not till almost 8, being much disquieted by little Peter's being so very ill this night, suddenly taken with vomiting. . . .

[2] There is an asterisk in the margin near here. 'Mr White' was possibly Josias White, author of *A Plaine and Familiar Exposition Upon the Creed, Ten Commandments, . . . by Question and Answer* (1632).

[3] Peter Newcome.

⟨Sabbath February 9.⟩ . . . ⟨Mercy.⟩ . . . Came home that night, and found my little boy hearty. He met me at door. Blessed be God for this mercy. . . .

⟨Wednesday February 19.⟩ . . . I had an occasion that might have sadded me this evening. My son Daniel in his passion spoke very irreverently and sinfully to me. I did desire to deal with him as well as I could to make him sensible of his sin, and I prayed to God to forgive him, poor child. . . .

⟨Sabbath February 23.⟩ . . . ⟨Parents' patterns.⟩ . . . The Lord hear prayers for our poor children and help us to do everything exactly, as not writing a running hand, but copying every line. For children will imitate what we do.

⟨Tuesday July 8.⟩ . . . After supper I helped the boy with his Latin. . . .

⟨Monday July 28.⟩ . . . I was forced to correct my son Daniel for his running out without leave, which is a very unpleasant work to me. The Lord sanctify it to him for the bowing of him unto God.

⟨Tuesday December 23.⟩. . . ⟨Mercy.⟩ . . . Have much comfort in the towardly studiousness of my son H[*arry*], which I have cause to bless God for and to pray earnestly about, that it may be continued, improved and sanctified.

[*1663*] ⟨Thursday May 21.⟩ . . . Mr Wickins . . . was with me. Harry was examined by him. The Lord hath showed me much mercy in his forwardness, and that his master takes such delight in him. . . .

[*1664*] March 21. (Monday.) My son Daniel went with his brother to bring John Russell and Ebenezer Fornace on their way to Oxford. He would not be persuaded nor commanded to change horses with his brother, but would ride on a fiery little mare, which was my Cousin Davenport's. The Lord did return him safe to us, but he was dangerously thrown.

⟨Thursday, October 6.⟩ I discharged my duty of correction to my poor child (Daniel), prayed with him after, entreating the Lord that it might be the last correction (if it were his will), that he should need.

October 16 (Lord's day.) I began the exercise in my family of having seven chapters of historical Scripture given account of, and to discourse of these sacred histories with the children according to their capacity; which we have kept on foot with profit and delight, and gone over all the history of the Bible.

[*1665*] January 31. (Tuesday.) The children shot at school for their cocks[4] this day, and I was moved much with fear about them, more than I had been; and I earnestly prayed that God would preserve them, and he did, and I desired to be thankful. And February 3 I understood I had cause, for Daniel's hat on his head was shot through with an arrow. The like care and fear was upon my wife's spirit also, and prayed also, and we spake of it at night, and concluded to bless God for their preservation, and now we saw that neither prayers nor praises were in vain.

Manchester, Chetham's Library, MS Mun.A.3.123, ff. 76, 83, 94, 96, 103, 163, 165, 176 and ff. 30–1 of supplementary extracts; MS Mun. A.2.140 (unfoliated).

50 HENRY NEWCOME'S MEMORIES OF HIS OWN CHILDHOOD, 1666–7

[*1666*] October 21. I was this day put in mind of some of the sins of my childhood by the weather, a softly rain. It made me freshly remember how at this time of the year, on the Lord's days ofttimes, in just such rainy days, we have played eagerly at bandy-ball.[1] We counted it fair enough for that sport, and we usually played at it on the Lord's day. Thus the Lord can by unthought of circumstances make one possess the sins of his youth. The time, the place, the person, the weather, may make one's heart sad in such remembrances.

[*1667*] September 6. Being abroad at Hulton Lane, we walked abroad and nutted. It put me in mind of my youth; and might have minded me of sin, in that sometimes on the Lord's day, when a child, I had done so.

Manchester, Chetham's Library, Mun.A.3.123, ff. 206, 218.

[4] Shooting at a cock tied to a stump or board: J. J. Bagley, *Lancashire Diarists: Three Centuries of Lancashire Lives* (Phillimore, London and Chichester, 1975), p. 33.

[1] Hockey.

51   A WIDOWED CLERGYMAN AND HIS
CHILDREN: OLIVER HEYWOOD AND HIS SONS
JOHN AND ELIEZER, 1666–72

On June 9 1666 being a Saturday when my maid was gone to Halifax market, and my two sons and I kept the house, in the chamber I set them both a praying, and then I went to prayer myself. My son John kneeled by me, and wept very sore; when I had done I asked him whether he understood me; he said 'Yes'. Then I fell a discoursing with them about the state of their souls, we all three wept sore, they were much affected with their state by nature, etc. It was a melting season. Who knows but some buddings may appear afterwards? 'They that sow in tears shall reap in joy'[1] – oh how many tears have been shed for them: they are dedicated to the Lord, oh for a little grace for their poor souls.

On Friday November 16 I returned to mine own house at Coley Hall, where I found my family in good measure of health, though my Eliezer had not been well of a swelling in his face, which now is fallen, blessed be God. My John on Lord's day sennight being November 4, I being from home and my maid out of the house, at her return found him weeping bitterly, sore bleared, having begun it as he was reading a chapter. She of a long time could not get from him the cause, he still sobbed and took on very heavily; at last he told her it was because he had sinned against God and had offended him. Blessed be God for this beginning of God's work upon his heart.

Upon Friday [*November 30*] I purposed a journey, but upon Thursday night my son John fell very sick and continued ill till Lord's day, which hindered my designed journey. We feared the smallpox, which are rife about us, but this day being Monday he is much better, I hope recovering. He hath been much affected in my discourse with him about good things – blessed be God. . . . came home to Coley Hall that night, safe and sound; found all well, being December 19 1666.'

---

[1] Psalm 126, verse 5.

As the Lord had blessed me abroad, so my poor family at home; they have been in health, my sons have been very towardly, plied their book, read chapters, learned catechisms, got some chapters and psalms without book; John repeated the 12th, Eliezer the 10th of Revelation last night in bed – blessed be God.

[*18 January 1667*] . . . when I came home I found my son John very sick of the smallpox (a raging disease through the country); he had been grievously heart-sick before they broke out: blessed be God that yet he is alive, and they come out pretty kindly; it was a week that day I came home since he begun. He speaks even beyond his age, and though he be in pain, yet he saith his heavenly Father takes care of him, etc. . . .

. . . upon Thursday (after five weeks' voyage[2]) October 24 67 we returned to Coley Hall, where we found my son John very sick of the measles, and that very day neighbours were called in to see him die, but God restored him. Eliezer had also passed that disease in our absence, and Martha my maid had been near death; but blessed be our God that hath not made a breach upon us, nor laid them all under sickness together, but successively, and now hath wonderfully raised their bodies: oh for a thankful heart.

[*1669*] On Saturday morning, my sons having not made their Latin in expectation to go to Halifax were loath to go to school, yet I threatened them, they went crying, my bowels worked and I sent to call them back, and I went into my study and fell on my knees and found sweet meltings – if God [set?] in a little they will occasion much good – this was February 13 68/9.

[*1671*] This day being August 24 71, called Black Bartholomew Day,[3] I resolved to keep a fast, and because I came home but last night, and could get no more company, I kept it with my family. The forenoon we spent in prayer, beginning at youngest. Eliezer prayed first very sensibly, though short, John prayed both a long time and exceeding pertinently and affectionately,

---

[2] A land journey in this case.
[3] So called because the Act of Uniformity had come into force on this day in 1662.

weeping much; I admired at it. God helped my maid, my wife and myself wonderfully – oh what a melting duty and day was it! . . .

[*6 May 1672*] On Monday I went to Morley to make way for my sons' going to school.

[*13*] On Monday I went with my sons to Morley, where they go to school to Mr David Noble, are tabled at Thomas Dawson's. . . .

British Library, MS Add. 45964, f. 61^v; MS. Add. 45965, ff. 29^v–31^r, 39^r, 49^v, 62^v, 82^v.

52 SOME DAYS FROM THE FIRST MONTH OF FOURTEEN-YEAR-OLD THOMAS ISHAM'S JOURNAL, NOVEMBER 1671[1]

⟨1⟩ My father first taught me the way to draw parallel lines and to divide a straight line. Father was godfather to the son of John Hanbury Esq., and the name given the child was John.

⟨2⟩ Thomas Hagady's wedding took place, and William, Mr Baxter's eldest son, lost his ribbon and burst into tears.

⟨3⟩ Toss was shut up to breed with Mr Richardson's little bitch, which has its name from its beauty.

⟨4⟩ Mr Guy came here and dined with us, and said he would send Father twenty fruit trees as a gift.

---

[1] In his edition (see appendix) Sir Gyles Isham included copious notes on the people mentioned in the diary. Nearly all those referred to in this extract fall into one of four broad categories: gentry, clergy, other professional men, and servants of the Isham family. The majority of those here called 'Mr', as well as people of the rank of Esquire and above, belonged to the local gentry. Others called 'Mr' were clergymen: Thomas Baxter, rector of Lamport, Richard Richardson, vicar of Brixworth (tutor to the Isham boys), and Gilbert Clerk, of Loddington, a distinguished mathematician who both taught the Isham boys and acted as an agent for the family. The Ishams also used the professional services of Mr Robert Guy, a lawyer, and Thomas Nuns, a surveyor. Among their servants were William Smith, Thomas Pole, Katharine Parry, Edward Holland (possibly Sir Justinian's valet), and Robert White. Thomas Hagady was a 'small yeoman farmer'.

⟨5⟩ The country feasts were celebrated according to custom. Father promised to pay me £6 each year if I would describe in writing whatever happened each day.

⟨6⟩ Sir William Craven and his wife, the daughter of Gilbert [*George*] Clerke Esq. of Watford, dined with us. Mr Wikes came with his hounds and challenged ours to a coursing match, but the beaters could not find a hare. The same day a very large hog was killed.

⟨7⟩ William Smith returned from London and said that John Chapman, our bailiff, had sold all the beasts. When asked whether he brought any news, he said that, being hindered by other business, he had not been eager for news, adding a proverb in the manner of countrymen: 'Go day, come day, God send Sunday.'

⟨8⟩ John Chapman returned home. The same day, labourers with a team of horses carried stones out of the orchard to mend the highways.

⟨9⟩ A great amount of snow fell and covered the countryside with a white mantle. We finished the first book of Caesar's *Commentaries*. The hound Sissa had eleven puppies, all of which however we drowned early next day.

⟨10⟩ . . . The carpenter set up new shelves for us to put the common books[2] on. A white cock of Brother Justinian's named Taffy, which was at Thomas Pole's, had one of his spurs violently wrenched off and died, from which it is clear that the men of Houghton are indeed rustic and completely ignorant of learning[3] not to remember that trite saying 'Never lay hands on a white cock.'

⟨14⟩ Katharine went to Northampton and bought cloth for Brother Ferdinando's[4] first breeches.

⟨15⟩ Mr Clerke of Watford came to dinner, and also Mr Palmer, domestic chaplain to the earl of Sunderland, with Monsieur Shatto.[5]

⟨16⟩ We finished off division in arithmetic.

---

[2] *libros communes*: the precise significance of the phrase remains obscure.
[3] *grammaticae*.
[4] Fifth son of Sir Justinian, b. 18 April 1663.
[5] Or Chattover, Frenchman and butler to the Earl of Sunderland.

⟨17⟩ Father, with Mother and Sister, set out to visit Mrs Syers of Loddington.

⟨18⟩ Father and I went into the fields to decide where new ditches should be dug and hedges set.

⟨19⟩ While we were at dinner Mr Clerk of Loddington called in.

⟨20⟩ . . . . Our cook, who had said he would give Holland five shillings if he played at dice with the Doctor,[6] was unable to control himself and played again. The same day a row of cherries was planted; where, while we were inspecting the workmen, we found two shillings, and since it was not clear whose they were, we divided them among the workmen. Cook returned from Mr Guy the lawyer's, and brought twelve fruit trees which ought to be planted tomorrow.

⟨21⟩ Today Thomas Nuns measured the fields near Haybrig, and near the spring commonly called Rodewell. A certain horse had strayed in Scaldwell Field, which the villagers shut in the pound for three whole weeks, and since no one claimed it they brought it here. . . .

⟨22⟩ Mr Wright dined with us, and at dinner asked for beer; he did not notice when it was brought to him, and while he was striking up a conversation with Mother, and officiously doffing his hat, he spilt it over the table and splashed the guests who were sitting next to him, especially the celebrated man Alexander Charles Curtius, Doctor of Medicine.[6] To make up for his fault he apologized profusely and invited him to his house in the most courteous fashion.

⟨23⟩ Cook went to Olney to buy all sorts of trees to plant in our new orchard.

⟨24⟩ The trees were planted in rows in the orchard in the form of a quincunx.

⟨26⟩ Our mastiff bit Squirrel, and because Trunk was thought to be the cause, he was banished to Maidwell.

⟨27⟩ Mr Poulton came with Major Hazlewood to dinner . . .

---

[6] Dr Alexander Charles Curtius, a noble Lithuanian whose doctorate had been conferred by the University of Leyden, 'a refugee, in whom Sir Justinian took a kindly interest': see Isham (ed.), *Diary of Thomas Isham*, p. 65 n. 41.

⟨30⟩ . . . White pruned the hanging branches which were causing trouble to the fruit trees. Twigden's ferrets were very nearly killed by a marten which hid in a cave near the Mount.

Northampton, Northamptonshire Record Office, Isham of Lamport MS, I.L. 527.

53 SIR RICHARD NEWDIGATE AND HIS CHILDREN, 1683

[*June 25*] . . . Sup[*ped*]. Finished reading *Elder B[rothe?]r*[1] to the children. . . .

⟨Wednesday 27.⟩ . . . Sup[*ped*]. Was pleasant with the children, but very weary. . . .

[*July*] ⟨Monday 2.⟩ . . . Dined with the two Mrs Parker and Nan Paul, the Countess of Essex her nursery maid. Walked with my wife and them and the children ith garden and saw the grotto, and Stephens vaulting and Phill[2] dance and play. Then I fenced with Stephen, and then looked about the works. Sup[*ped*]. Bowled with Mr Wyat and Dicky.[3] . . .

⟨Friday. 27.⟩ . . . With our company till 3. Then counted my money and taught Phill to do so till 5. . . .

⟨Sunday. 29.⟩ . . . Dined with my wife and all the children. . . .

[*August*] ⟨Sunday 5.⟩ . . . Went into the garden and eat (rather) too much fruit with Dick. Gathered some for my aunt and cousin and the girls, to whom I gave sparingly. . . .

⟨Monday 6.⟩ . . . Paid Mr Wyat 15*l* for the four boys' teaching and diet. Dined. . . . Walked ith garden with the girls. . . .

[*September*] ⟨Friday 28.⟩ ⟨Mr Wyat and my 4 boys⟩ . . . I supped with Mr Wyat and the children and discoursed with him till prayers. . . .

Warwick, Warwickshire Record Office, Newdegate of Arbury MSS, CR 136/ B 1307, D–F.

---

[1] Perhaps this was *The Elder Brother, a Comedie*, attributed to John Fletcher on its first publication in 1637, and to Francis Beaumont and John Fletcher in the edition of 1651.
[2] Amphilis, his eldest daughter, b. 1669.
[3] Richard, his second, and eldest surviving son, b. 1668.

54 MERCIES RECEIVED: SOME OF THE HAZARDOUS EPISODES IN THE LIVES OF WILLIAM COE'S CHILDREN, 1693–1714

⟨Jan⟩uary 9 1692/3. My daughter Judith escaped a great mischief by the fall of a spit which narrowly escaped her head. She was then a little above five years of age.

⟨F⟩ebruary 11th 1693/4. My daughter Betty escaped choking by a pin in her victuals. The Lord make me truly thankful for this and all other his mercies.

[*1695*] ⟨October 7⟩th My son William escaped choking with a pin at dinner.

[*1696*] ⟨December 6.⟩ He escaped burning, his cap on his head being set on fire by a candle.

[*1700*] ⟨May⟩ 12. My son William fell into the creek¹ up to the knee and nobody with him: it was through God's great mercy he did not fall over head and ears and be drowned.

He was then a little above six year old.

[*1701*] ⟨July⟩ 26. My son William got a fall off Mr Meadows mare with Thomas Meadows and she did tread upon his thigh and made it black and blue. But (God be thanked) got no further hurt.

[*1702*] ⟨Nov⟩ember 3. My son William had a dangerous blow upon his eye with the end of an oaken rail, but, God be praised, it did not perish his eye. It was at Tuddenham.

[*1705*] ⟨April 12.⟩ My great bitch Surly which I had from London flew upon my daughter Sarah and bit a hole under her right eye, but, I thank God, she had no further mischief.

⟨June⟩ 3. The same bitch snapped at my daughter Barbara and bit her under her left eye a little hole, but, God be praised, she had no further damage.

[*1706*] ⟨Marc⟩h 2. My house escaped burning by a boiler of fat hanged over the fire and was forgot, but my wife happily saw it just as it began to boil over, and with hastily taking it off as it boiled over and flamed up into chimney some spilled upon

---

¹ *Crick.*

my son Henry's frock as he sat by the fire but by God's mercy did not scald him, so we escaped two great dangers.

[1707] ⟨December⟩ 25. My son Thomas got a sharp awl which I happened to leave about the house and was playing with it and at last run it at my daughter Barbara and thrust it into her arm, but, I thank God, did himself nor her no further harm: it was God's great mercy he did not thrust it into his own eyes or body, or hers.

⟨July⟩ 7, 1709. My son Tommy did hang by the neck in the hall window endeavouring to get out there, being left alone in the house, and it was God's great mercy he was not killed, for there was nobody near to save or help him if he had not scrambled in again of himself, being then between four and five years of age.

⟨171⟩0. November 8. My son Thomas fell backwards into a kettle of scalding water and scalded all his back: it put him into a high fever so that we thought he would have died, but, blessed be God, he grew well again and his back healed in less than a month.

[1711] December 10. My two little boys Henry and Thomas was at play in the cowyard, and Thomas was reaching into a cow bing[2] and a cow on the other side of the bing run her horn into his mouth and ranched the inside of his right cheek, and did him no further hurt: for this and all other thy mercies to me and mine my soul doth magnify thee O Lord.

[1712] ⟨April⟩ 11. My son James went into cart horse stable, and playing too near the horses the Delph horse struck him and broke his thumb: it was God's great mercy he did not strike him on the body or head.

⟨July 13.⟩ My two little boys Henry and Tommy on the little hobby came galloping into yard as they came from church and rode against a ladder that stood up against the malt-house (as the thatchers left it) and were both thrown down, but by God's great mercy they got no harm.[3]

⟨December⟩ 15. I lent our coach without the doors to carry Goody Hibble to be buried, and my two sons Henry and Thomas

---

[2] Bin.
[3] One of several accidents involving the hobby.

came home in it; and because it jolted going over wheat ridges Henry jumped out and by God's great mercy got no hurt; if he had jumped short or his clothes had hung on anything the wheel had gone over him.

[*1713*] ⟨December⟩ 26. My son Thomas had a desire to go with my man to the wheelwright's to fetch home two carts that were there to mend, and they were tied one to the other and my son in the foremost; it was night before the man could get away, and my son being cold said he would get down and walk. The[4] man bade him not come down, but by God's good providence the boy would get down, for the cart very soon after overturned, and there was an old wheel in the buck[5] of each cart and that might in all likelihood have killed him or done him some great mischief: for this and all other thy mercies my soul doth mag⟨nify thee O Lord.⟩

[*1714*] ⟨December⟩ 26. My son James fell down the kitchen stairs, made his nose bleed and swelled his cheek a little, but, God be praised, got no further harm. He was then about five years old.[6]

Cambridge University Library, MS Add. 6843, ff. 4ᵛ, 5ᵛ, 6ᵛ, 9ᵛ, 10ᵛ, 12ᵛ, 15ᵛ, 18ᵛ, 22ᵛ, 32ᵛ, 39ᵛ, 40ᵛ, 42ᵛ, 44ᵛ, 47ᵛ, 49ᵛ.

55   CLAVER MORRIS AND HIS DAUGHTER BETTY, 1709–10

[*1709, August*] ⟨20⟩ I writ a letter to my daughter Betty, the first I was able to write. [*Morris was recovering from a dangerous attack of spotted fever; Betty was at boarding school in Salisbury.*]

⟨September 9⟩ I dined and my daughter at Mr Brockwell's; thence I went to a concert[1] at Mr Harris's; afterwards to church, and then back with my daughter to the concert. . . .

⟨December 13⟩ I went to Salisbury to fetch home my daughter from Mrs Deer's boarding school.

---

[4] Or possibly *that*.
[5] The body or back.
[6] Several more accidents were recorded after this date.

---

[1] *Consort.*

[*1710*] ⟨January 2⟩ My dear daughter Betty refused to speak French with Mrs Keen; and I taking it unkindly from her, she fell into tears, and continued grieving in that way even after she came home, so long that I was doubtful of her hurting her constitution; and upon her being sorry for refusing what was desired from her and promising it should be otherwise another time, I forgave her, and she was extremely pleased with the reconciliation.

⟨February 1⟩ My daughter had a ball; at which were Mrs Katherine, Mrs Anne, Mrs Mary and Mrs Hannah Webb; Miss Hooper, Mrs Wiggon, Miss Hughes, Mrs Fanny Pain, Mrs Cannington and her daughter, Miss Mattocks. And Mr Rabatier and Mr Gapper were spectators. They all went off betwixt 12 and 1 a clock.

Hobhouse (ed.), *Diary of a West Country Physician*, pp. 55–6, 58, 60–1.

V

Adolescence and Departure from Home

Some children left home before adolescence, but a very much larger number did so during their teens. Entry into service or apprenticeship took many no further away than a nearby town or village, others to London or a provincial capital. (The dramatic economic development of the metropolis and its terribly high mortality made it dependent on an influx of young immigrants.) The passages which follow show how intimately some parents were concerned in their children's advancement. In this they were probably atypical: the majority would not have had the means or leisure to involve themselves so thoroughly in the business of launching their children in the world. Furthermore, a substantial proportion of those who survived to reach adolescence would already have lost one or both parents.

In the diary of William Carnsew (56), we are able to observe an Elizabethan squire during the very time when provision for his children was becoming his foremost preoccupation. Yet Carnsew's efforts in this direction were only partially successful. In 1576 his three sons were still at home, though two of them had already been at Oxford. His second son, Matthew, and his two girls, died unmarried; none of the five left any children of their own. Perhaps Carnsew's protective solicitude made it harder for his children to spread their wings.

Those anxiously affectionate clerical fathers Ralph Josselin and Henry Newcome also had difficulty in placing sons (57, 58). Both went to some trouble to find suitable masters in London and accompanied sons to the capital in person – a considerable journey for Newcome. Yet of three boys apprenticed by the two men[1] only Thomas Josselin completed an apprenticeship successfully, and that was at the second attempt. The more familiar world of academic learning could also give rise to worries in the minds of conscientious parents (58, 61, 62), which were particularly acute in Oliver Heywood's case. Perhaps the fact that Josselin, Newcome and Heywood each had trouble with at least one of their sons (which was serious in the cases of Josselin and Newcome) was largely due to the unfortunate combination (common to all three) of a stern creed, an anxious temperament and a reluctance to take harsh measures.

The experience of the Derbyshire yeoman Leonard Wheatcroft (60) was probably much more typical of the 'middling sort' of seventeenth-century parents than was that of our three puritan ministers. He took some care in placing his numerous offspring (a task in which he was given valuable help by kinsfolk). Yet the genial and easy-going Wheatcroft seems never to have suffered on this score the terrible worries which tormented some of the pious clerical diarists. That none of Wheatcroft's children went to the bad, so far as we can tell, or caused their father much anxiety, was due in some measure to his own temperament – equable, resilient and affectionate.

Binding a son apprentice or supporting him at the university were both expensive. Some impression of these costs can be obtained from the accounts kept by James Jackson (59), especially those which record the flow of supplies to Joseph Jackson at Oxford. A number of friends and neighbours seem to have contributed to a collection on his behalf when he first set out for the university. After apprenticeship had been completed, both James Jackson and Ralph Josselin had to make substantial further investments in order to enable sons to establish themselves as independent tradesmen.[2]

---

[1] For Josselin's difficulties with his son John, see A. Macfarlane, *The Family Life of Ralph Josselin, a Seventeenth Century Clergyman. An Essay in Historical Anthropology* (Cambridge University Press, 1970), pp. 120–3.

[2] See ibid., pp. 46–51, esp. p. 46, for a very useful analysis of Josselin's investment in his sons.

The continuing importance of contacts between one father and his children once the latter had left home is particularly well illustrated by Leonard Wheatcroft's chronicle (60). An indefatigable tramper, Wheatcroft readily visited on foot those of his grown-up children who lived within walking distance, and they were always welcome back to the paternal hearth between periods of service. The process of dispersal was a very gradual one in this family. Many parents, like Wheatcroft, had at least one child still at home to help look after them in old age.[3] Elias Pledger's experience (63) was at the opposite end of the scale from Wheatcroft's. After his wife's death in 1709 and his only surviving son's departure from home he faced a lonely middle and old age. Such a pattern may have been commoner in London, with its high mortality, than it was in the countryside, though the Pledgers had also had an unusually small number of children.

The arrangements made for the training and education of daughters tend to occupy less space in diaries than the launching of sons in the world. Leonard Wheatcroft certainly went to some trouble to place his girls well (60), and other parents worried about their daughters' health, or the risk of their forming unsuitable attachments. But the costs of training girls were usually far less than those of advantageous apprenticeships or higher education for boys. The latter also usually involved a much longer commitment than service for girls. In the case of daughters (at least in the middling ranks of society) parental concern was concentrated above all on the moment of marriage, when heavy investment in a dowry coincided with the tying of a knot which only death could unravel.

[3] P. Laslett, *Family Life and Illicit Love* (Cambridge University Press, 1977), pp. 201, 203–4.

56 WILLIAM CARNSEW AND HIS CHILDREN, 1576

[*January*] ⟨B¹ 16⟩ Read to Mathye and Richard. . . .

[*February*] ⟨E 16⟩ Talked with Richard for his going to London.

⟨F 17⟩ Frances Carnsew very sick.

⟨B 20⟩ Richard and Matthew went to St Germans.² . . .

⟨E 23⟩ Conceived matter in writing to convey Matthew forth.

⟨G 25⟩ Gave Frances Carnsew stybye³ wherewith she was not much molested, but wrought so as she had three vomits, one stool and amended.

⟨*A 26⟩ At home all day. Frances amending; complained of her head and stomach. . . .

⟨B 27⟩ Delivered Matthew letters⁴ to carry to Lord Treasurer, to Earl [*of*] Hertford, to Edmund Tremayne. Richard and he rode both away, Richard to bring him on his way.

[*March*] ⟨D 7⟩ Went with my family to the church, whence John Roscarrock had Richard Carnsew home with him. . . .

⟨B 12⟩ Matthew Carnsew delivered my letters to the Earl of Hertford and had answer.

⟨F 16⟩ At home all day; gave my horse medicine for the botts;⁵ chid Richard for his sloth.

⟨C 20⟩ Read to Richard Littleton, *Tenures*; read to him and William Carnsew Vegetius and Whythorne.⁶

⟨D 21⟩ Read to Richard. . . .

---

¹ Letters A–G stand for the days of the week. A stands for Sunday until 1 April, when, owing to a mistaken repetition, G becomes the Sunday letter. From 5 February onwards, Sundays are also distinguished by a flower-like symbol here printed as an asterisk.

² Where Carnsew's brother-in-law John Eliot lived: see A. L. Rowse, *Court and Country: Studies in Tudor Social History* (Harvester, Brighton, 1987), p. 139.

³ 'Probably a concoction of antimony, the common ore of which was stibnite. It was once used as an emetic.' Pounds, 'William Carnsew of Bokelly and his Dairy', p. 34 n. 39.

⁴ 'These letters concerned mining prospects in Cornwall.' Rowse, *Court and Country*, p. 147.

⁵ Worms.

⁶ Vegetius was author of *De Re Militari*. Perhaps this was J. Sadler's translation, published in 1572. Peter Whitehorne's *Certain waies for the orderyng of souldiers*, was a supplement to his translation of Machiavelli's *Libro dell'arte della guerra*, published in 1560–2.

⟨E 22⟩ Did nothing but read to Richard and saw my hedgers.
. . .

[*April*] ⟨B 17⟩ . . . received letters from Matthew, but not the first he sent me.

[*May*] ⟨B 1⟩ . . . received letters of the 3 of April from Matthew.

⟨C 2⟩ . . . wrate to Matthew Carnsew and Doctor Kenall.[7]

⟨*G 20⟩ Wrate to Matthew by John Roscarrock who supped here.

⟨B 22⟩ Mathye came home. . . .

[*June*] ⟨E 8⟩ Read with Matthew in Orontio.[8] . . .

⟨*G 10⟩ Grace was very evil at ease, of whom I mistrusted.

⟨A 11⟩ She amended. . . .

⟨*G 17⟩ Sent Matthew to serve a subpoena to Francis Penkevall, but he missed him. . . .

⟨B 19⟩ William Persis wife dead;[9] sent Richard thither to fetch me two heriots.[10] . . .

⟨E 22⟩ . . . made conserve of roses for Grace and [Agnes?] Wclys.[11] Richard Carnsew fetched home another heriot.

[*July*] ⟨C 18⟩ . . . Richard bought a colt of William Calwaye. . . .

⟨D 26⟩ Talked with John Tregose[12] for marriages, who promised me that his son should come hither. . . .

[*August*] ⟨D 9⟩ Wrate and sent to Thomas Coswarth for money by Matthew Carnsew. . . .

⟨B 14⟩ Matthew rode westwards to do divers errands and to look for moneys.

⟨F 18⟩ . . . Matthew came home and brought me moneys. . . .

[*September*] ⟨A 17⟩ . . . Richard and Matthew went a hunting.

---

[7] Archdeacon of Oxford, canon of Exeter Cathedral, rector of Carhayes and St Columb Major in Cornwall: A. L. Rowse, *Tudor Cornwall: Portrait of a Society* (Jonathan Cape, London, 1941), pp. 22–3.

[8] Rowse, in *Court and Country*, p. 156, suggests 'probably Oronce Finé who wrote on geometry and astronomy'.

[9] *deed.*

[10] A tenant's best beast or chattel, due on his death to the lord of whom he held his land.

[11] *Annys Welys.* Carnsew's sister Mary married as her second husband Richard Wills of Saltash.

[12] A cousin of Carnsew's: Rowse, *Court and Country*, p. 160.

[*October*] ⟨E 19⟩ Lord Mountjoy's letters for Matthye. . . .

⟨F 20⟩ Matthew departed towards Lord Mountjoy with weeping tears. . . .

⟨B 23⟩ . . . Devised medicine for Richard's toothache.

⟨A 29⟩ Matthew Carnsew came home. . . .

[*November*] ⟨★G 4⟩ John Kenalls with me for to have William go to Oxford, and lent me a nag; promised to write his letters for placing of him. . . .

⟨C 7⟩ Matthew and William went away towards Oxford.

[*December*] ⟨E 14⟩ John Teage of St Mabyn came to move me for marriages for young Hill, but secretly. . . .

⟨★G 16⟩ Received letters from Oxford.

[*The diary covers two further months.*]

London, Public Record Office, SP 46/16, ff. 39ʳ–50ʳ.

57   THOMAS JOSSELIN'S APPRENTICESHIP, 1657–64

[*1657, February*] ⟨21:⟩ . . . spoke to Mr John Cressener of my son being an apprentice: God in mercy look after my child.

[*1658, March*] ⟨26:⟩ . . . I have gathered 36*li* towards Tom's prenticeship . . .

⟨June⟩. 6. . . . Henceforward Lord help me not to forget the condition of my son Thomas in my daily prayers, that thou wouldst choose his master, trade, and bless him in his way.

[*November*] ⟨13.⟩ Received a letter from Mr Cressener, wherein he seemeth inclinable to take Tom, but his demands are very high. God Almighty show favour to him therein . . .

⟨18:⟩ . . . I writ up again to Mr Cressener . . . wherein I manifest my hope he will be a good servant and my assurance to be willing to do considerably for my child.

[*1659, May*] ⟨16.⟩ Mr Cressener brought me a letter from his brother to send up my son to him; the Lord make him a blessing, and bless him, oh my God.

⟨25:⟩ I and my son being Wednesday in Whitsun week set forward for London. We had sweet showers before, and so cool but dry riding all the way; we came safe to London 26. on

Thursday; that afternoon Tom at Mr John Cressener's put on his blue apron.[1] . . . My son is to serve eight years; his time will expire May 1 1667, in a good time I hope, the Lord sparing his life: Lord make him like Joseph a blessing to his master, and be thou his blessing and portion.

[*June*] ⟨10:⟩ . . . amazed in spirit about Thomas not liking at London. I leave events to God: Lord I trust thou wilt show favour unto me.

⟨11:⟩ This day Tom returned from London; it was a sad amazing providence to me, but more to my dear wife: God sanctify all. I hope there is good in it; I must learn in patience to possess my soul.

⟨16:⟩ Heard so much of Tom's foolishness at London that cut my heart . . .

⟨July.⟩ 17. In some perplexity about my son, his master not being willing to take him. I read in course 1 Samuel 9; Saul, seeking lost asses, found the kingdom, and this was some stay: God can order good out of our evil. Lord, I roll my soul on thee, I commit myself unto thee, I pray bring things about for thy glory and our good. . . .

[*October*] ⟨10:⟩ . . . offered a place for my son at London: the good Lord direct me therein for his tender mercy sake.

[*November*] ⟨5:⟩ . . . By letter I find a place provided for my son at London: God command his blessing therein for him.

⟨8:⟩ This day, my dear son Thomas rid towards London to be an apprentice; the God of heaven be with him, and merciful to him, and give him an heart to fear him, and make him industrious. . . .

⟨November⟩: 20. . . . my son Tom arrived safe at London: God be merciful to him and me in that affair . . .

⟨26:⟩ Heard of my son; he liketh well at London; God grant he be liked and do well: I bless God for his providence thus far towards me for good.

[*December*] ⟨12.⟩ Rid towards London . . .

⟨15. being Thursday⟩ <u>I bound also</u> Tom to Mr Tooky; his time expireth, if God lengthen his life, and he do well, June 24

---

[1] The words 'Tom: apprentice.' with a pointing hand are in the margin near here.

1667, the day the new parliament was proclaimed. Oh Lord, give him grace, wisdom, and make him industrious . . .

[*1660*] ⟨April:⟩ 14: When I come to view my outward estate I find my lands as formerly; I have paid off divers great debts, put out my son Tom prentice, which cost me in money and clothes about an 100*li* . . .

[*1664, March*] ⟨12.⟩ Heard from my son of a loss of cash of 20*li*, I praise God not by his unfaithfulness. But it's a trouble to me: oh Lord watch over us for good.

⟨19.⟩ Heard Tom had recovered the money lost. Blessed be God for this merciful providence. . . .

[*July*] ⟨16.⟩ Heard my son Thomas could not come down this summer; a hard master not to give a little respite in four years, when also promised: Lord be thou his friend I pray.

Macfarlane (ed.), *Diary of Ralph Josselin*, pp. 391, 421–2, 426, 434–5, 445–7, 449, 452–5, 462, 506, 510.

58 TWO OF HENRY NEWCOME'S SONS LAUNCHED IN THE WORLD, 1667–72

Henry at Oxford; his first cure

[*1667*] March 17., being the Sabbath day (and the day before we set out [*on*] our journey with Harry), I insisted on Job 1. 5 among my children, now in their beginning to part asunder. The notes of which sermon Harry desired, and so he hath them.

[*22 March*] . . . came in to Oxford about two of the clock. . . .

March 23. Harry was admitted by Dr Tully in Edmund Hall. I had much satisfaction in the Doctor, the government of the house, and the good tutor I hope I had for him, Mr March. I had many thoughts of heart, and fears, when I saw the looseness of many. . . . Harry put on his gown on the Monday, and was matriculated on Friday. The carrier not coming in as was expected, we resolved to stay in Oxford till Monday; on which day, being April 1, having settled matters as well as we could, we set out of Oxford about eight . . .

[*Newcome and his wife went on to visit a number of friends and relatives in London and elsewhere before returning to Oxford in May for a four-day stay on their way back to Lancashire.*]

August 10. I had letters from Oxford. One from Mr March, which gave me a comfortable account of Harry, which was a great refreshment to me. Blessed be God!

[*1672, November*] My son Harry now with me. I was necessitated to have thoughts of getting some place for him, not being able any longer to maintain him at the university. My Brother Leadbeater had thoughts of motioning him to Sir Samuel Barnardiston, but that place proved not. Mr Eccleston had written to me formerly about Mr Paul Foley, but that also swerved. He then had also motioned his going to Mr Avenant, to supply a small cure, and to have 20*li* and his diet. He was unwilling to undertake to preach twice a day, as being more than he thought he could perform; yet he said once a day he would adventure upon. This answer I returned to Mr Eccleston, which I judged a conclusion to that offer, by reason I judged the cure could not be supplied but by twice preaching; and so wrote to Mr Ashurst to think of him, if a place came to his knowledge. Whilst my letter was going to him, he wrote to me that if Harry was unsupplied, he thought he could provide him with one of 40*li* per annum, etc. This place I forthwith writ to fasten for him, desiring to know the particulars about it. Mr Thomas Sergeant, my good friend, had interest in it, and he forthwith secures it for him, and sends for him to hasten speedily away to Colonel Norton's. It was to be household chaplain to him, to have that noble allowance, and to preach but sometimes, when they did not go to church. That very Saturday night, which was November 30, that the letter came to assure us of that, came one from Mr Eccleston, which revives the other motion for Mr Avenant's; he being content to accept of once a day preaching, and pressing it with encouragements from worthy Mr Foley to accept of it. It was somewhat difficult to us to know what course to take. I concluded to deal uprightly and plainly in the case: and so, though the work was more suitable, and the wages double with Colonel Norton, yet I considered, 1. The expectation might be what he could not answer, the Colonel having had an able nonconformist to go before. 2. The family great, and so temptations more, and the attendance greater, which his weak body might not be so well able to answer. 3. The distance great, he living near Portsmouth; and so we could persuade ourselves of less opportunity of seeing him. Thomas Topping's son cast into those parts, and is almost as dead to his aged father, not hearing from him once in half a year. If no other place had been offered, Providence had chosen for him, and we should cheerfully have closed; but this other place thus offered, and coming at this very time (for another post had put it past recall), I thought it was a direction to consideration and taking advice in the case. And so I took this above board way in the case, to acquaint my friends at London with what had intervened, and to desire their advice in the thing, and withal to tell them, that if it would be any disappointment to the Colonel (having proceeded so far), I should take it as a determination from God to close there. Mr Sergeant wrote to me, October[*sic*] 9th, that he would advise me to the nearer place, and that he could without any prejudice excuse him to the other. And so when I understood this, I sent to Mr Eccleston of our acceptance of their offer. And so on the 20th of January we parted with him into Worcestershire, to Shelsley, where he was received kindly, and I hope to his comfort at present, and that it will be to his future great advantage. But that which added to my comfort on this account was that I had account that he preached plainly and seriously to the good content of the persons concerned.

Daniel Newcome's abortive apprenticeships and departure overseas

[1668] And now I received letters from Mr Ashurst the younger (my cordial friend), of a place that he had provided for Daniel, and he must be got ready as fast as we could. We sought God in the case and prepared for it . . . My wife and I double set out with him from Manchester on Monday September 7.

[*The Newcomes arrived in London on 16 September.*] On Tuesday after, being September 22, Daniel went to his place, to Mr Grant, a milliner, in Redcross Street, at the Half Moon and Seven Stars. He proved brother to my dear friend Mr Richard Grant, my contemporary in Cambridge, and afterward my singular bosom friend. The man one of a very good temper, quiet and kind natured, and I saw the boy was like enough to be well used. And here he continued, liked well, and soon was master of his business, and was very cheerful.

On October 14. (Wednesday), I fell into a new exercise; for I perceived and suspected lest the place designed for Daniel should not prove right. (1) This I found: the master civil and well natured, but, I doubt, not careful for religion. No prayer in the house since the boy came to him, and this troubled me much. (2) He dealt by wholesale, and only with gloves, a trade the boy could not think how to set up of, without such a stock as I could not, in an ordinary way, presume to have for him. (3) Little employment, so that for want of stirring, he began to be unhealthy; and further, I feared it would expose him to idleness and company, even want of employment, and the too much goodness (as some call it) of his master, to let him go when he asked, etc. . . . And now I saw the providence of God in bringing me up to London; for at a distance I should have laid the fault on the boy, and not have thought it could have been otherwise . . . But with my own eyes I saw, and was forced to advise and bestir myself. Mr Ashurst was presently aware of the business. And my dear friend Mr H. Ashurst Junr put it into his father's thoughts to motion him to Mr Langworth, a factor at Blackwell Hall; an employment of trust, needs no stock to set up with; the gentleman an intimate friend of Mr Ashurst's, a godly man.

[*Langworth met Daniel and ultimately agreed to accept him, while Mr Grant released him.*]

November 4. (Wednesday) Daniel went to his new master, Mr John Langworth, a factor in Blackwell Hall. . . . I daily hearkened after Daniel, and found him under difficulties in his new place. But I still hoped that the Lord would arm him against them, and bear him up under them, and finally do all things well. I humbly hoped, that since it is a place so good for the soul and for employment, the Lord make it his place, and every way good and best for him; for it did greatly satisfy me that his master told him of catechizing and Sabbath keeping and constant business. . . . He was sensible of cold, and desired a gown, his master not willing of it, and my wife took the boy off that. This was before the week's end after his first coming thither.

November 23. I had a letter from Harry which acquainted me with Daniel's desire that he might go to school again that he might be a scholar, so much he began to be prejudiced against being an apprentice, and this troubled me much. Yet a day or two after he seemed to be off this.

December 1. (Tuesday) . . . at night I found Daniel had been with his mother, and told her more of his troubles; and had declared so much, that we concluded, unless we could have some things changed it would be impossible to settle him. I had hitherto moved Mr Ashurst to get his master to bind him as soon as he could, that I might be free to prepare to get home. Mr Ashurst very lovingly had himself (being one of the assistants) presented him to the Master of the Company on Friday December 4, that so he might be bound at any time when his master could come with him. His master that day, in pursuance of my request to hasten his binding, went with him to dispatch it. As he went towards the Hall, he turned and asked him whether he was willing. The boy wept, and desired to speak with his father first, and so came back. This the boy took for a design upon him, that they would have bound him without my consent, etc., and the prejudice was so great that everything was taken in the worst sense; and this was settled in his mind, that when he was bound, they would then use him at their pleasure; and settled in these conceits by the discouragement that was upon his spirit, by which he saw everything in wrong colours, and also by a naughty boy in the house, that told him some lies, and made him still believe how sad it would be to be bound. On the Saturday morning he came to us and told us his thoughts, and very stiff he was, that he could not be bound, he should never give content, etc. And we could hardly get him to consent to be bound if we could get things remedied. . . .

. . . And by much importunity they had prevailed with me to let Harry come to London, now we were like to stay. His uncle[1] thought he [*Henry*] might do good with Daniel; but God had

---

[1] Almost certainly Newcome's brother Thomas, with whom he was staying while in London.

done it before he came. On the Tuesday after, he came to London. Daniel got leave, and met him in Holborn; was very cheerful; and the next day, December 16, came to see us with his indentures in his hand. He had gone himself and was bound. I desire I may never forget this wonderful mercy. December 18, we sealed the bonds and covenants, and all things were smooth and well; and December 26 (Saturday), we were all invited to his master's house to dinner, and exceeding much made of. Great content God gave us in this affair after all our fear and sorrow about it. . . .

[*1669*] February 1, being Monday morning, we set out of London. Took leave of Daniel and friends at the George in Aldersgate. . . .

November 20 (Saturday.) This night I had a letter from my friend Mr H. Ashurst Junr which brought me the saddest news that ever I had in my life, viz. of the miscarriage of Daniel; and in such general terms that we had sorrow without bounds. It is a great sorrow, bitter, reaches to the very heart, and it is a sorrow I can see no end of. . . .

[*Newcome remained for the next few months torn between hope and fear about Daniel, some letters from London reassuring him, others renewing his worries*].

. . . [*1670*] April 4, being Easter Monday, I received two letters which brought me the sad news of Dan's being gone away from his master, and could not, when those letters were writ, be heard of. They also seemed not willing I should come till he was heard of. Upon this I waited all the week, and could hear nothing. . . . The poor lad was found and brought back again to his master . . .

[*21*] . . . This night, in much sorrow and with trembling hearts at our coming to London, I sent for my brother (whom we found newly married), and with him we went, seeing our poor child in the way. I was supported from sinking sorrow by the Lord's own hand. Matters I found bad, yet not so bad as I feared. . . .

April 25. (Monday) I took Daniel to us at his uncle's. This week passed in taking advice what to do with him. My best friends were positive in it, that the best way was to send him beyond seas. And when we were thus resolving in the general, and fixed on Jamaica as the fittest place, the Lord wonderfully set us to enquire after Mr Jonathan Ashurst, a merchant, going himself thither, and by the solicitation of friends, he was easily induced to take him with him, a trading voyage, by Tangier, the Madeiras, Barbados, and so to Jamaica, which all judged much to his advantage. . . .

On Lord's day night, May 8, we sat up till 3 of the clock, and spent some of the time in prayer; and about two on Monday morning, my dear child took boat for Gravesend, and so I took leave of him with a rueful heart; and the sad cries of his poor mother I shall not quickly forget, and I pray God he may remember them. We had several letters from him, from Deal, and after from Portsmouth, and there they stayed for their convoy till we came from London.

Manchester, Chetham's Library, MS Mun.A.3.123, ff. 211–12, 217, 225–6, 228–9, 232–6, 238, 242, 255, 259–61, 282–3.

59   THE EDUCATION AND TRAINING OF JAMES JACKSON'S SONS, 1674–80

The boys at Bromfield grammar school

April xvth 74.

⟨P⟩aid for Joseph's and John's table for a xi weeks and three days il*i* vii*is* vj*d* and given little Jane vi*d* per John. Both came home the abovesaid day: fetched home per self. ⟨P⟩aid to Mr Bolton quarter wages per both ended the same day they came home —— vs at Cannonby Beckfoot. Witness Mr Lamplugh.

John and Daniel went to Bromfield School May 4th 1674 to Mr Jonathan Bankes.

Paid John Ritson of Bromfield for Samuel Munke,[1] John and Daniel's table December 6th 1674 per six weeks' time:

First week, 2 boys at 1*d* ob[2] a meal, 5 days	00.03.09
2: week, 3 boys, 5 days	00.05.07½
3. week, 3 boys, 4 days comes to	00.04.06
4. week, 3 boys, 4 days	00.04.06
5. week, 3 boys, 5 days, comes to	00.05.07½
6. week, 3 boys, 5 days, comes to	00.05.07½

Meals in that time } 237.

	01.09.07½
but paid	01.10.00

Ending December 12th 1674
at breaking up per Christenmas.

September 21th, 1675.

⟨M⟩emorandum the day and year abovesaid was the last day of my son's William's prenticeship in Carlisle bound to Mr Richard Munkes, Merchant; and upon the 24th of the same month was he made freeman at Guild Hall and sworn before Mr Stanix then mayor and the rest of the brethren and had his treatment and the company at Chamberlain Thomas Jackson. Charges then ii*li* xi*s* . . .

John apprenticed

⟨M⟩emorandum March 21th, 1675[*6*], did I send[3] to Mr Gawin Chamber per John Stamper ten pounds and four crowns for his wife upon promise for my son John's apprenticeship and an acquittance for the same. Witness John Stamper younger and my son John Jackson.

---

[1] Son of the Richard Munkes to whom William Jackson was apprentice.
[2] *obolus*: halfpenny.
[3] *sent*.

Joseph goes to Oxford

March ith, 1676[7].
My son Joseph went towards Oxford the day etc.
his brothers (to wit) Richard, William, John and Daniel
altogether over Crumbeck Bridge and John Stamper.

Money given to my son Joseph when he went to Oxford per
friends.

	s . d		s . d
Mr William	01 . 00	John Benson	01 . 00
Chamber		John Stamper	01 . 00
My Brother[4]	02 . 00	Mary Huddert	01 . 00
Simson		Anne Kendall	01 . 00
John Simson	02 . 06		
Henry Currey	05 . 00		04 . 00
Old Blackdike	02 . 00		01 . 16 . 00
Son Richard	01 . 00	My self	00 . 12 . 00
Brother William	02 . 06	His mother ⎫	00 . 05 . 00
Brother John	02 . 06	in gold ⎭	
Brother Daniel	01 . 06		
Daniel Dickenson	01 . 00	in his pocket	2 . 17 . 00
Francis Threlkeld	03 . 00	to his tutor	6 . 00 . 00
Robert Farish	02 . 06		
Robert Wilson	01 . 00	in all	8 . 17 . 00
Joseph Brisco	01 . 06	besides his ⎫	[*space left*
Jane Brisco	01 . 00	mare price ⎭	*blank*]
Thomas Jefferson	01 . 00		
Thomas	01 . 00	his mare sold at ⎫	3 . 10 . 00
Wilkinson		Oxford per ⎭	
Mr Head	01 . 00	in all with him	12 . 07 . 00
Thomas Barne	01 . 00		
Anne Dalton	02 . 00	his first letter from Oxford	
John Parkin	00 . 06	received March 25 (77)	

01 . 16 . 06

[4] His daughter Isabel's father-in-law.

William sets up in business at Carlisle

February 9th 1677[*8*]

⟨Sen⟩t John Stamper to my son William
Jackson to Carlisle the day etc. with a
100*li* for his portion to begin his trade } 150*li* 00 00
with and 50*li* he is to have from his
master owing to me per bond, in all

Joseph at Oxford[5]

May 28th 77, paid to Burnyeats[6] etc. for carrying Joseph's clothes
and books to Oxon. 8*s* 3*d* and for 6*li* of money [*figure illegible*]
in all x*s* and vi*d*.

March 17th 1678[*9*]
⟨Sen⟩t to my son Joseph to Oxon. per Burnyeats forty shillings
and in his new breeches pocket vi*s*, whereof sent per his mother
i*s*, in all ii*li* vi*s*. Borrowed of Burnyeats at Oxon. x*s*, in all ii*li*
16: 0.

September 29th 79
⟨S⟩ent to my son Joseph at Oxon. a suit and a coat with trimming
for his coat, and x*s* in money for a token per Richard Burnyeats,
per Tom Crosse.

September 20th 1680
Memorandum I went to Carlisle to meet with Mr Mills, my son
Joseph tutor at Oxon. who was both civil and kind to me, giving
a good character upon my son. In company at Carlisle with Mr
Mills, Mr Chancellor, Mr Feilding, Mr Thomas Nichols, Mr
How, my son William and myself. Spent then in Rhenish wine
iiii*s*. ⟨Spent then ii*s*⟩
    Sent Joseph per token per Mr Mills — 5*s* piece./ in all xi*s*.

---

[5] A small selection from a very large number of entries.
[6] Richard, a carrier: Grainger (ed.), 'James Jackson's Diary', p. 125n.

September 29. 80 Michaelmas Day
⟨Se⟩nt to Oxon, to my son Joseph per Burnyeats a feather[7] bed, tick, a waistcoat and two pair of stockens and in money 30s to Cockermouth per Thomas Crosse. —— *ili xs.* ⟨paid to him 4s [6?]d.⟩[8]

Carlisle, Cumbria Record Office, microfilm no. JAC 257, section TL/702.

60 LEONARD WHEATCROFT AND HIS CHILDREN: THEIR DEPARTURES FROM HOME AND HIS SUBSEQUENT ENCOUNTERS WITH THEM, c.1675–1701

[*c.1675*] . . . I put Leo and Ester to Derby to learn some better work and breeding, after that to Nottingham etc. . . .

   [*1679, after 18 October*] . . . After that I went to Lenton Fair, to see two [*of my*] children that lived at Nottingham . . .

   Then did fortune so favour my daughter Ester. . . that upon April 9 1679 [*sic*], I went with her to service to a place call[*ed*] Rowthorn near Hardwick Hall, where she lived with one John Hardwicke for the space of two years. From thence I went along to a town called Carlton in Nottinghamshire, where my daughter Anna lived. From that place I brought her to one Mr Horn's of Butterley, April 13. . . .

   [*1681*] . . . Then did my son Leonardus[1] desire me to suffer him to take a journey to London, to which I granted; and upon Monday, March 11 1680[*1*], I went with him agateward for the space of seven or eight miles, and Ester with me. So when we parted, I went with Ester to her master's house, that was eight miles more. . . .

---

[7] *fedder.*
[8] Joseph became fellow of Queen's College in 1685; died rector of Bramshott, Hants., in 1729: Grainger, 'James Jackson's Diary', p. 121n.

---

[1] Wheatcroft's son Leonard had evidently returned from Nottingham.

After this, my daughter Anna came from Mr Horn's, having served her whole year, and staying awhile at home; I went with her to service again to Mr Wollhouse's of Glapwell, being April 20 1681, where she was liked very well, and so much of her. . . .

After a while I went to see my daughter Anna again, but not before August 11. . . .

And upon September 5 1681 I had occasion to go to Chesterfield, where I met with a bone-lace-weaver, with whom I bargained to take a daughter of mine apprentice, Elizabeth by name. So for three pounds ten shillings we agreed, and bound she was, September 14, being Chesterfield Fair day, for four years. But of her more as occasion serves.

October 18 after, both I and my wife went to see our two daughters, Anna and Ester, at Glapwell and Rowthorn, where we was very rarely entertained, and our children very much made of, to our joy and comfort.

And . . . [*in December*] came both our daughters to see us, it being Christmas after, and after three or four days[s] sporting was ended amongst their brethren and friends, they all parted to their several places of abode.

[*1682*] After that I heard from my son which lived in London that he lived so well that he had a mind to have his brother John to come up to him, and that he would provide him a master, to which I and my wife gave consent to his journey, and with all speed we got him ready, and towards London he went, April 6 1682. He had a very good journey thither, and was well entertained both of his uncle and brother and other friends. So after a little trial he bound himself for four years, as appears by his letters to me. He was bound April 20 1682. He was to have two pounds the first year, and three the second year, and four the third, and five pounds the last year, meat, drink, washing and lodging, and some of his master's old clothes,[2] all which I liked well; and so much of him at present.

---

[2] *close.*

But again, John had not lived with his master above half a year but he died. Then did his Uncle John take to him, and as a club[3] he served him for three years. All that time he was with him till he come down with his brother Leonard to see his relations in the country. In the interim all my daughters came to see me . . . [*1683*] In that year my daughter Elizabeth[*'s*] dame died. Then was I at an onplus [*sic*] to seek for another for her. And upon February 28 I went to Chesterfield Fair, where I light of another dame, one Mary Jenings, to whom I bound her for two years, and soon after she died; then she came home almost half a year. Then I went to see my daughter Anna at Glapwell, where I stayed grafting and planting for the space of three days.

And upon May 26 I went with my son David to Chesterfield to be a tailor with one William Webster, with whom he stayed one year. This was in September 8 in the year 1684.

After that I followed my occasions at home till at last I, not finding myself well, I sent to my sons at London, desiring to see them before I died. So according to my desire and their mother's they came down to us August 15 in 85. Then all the rest of my children come from their services to give them the meeting, whom they had not seen in four years' time.

So after they had rested awhile with me and told me all their travels and adventures, and cheered up their parents' mournful spirits,[4] we all concluded to go to our brother Robert Hawley's to a wakes which was there at that time, September 4.

After that, Anna went to live at John Thweates, July 6 1685, where she stayed for one year.

Then did my daughter Betty go to live with one Catrin Balme for two years. She was hired October 26 1685.

And David was hired again by my son Leonardus to one Samuel Higgens, a London tailor, for two years, December 30 1685.

Again March 7 1685[6] it pleased God my son Leonardus was minded to go towards London again,[5] and then did all my

---

[3] A heavy, clumsy fellow, so presumably here an unskilled servant.

[4] *sperits*.

[5] The younger Leonard had accompanied his father on a journey to Hathersage in February.

children come together again to take leave of him with several more relations to all our comfort. . . .

[*1687*] . . . and February 3 John went to London again where he stayed.

And after him David went February 24 86[7], where he stayed, waiting on King James the 2, to be touched by him of his infirmity called the King's Evil. There was he touched twice by him, but never the better at his return. [*After his return, David and his father visited Leonard's sister Sarah, at whose suggestion, on 26 December 1687, David tried the remedy of touching with a dead woman's hand.*] . . .

But he being so far gone by that distemper continued till October 15 1688, then died. . . .

And upon October 9 [*blank*] did my daughter Ester go towards London, and I went with her as far as Nottingham. . . .

Then did another daughter of mine, Anna by name, take a journey into Yorkshire, August 15 1687, where it pleased God she had not lived above two years but she was married to one John Ingle, a farmer living in the town of Barwick near Castleford.

In the same year 87 did I bind my son Solomon to my cousin John Wheatcroft for two years to be a tailor. . . .

My son Titus began to work of the tailor trade in the year 1690. . . .

And my eldest son Leonardus was wed to one Ellen[6] Pirkin of London, a widow, February 9, 1690[*1*] . . .

In the year 1691, my daughter Anna and her husband John Ingle came to see me at Ashover Wakes, and I was as glad to see them as they me. . . .

That year also was my second[7] son John wed to a widow in London, her name was Anne (*blank*), December 22 1691. . . .

In the year 1692, my son Leonardus and Hester came from London to see me, for they had never seen me since their mother died.[8] So in sorrow they came to the place of their birth. They came August 7, and upon August 26 we went to see my daughter Anna at Barwick in Elmet in Yorkshire, where we found all

---

[6] *Eling.*
[7] *seckand.*
[8] She had died 3 March 1688/9.

very well and in good health, blessed be God for his mercies to us all, but we did not return home till August 31 92. And after our return home I went with Hester as far as Mansfield towards London, which was September 19 1692. . . .

[*1693–4*] . . . In that year did my daughter Sarah as a servant go to live with her uncle William Wheatcroft. And Titus and I kept house together in 1694 till June 26 1695, almost two years. Blessed be God we lived very quietly together, and he ordered all things very handsomely both within doors and without. And after Sarah came home I had more liberty, and Titus too, to walk abroad to see our friends and relations etc. . . .

September 12 1696, my son Leonardus came from London to see me and all his relations, and I at his return went agateward[9] with him as far as Holbrook, and there we parted, September 28.

Then . . . [*June 17 1697*] did my daughter Sarah and I take a journey into Yorkshire on foot to see my two daughters Anna and Elizabeth at a town called Barwick, above fifty miles from Ashover. We was three days in going thither, and three days in coming home again, but, blessed be my good God, we found them all in good health and prosperity; and for six days we were very merry together, and the Lord make us all thankful. We found all well at our return, which was June 28 1697. . . .

[*1700*] And, unexpected, my son Leonardus came from London, which was August 23 in the year 1700, who stayed with me till September 9. In which time he bought that house and land which I sold, which was to the value of one hundred and twenty pounds, which was great joy to me and all my neighbours and relations etc.

[*1701*] . . . about June 20[10] my daughter Hester came down from London to see me, who at that time was very lame, but it pleased God she brought me an ointment which gave me much ease – blessed be God!

Matlock, Derbyshire Record Office, D2079/F1.

---

[9] *Agaterd*: on the way.
[10] Possibly *26*.

61   OLIVER HEYWOOD'S ANXIETIES ABOUT HIS
ABSENT SONS, 1676–7

[*Heywood's two sons John and Eliezer left home in 1672 to study first at Morley (Yorks.), then near Droitwich (Worcs.), at Rathmell (Yorks.), and finally in Scotland before their return home in April 1677. The first of the following extracts comes from a list of meditations, the second from a list of temptations.*]

I have within this week met with more fears about my two sons abroad at learning, and sustained more bitter agonies of soul than ever I did in all my life that I remember upon any account, occasioned upon some reports that I heard concerning them, which multiplied in my imaginations, and exceedingly aggravated by my own jealousies and suspicions so that I was almost distracted, could not sleep quietly, nor take content in anything, though I concealed it so from my wife and family that nothing was discerned; however God made good use of it to humble my heart more effectually for mine own sins, to be importunate with God for mercy. Upon Friday night, January 14 1676, I was in great bitterness of spirit, so on Saturday night, yet God helped me comfortably through my Lord's day work; Monday, Tuesday, Wednesday, still God bore up my heart in hopes and frequent wrestling, so that this day, being Thursday morning, January 20 76, I am inclined to issue my sad thoughts that I have had into these meditations, vows, covenants and resolves.

. . . Lord, my sons are thine, more thine than mine; thou gavest them me, and I have given them back again to thee, not only in the ordinance of baptism, and many a time since in prayers and tears, but in a peculiar manner I have, upon May 15 1673, when they were to go abroad,[1] given them up to God in a most solemn ordinance with much affection, before many witnesses; the remembrance of that day bears up my heart with much encouragement that God will hear and answer, in giving grace to mine: Lord, my children are part of myself, and in giving up myself to thee I have also given them to thee, and

---

[1] To Worcestershire, their first journey far from home.

wilt thou not accept of this loan which is lent to the Lord? Are not children thy peculiar heritage? . . . Lord, is there no difference betwixt covenanted children and such as are out of covenant? Shall children of so many prayers and tears miscarry? Wilt thou not take possession of thine own right and of thy son's purchase? . . . Lord, leave them not to conform to ceremonies, or turn formalists or persecutors of thy people, let it appear there is a blessing in their education in a private college more than in the public universities, and that God hath peculiar ways to store his church in the day of academical and epidemical corruptions. I have committed them more to thy tuition than man's; if thou wilt own them with special sanctifying grace, and useful gifts and learning, and fit them for public work amongst thy people, I will by thy grace bless thy name while I live, yea I do solemnly promise to devote every year a day to the work of solemn thanksgiving to God peculiarly for that mercy whiles I have a day to live amongst saints, and to spend some time monthly apart by myself to praise thy Name. . . .

January 6 77 at night after I was gone to bed, at my first sleep, I had a terrible dream concerning my son John, that he was fallen to the study of magic or the black art and that he had books of that sort, and that he played some tricks in my sight. I was so affrighted that I wakened, fell a sweating, trembling; begun to ponder of it, could not tell how God might leave him, they being in Scotland a great distance from me; it awakened me before 12 and I lay tossing with that dreadful apprehension till almost 2 a clock, and was ready to faint under it; oh what a night had I! . . .

British Library, MS Add. 45966, ff. 14ʳ–16ʳ, 30ᵛ.

62 MARY WOODFORDE'S SONS AT SCHOOL AND UNIVERSITY, 1687–8

[*1687*] March 6. This evening I had the cutting news that my second boy John was in rebellion at the College at Winton, where he and all his companions resolved not to make any verses, and being called to be whipped for it several of them refused to

be punished, and mine among the rest, though some of them did submit, among which was Cousin John [*Woodforde*], and if the other do not, they must be expelled. God I beseech thee of they great mercy subdue all their stubborn hearts, and give them grace to repent and accept of the punishment due for their fault, and let them not run on to ruin, for Christ's sake. Amen.

March 8. Yesterday my dear husband went to Winton about Jack, and I have received this afternoon a letter from him which gives me hopes he has humbled himself, for which I from the bottom of my heart give most humble thanks to Almighty God . . .

March 13. This evening we had a letter from Sam wherein he expresses a great deal of dullness and indisposition to his studies, and a desire if his father think fit to change the air to see if that will do him good. Now we are in a strait which way to incline, but we beg direction of thee, O All wise and Almighty God, what to do, and beseech thee to satisfy our child to submit to whatever shall be prudently concluded on for him. . .

June 1st. My husband had a kind letter from the Bishop of Ely in order to carry Sam to Cambridge to St John's College, to be admitted scholar. God bless all our proceedings in this affair, so as may be for his glory, and our child's good

The beginning of June I went to London with my husband and Sam; they went to Cambridge, where Sam was admitted scholar at St John's College, where may he do virtuously, and bring a great deal of honour to the Name of God, and comfort to himself and his relations. . . . [*He went up on October 13.*]

May 20 1688. We had a letter from Sam which tells us he is not very well, and that his mind hangs much towards home. God restore him to his health again (and as he prays in his letter), keep us all in his true fear and love, and give him a cheerful spirit and make him content and pleased to stay till it is convenient for him to come home, and let us see one another with joy and comfort again. . .

July 24 1688. I had a letter last night from my son John wherein he tells me he is chosen tutor to Sir Thomas Putt and to two more, Carter and Wotton. God give him grace and wisdom and faithfulness to discharge his duty to them. . .

August 16 1688. My son Samuel came home from Cambridge to see us. I hope bettered in his learning, and not drawn away from sobriety and honesty. . . .

[*September*]. Cousin brought a kind letter from our good friend Doctor Nicholas, the warden of Winton College, giving us great hopes of our son John's being in a good way towards New College in Oxford. God order all for the best and make him worthy of the favour intended towards him . . .

October 22. This day my dear Sam is gone again toward Cambridge. . . . I bless God I hear my son is safe at Cambridge.

December 14. This evening we had a letter from poor Sam's tutor which tells us he has a dangerous cut in one of his fingers which makes them fear a gangrene, which God of his mercy prevent. He is at a great distance from us and all his relations, but oh, my dear Lord, do thou supply all our love and care in taking him into thy special protection . . .

December 18 1688. We had a letter from Mr Brown which gives us great hopes my poor Sam's finger is in a good way of curing, which God of his mercy grant. . .

Oxford, New College Archive, Steer 9507, ff. 21–6, 34, 39, 41, 43, 48, 50, 51, 53.

63   THE WIDOWER ELIAS PLEDGER LEFT ALONE ON THE COMMENCEMENT OF HIS SON'S APPRENTICESHIP, c.1709[1]

My son in a week or two is to go apprentice to Mr Walter Cock, a Dutch merchant, and my wife's shop at the Royal Exchange will be put off to her kinswoman[2] and another in partnership, and then I shall be left alone. Lord grant I may be never less alone than when I am most alone as to the world, that then God may be with me, that I may walk more closely with him, as I shall have more leisure for retirement and study, which I have

---

[1] This entry is undated. It follows directly after the record of his wife's death on 15 February 1708/9; his son Elias was then sixteen, a good age at which to be bound.

[2] Or possibly *kinswomen*.

always taken much delight in, and now I hope shall have an opportunity to make use of[3] to advantage, having a design to leave off housekeeping and to live retired in lodgings.

London, Dr Williams's Library, MS 28.4, f. 84ᵛ.

---

[3] *it* follows here, apparently deleted.

VI

Parents' Old Age and Deaths

The passages in the previous section presented the relationship between parents and their adolescent children from the parents' point of view. This one conveys some impression of the enormous variety of children's often complex feelings towards their parents. Among the diarists represented here, the closest relationships seem to have involved parents and children of the same sex. Daughters inherited both social and economic roles and skills from their mothers; but the strongly positive feelings between fathers and sons recorded in this section, which were perhaps less typical, were primarily due to the elusive chemistry of individual personalities. Two of the three diarists who enjoyed close relationships with their fathers (66, 71) did not follow the latter in their callings.

Widowhood (when not followed by remarriage), and being an only child or lone survivor from a larger brood, may also have reinforced the bond between parents and children. Lady Anne Clifford and Samuel Jeake were both the only, or only surviving, children of widowed parents. In addition, Lady Anne Clifford experienced, during the years when she kept her diary, an intermittently stormy relationship with her husband which made the love and sympathy of her mother doubly valuable to her, while the Jeakes belonged to a persecuted religious minority (64, 70).

In this group of writers it was Lady Elizabeth Livingston who expressed the strongest feelings of hostility towards a parent – her father (68). She had continued to hope for his affection and approval despite their long separation and his second marriage, but his arrangement of an uncongenial match for her, doubly distressing because it followed the failure of an intense though unconsummated love affair, aroused her deep resentment. Samuel Pepys and Dudley Ryder were also critical of their parents, though in neither case was there that element of bitterness which sharpened Lady Elizabeth's feelings towards her father (66, 71). Both men were irked by their elderly parents' quarrelsome behaviour towards each other, and both believed that their mothers were to blame in the first place. In addition, Pepys was probably ashamed of his mother's humble origins, which her demeanour continued to betray. But Ryder, while feeling that his mother's conduct was usually responsible for starting trouble between his parents, blamed his father's obstinacy and lack of judgement for continuing it. He was critical of his father's irascibility and tendency to harp on trifles. Usually, however, he was readier to confide in his father (even in the matter of his love for Sally Marshall), though it was to his mother that he intended to broach the very intimate problem of his 'stinking breath'.

Ryder was in the position, common in the middle and upper ranks of society, of continuing dependence on paternal help for his advancement, and a current of dissatisfaction runs through his comments on his father's financial provisions for him. Pepys, on the other hand, enjoyed an exceptional independence. The patronage of his distant relative Lord Sandwich and his own outstanding drive and ability freed him from reliance on his father long before the latter's death. Furthermore, he had no need to please his father in order to ensure his succession to the country estate entailed upon him by a childless uncle. So this was a relationship unusually free of any element of paternal power or filial subservience, whose strength lay in genuine mutual affection. Indeed the customary positions of father and son were partially reversed, for John Pepys needed his eldest son's help in advancing his other children.

Alice Thornton's and Samuel Jeake's descriptions of their parents' last hours on earth underline the immense importance of the 'good death' for survivors (65, 70). Their passing certainly caused anguish, yet also brought parents and children together in moments of intense emotion which facilitated the natural process of grief while also helping the bereaved to come to terms with loss. These parents' last blessings, heartfelt expressions of love, and belief that they were bound for a better world, were potent sources of consolation. Lady Anne Clifford's grief was probably deepened and prolonged by her inability to attend her mother's death-bed (64). Lady Elizabeth Delaval (née Livingston), still smouldering with animosity against her father, neglected to visit him in his last sickness, but later paid a high price for her wilfulness in sharp regret and vain remorse (68). Samuel Pepys, who had long expressed a marked coolness towards his mother, was nevertheless troubled by the stirring of a former attachment as her death approached, most notably in a curious dream the night before she died. Pepys's reactions constitute a good example of the beginning of adjustment in advance of an expected death. He appears to have weathered his bereavement fairly easily; some immediate tears and the donning of the customary mourning were the only recorded tributes Margaret Pepys received from her eldest son after her departure, and reflection led him to the conclusion that she had died at a convenient time (66).

Some diarists recalled their parents long after they had gone. Nearly eighteen months after she had lost her mother, Lady Anne Clifford's return to the house where she had been married aroused memories which made her weep 'extremely' (64): Many years later, she was to erect the Countess's Pillar on the spot a mile east of Brougham where she and her mother had last parted. The Lancashire apprentice Roger Lowe recorded in his diary two visits to his parents' grave; during the second, in January 1665, he wept together with his sister (67).

Diaries and autobiographies treasured by the writers' children sometimes helped to keep their memories alive. A number of autobiographers intended their accounts to be read by the next generation. Leonard Wheatcroft's chronicle was continued for a time by his youngest son Titus, an altogether more shadowy figure. But Isaac Archer learnt of a side of his father's character previously hidden from him through his chance perusal of a volume not designed for his eyes. The moment of discovery is recorded in a passage probably without a parallel in any other English journal (69). He faced the unexpected revelation that his father had battled with the same temptations that he himself had faced. Perhaps it kindled a spark of fellow feeling which offset in some small measure the sadness of their estrangement and Isaac's bitter disappointment with the seemingly punitive provisions of his father's will.

64   LADY ANNE CLIFFORD AND HER MOTHER, 1616–17

[*1616, March*] Upon the 20th in the morning my Lord William Howard with his son, my coz. William Howard and Mr John Dudley came hither to take the answer of my mother and myself, which was a direct denial to stand to the judges' award. . . .

Upon the 22d my Lady and I went in a coach to Whinfell[1] and rode about the park and saw all the woods.

Upon the 31st being Easter Day I received with my mother in the chapel at Brougham.[2]

⟨April 1616⟩ Upon the 1st came my coz. Charles Howard and Mr John Dudley with letters to show that it was my Lord's pleasure that the men and horses should come away without me, and so after much falling out betwixt my Lady and them, all my folks went away, there being a paper drawn to show that they went away by my Lord's direction and contrary to my will.

At night I sent two messengers to my folks to entreat them to stay. For some two nights my mother and I lay together and had much talk about this business. Upon the 2d I went after my folks in my Lady's coach, she bringing me a quarter of a mile in the way, where she and I had a grievous and heavy parting. . . .

[*May*] Upon the 9th I received a letter from Mr Bellasis how extreme ill my mother had been, and in the afternoon came Humphrey Godding's son with letters that my mother was exceeding ill and as they thought in some danger of death – so as I sent Rivers presently to London with letters to be sent to her and certain cordials and conserves.

Upon the 13th being Monday, my Lady's footman Thomas Petty brought me letters out of Westmorland by which I perceived

---

[1] *Whingfield.*
[2] *Broome.*

how very sick and full of grievous pains my dear mother was, so as she was not able to write herself to me and most of her people about her feared she would hardly recover this sickness; at night I went out and prayed to God my only helper that she might not die in this pitiful case.

Upon the 29th Kendal came and brought me the heavy news of my mother's death, which I held as the greatest and most lamentable cross that could have befallen me. . . .

[*July*] Upon the 11th . . . About 5 o'clock came my coz. William Howard and five or six of his. About 8 we set forward, the body going in my Lady's own coach with four horses and myself following it in my own coach with two horses and most of the men and women on horseback, so as there was about forty in the company; and we came to Appleby about [half?] an hour after eleven, and about 12 the body was put into the ground. About 3 o'clock in the morning we came home . . .

[*1617, May*] The 24th we set up a great many of the books that came out of the North in my closet, this being a sad day with me thinking of the troubles I have passed. I used to spend much time with Mr Wolrich[3] in talking of my dear mother and other businesses in the North. . . .

[*November*] The 3d . . . I went to Austin Friars, where I wept extremely to remember my dear and blessed mother. I was in the chamber where I was married and went into most of the rooms in the house, but found very little or nothing of the stuffs and pictures remaining there. . . .

Maidstone, Kent Archives Office, MS U269. F48/1, 2.

65   LADY WANDESFORD'S LAST FAREWELL TO HER CHILDREN, DECEMBER 1659, DESCRIBED BY HER DAUGHTER ALICE THORNTON

. . . For no thing of this world, nor in it, could hinder her fixedness for heaven; nor indeed did the concerns of this life

[3] Or Wooldridge, a servant of Dorset's listed in Sackville-West (ed.), *Diary of the Lady Anne Clifford*, p. lvii.

come into her thoughts, saving to leave her pious and Christian instructions and holy admonitions amongst us her children and servants; and to learn by her how to live well, and die happily, joyfully and comfortably, embracing and often calling for death, to let her into the enjoyment of her Lord. . . . She poured out her fervent, admirable prayers to her God for all her children and relations, begging to each particular child those graces and gifts they wanted . . . As to my own private concerns, she petitioned God that I might find comfort in my husband's family, and be rewarded with the same blessing that God had been graciously pleased to give me in my children as (she was pleased to say) I had been to her; and that I might be strengthened by his grace to endure those afflictions with patience which I must find in this world after her death; and that I might have hope in God's mercy that he would lay no more on me than he would enable me to undergo; and that they were signs of his love to me; and that I must not grieve too much for her loss, since the Lord had continued her so long to me, for he could make up her loss in a greater comfort by giving me a son, which I wanted, and that I was then with child of one. Wished me continue as I had begun, and then we should receive each other with joy in heaven, which she was confident of through the merits of Jesus Christ . . .

She told me she had fully finished her will and settled her estate according as she desired, and she hoped with a good conscience, settling all she had in such a manner as would breed no trouble; and that she hoped her son Christopher would be satisfied with it, because she had not been a wanting in the discharge of a good conscience towards him ever since he was born, by taking pains with him and care of him in his minority, and disbursing the greater part of her widow's estate upon him or for his brother John, or the other part of Kirklington, whereby he had the benefit of her maintaining the children; and that now he would let me enjoy with my husband and children what she had done for us, considering my husband's estate needed it; and he was heir of a great large estate of his father's, and by her death the jointure came in clear to him. All which estate would amount to yearly to him in England and Ireland three thousand pounds, which she prayed God to bless to him and his posterity, that they might enjoy it in righteousness so long as *the moon and sun endureth*.[1] . . .

About Thursday night[2] she sent for her children to take her last farewell in this life, when Mr Thornton and myself came with our two children Alice and Katherine, she desiring my husband to pray with and for her, as he had done several times; in which she was much pleased and satisfied, ever joining most devoutly, reverently praying with her heart and soul in each petition, finding great joy and refreshment upon such occasions. After which prayer, she embraced us all severally in her arms, and kissed us, pouring out many prayers and blessings for us all; like good old Jacob, when he gave his last blessing to his children, she begged of God Almighty for us all. After which I took the saddest last leave of my dear and honoured mother as ever child did to part with so great and excellent a parent and infinite comfort. And yet the great grief I had was increased by reason of her exceeding torment which she endured, which made me more willingly submit to part with her, who I saw endured much pains and extremity, not desiring she should long endure that which it was the pleasure of God, for the exercise of her patience, to lay on her. Also, when she see me weep much, for this affliction of hers did indeed concern me nearly, she said, 'Dear child, why will you not be willing to part with me to God? Has he not lent me to be a comfort to you long enough? O part with me freely, as I desire to enjoy my Saviour in heaven. Do not be unwilling that I should be delivered from this miserable world; give me willing and freely to him that lent me thus long, and be contented in every thing. You never have been disobedient to me in all your life; I pray thee obey me in this, that you submit cheerfully to the wise and good determination of our Lord God. And fill your heart with spiritual comfort instead of this in me he takes to himself. And so the blessing of God Almighty be upon the head of you and yours for ever. Amen.' Certainly the words of a dying friend prevails much; and I do believe the Lord had put words of persuasion into her mouth which prevailed more than all the world with me to moderate

---

[1] Psalm 72, verse 5.
[2] 8 December 1659.

my excessive sorrow, and build me up in hopes, as she said, of our meeting again never to part; which so happened, for I was after this even desirous that if it were the determinate pleasure of God to take her from my head, that I might patiently submit when he should free that sweet soul from all those burthens of pressures and extremities. . . .

Jackson (ed.), *Autobiography of Mrs Alice Thornton*, pp. 110–13.

66 SAMUEL PEPYS AND HIS PARENTS JOHN Sr AND MARGARET, 1661–7

[*1661, September*] 23. Up, and sad to hear my father and mother wrangle as they used to do at London,[1] of which I took notice to both; and told them that I should give over care for anything unless they would spend what they have with more love and quiet. . . .

[*1663, April*] 4. . . . So to my office about writing letters by the post – one to my Brother John at Brampton, telling him (hoping to work a good effect by it upon my mother) how melancholy my father is, and bidding him use all means to get my mother to live peaceably and quietly, which I am sure she neither doth nor I fear can ever do – but frighting her with his coming down no more and the danger of her condition if he should die, I trust may do good. . . .

[*Pepy's father had come to visit his sons in London on his own, and had complained to Samuel of Margaret's 'unquietness'.*]

23. . . . I up betimes and with my father, having a fire made in my wife's new closet above, it being a wet and cold day; we sat there all the morning, looking over his country accounts ever since his going into the country. I find his spending hitherto hath been (without extraordinary charges) at full a 100*l* per annum – which troubles me and I did let him apprehend it, so

---

[1] Pepys's father had just retired to Brampton House (Hunts.), which he had inherited from his brother Robert on the latter's death in July 1661.

as that the poor man wept, though he did make it well appear to me that he could not have saved a farthing of it. . . .

[*1664, April*] 12. [*Samuel's brother Tom had died on 15 March, leaving his affairs in serious disarray. John Sr had come to London to help sort them out.*] . . . So home and find my father come to lie at our house; and so supped and saw him, poor man, to bed – my heart never being fuller of love to him, nor admiration of his prudence and pains heretofore in the world than now, to see how Tom hath carried himself in his trade – and how the poor man hath his thoughts going to provide for his younger children and my mother. But I hope they shall never want. . . .

[*October*] 14. Up by break of day and got to Brampton by 3 a clock – where my father and mother overjoyed to see me – my mother ready to weep every time she looked upon me. . . .

15. . . . And then my mother called me into the garden and there, but all to no purpose, desiring me to be friends with John; but I told her I cannot, nor indeed easily shall; which afflicted the poor woman, but I cannot help it. . . .

[*After Tom's death, Samuel had found among his papers 'many base letters of my Brother John's to him against me'.*]

[*1665, June*] 22. [At the end of a visit to London by Margaret Pepys.] Up pretty betimes, and in great pain whether to send my mother into the country today or no, I hearing by my people that she, poor wretch, hath a mind to stay a little longer; and I cannot blame her, considering what a life she will, through her own folly, lead when she comes home again; unlike the pleasure and liberty she hath had here. At last I resolved to put it to her, and she agreed to go . . . So I did give her money and took a kind leave of her – she, poor wretch, desiring that I would forgive my Brother John, but I refused it to her; which troubled her, poor soul, but I did it in kind words and so let the discourse go off, she leaving me, though, in a great deal of sorrow. . . .

[*1666, June*] 13. . . . Here [*i.e. at the house of John Hayls, who had already painted portraits of Pepys and his wife*] I find my father's picture begun; and so much to my content, that it joys my very heart to think that I should have his picture so well done – who, besides that he is my father, and a man that loves me and hath ever done so – is also at this day one of the most careful and innocent men in the world. . . .

17. *Lord's day.* . . . Thence my father and I walked to Gray's Inn Fields and there spent an hour or two, walking and talking of several businesses. First, as to his estate, he told me it produced about 80*l* per annum. But then there goes 30*l* per annum taxes and other things, certain charge – which I do promise to make good, as far as this 30*l* – at which the poor man was overjoyed and wept.

As to Pall,[2] he tells me he is mightily satisfied with Ensum;[3] and so I promised to give her 500*l* presently, and to oblige myself to 100*l* more on the birth of her first child, he ensuring her in 10*l* per annum for every 100*l*. And in the mean time, till she doth marry, I promise to allow her 10*l* per annum. Then as to John, I tell him I will promise him nothing, but will supply him as so much lent him – I declaring that I am not pleased with him yet. And that when his degree is over, I will send for him up hither, and if he be good for anything, doubt not to get him preferment. This discourse ended to the joy of my father, and no less to me, to see that I am able to do this . . .

23. My father and sister very betimes took their leave; and my wife, with all possible kindness, went with them to the coach – I being mightily pleased with their company thus long, and my father with his being here; and it rejoices my heart that I am in condition to do anything to comfort him, and could, were it not for my mother, have been contented he should have stayed alway here with me – he is such innocent company. . . .

[*1667, March*] 25. *Lady day.* . . . Thence home, and there I find letters from my brother which tell me that yesterday, when he wrote, my mother did rattle in the throat, so as they did expect every moment her death, which though I have a good while expected, did much surprise me; yet was obliged to sup at Sir W. Penn's, and my wife; and there counterfeited some little mirth, but my heart was sad; and so home after supper and

---

[2] Pepys's sister Paulina.
[3] This projected match with Robert Ensum (d. 1666) came to nothing.

to bed, and much troubled in my sleep with dreams of my being crying by my mother's bedside, laying my head over hers and crying, she almost dead and dying, and so waked; but which is strange, methought she had hair on her face, and not the same kind of face as my mother really has; but yet did not consider that, but did weep over her as my mother – whose soul God have mercy of.

27. . . . I being desirous to be at home to see the issue of my country letters about my mother, which I expect shall give me tidings of her death, I directly home and there to the office, where find no letter from my father or brother; but by and by the boy tells me that his mistress sends me word that she hath opened my letter, and that she is loath to send me any more news. So I home, and there up to my wife in our chamber; and there received from my brother the news of my mother's dying on Monday, about 5 or 6 a clock in the afternoon, and that the last time she spoke of her children was on Friday last, and her last words was, 'God bless my poor Sam!' The reading hereof did set me a weeping heartily; and so, weeping to myself a while and my wife also to herself – I then spoke to my wife, recollecting myself, and indeed having some thoughts how much better, both for her and us, it is than it might have been had she outlived my father and me or my happy present condition in the world, she being helpless, I was the sooner at ease in my mind . . .

[*April*] 13. . . . Wrote to my father, who I am glad to hear is at some ease again; and I long to have him in town, that I may see what can be done for him here, for I would fain do all I can, that I may have him live and take pleasure in my doing well in the world. . . .

[*December*] 5. . . . This day, not for want but for good husbandry, I sent my father by his desire, six pair of my old shoes, which fit him and are good; yet methought it was a thing against my mind to have him wear my old things.

Latham and Matthews (eds.), *Diary of Samuel Pepys*, vol. II. p. 183; vol. IV, pp. 96, 108; vol. V, pp. 120, 298; vol. VI, 133–4; vol VII, 164, 169–70, 175; vol. VIII, pp. 134, 166, 565.

67   ROGER LOWE VISITS HIS PARENTS' GRAVE,
1663 AND 1665

[*1663, September*] 13. – Lord's day. . . . I was at this time very
sad in spirit by reason of myself and seeing my father's and
mother's grave and pondering of other deaths, for I went round
about church to look at graves of such as I knew.

[*1665, January*] 1 . . . At noon my Sister Ellin came to me in
the churchyard and we went, both of us, to my father and
mother's grave and stayed awhile, and both wept. Went to my
sister's, Katherine's, and we had 2*d* in ale and so parted. . . .

Sachse (ed.), *Diary of Roger Lowe*, pp. 29, 77.

68   LADY ELIZABETH LIVINGSTON AND HER
FATHER, *c.*1668–70

[*1668 or 1669?*][1] O dear God forgive, I beseech thee, my father's
unkindness to me (if he displeases thee by it). O let me be no
occasion of increasing his sins, which are I much fear (though a
burden too heavy for him to bear) what he feels[2] not enough
the load on. O for Christ Jesus his sake, the Son of thy love,
have mercy on him, and give him true repentence, that the devil
may not rejoice at his ruin, but good angels at his conversion.

[*1670, October 10*] . . . I am commanded by God to honour
my parents, and yet without regard to this divine law (unworthy
as I am), though the blessing of long life is annexed to it, I fail
not with bitterness to censure my father for all his failings, and
to discourse of them to many hearers, which now I am sensible

---

[1] This prayer is one of eight preceded by undated 'Meditations upon the unkindnesse
off my father and the treachery of a friend'. They are immediately followed by the
words 'Here ends the prayers and meditations writ from my 14th yeare to my 20th'.
Lady Elizabeth was twenty about October 1669.
[2] fell's.

is a very great wickedness in me; the Lord in much mercy pardon it. I will now endeavour to lessen his faults in the esteem of others, and will proclaim his virtues, which may justly challenge love from all who know him well. This way will I begin to honour him and endeavour he may be as I wish: no way but by daily prayers to my God and by paying of an humble, constant duty to him.

[*Lady Elizabeth's anger with her father was probably due to his arranging a marriage for her with Robert Delaval against her will.*]

Christmas Eve, 1670, the first meditation writ after my marriage with Mr Delaval

. . .I am amazed and confounded at the intolerable number of my sins, and chiefly at my horrible iniquity in breaking those resolutions I made not three months ago of paying always an humble duty to my father. O miserable wretch that I am, I have so far broke them that, quite contrary, I have scarce paid him any duty at all but out of a wicked revengeful spirit. Even in his sickness, nay what is yet more heinous upon his very death-bed, have I peevishly expressed my sense of his unkindness to me in things which I had reason to believe he bitterly repented of; yet I then slighted him and stuck to the interest of a father-in-law who daily flattered me, and did not only neglect to visit my father the last eight or ten days of his life, but did also neglect some of those days so much as to send and enquire after his health, though I could not be ignorant that my undutiful behaviour would grieve his soul, which certainly it did to the very quick.

I knew he had so much natural affection for me, and withal I may say (with truth) so much esteem, that he would readily have hearkened to me in anything, but rashly and inconsiderately I suffered the height of my spirit to sway me and did not endeavour to do the least service to his decaying body, ruined fortune, or afflicted soul; and now whilst I am meditating upon my unworthy neglect of the last duties I should have paid him and my unexpressable loss in not being near him to receive a blessing from him in his last hours, he is resting in his grave, and 'tis (alas) too late for me to beg his pardon for faults which I am but newly sensible of.

'Tis only to my God that I can fly for mercy, whom I have also offended in the breach of his laws and in the breaking of my vows, and to whom I can never make any recompense for the least of those sins I have committed against his infinite majesty, and much less for all the transgressions of my whole life heaped up together. But what I can do now which may look well to my father's memory (through the grace of God assisting me), I will not fail to do, and that is to excuse what I have thought great unkindness to me as well as possibly I can, to put the best construction that may be upon all his actions, and to condemn myself to others for having resented them so ill; and to my heavenly Father I will humbly pray that all my iniquities may be blotted out and my transgressions no more remembered, for his sake who came into the world to save sinners, even Christ Jesus my blessed Lord and Saviour.

Oxford, Bodleian Library, MS Rawlinson D. 78, ff. 239, 278–9, 312, 314–16, 14–16.

69 ISAAC ARCHER'S DISCOVERY OF A CONFESSION MADE BY HIS FATHER, 1670

[*Archer's father had died just over two months before the discovery described here.*]

November 6. Having my father's books and writings, I found an old written book of experiences of God to him, in which he confesseth some infirmities which he was guilty of; I knew nothing of it till now. And I find Satan got the better of him in the same sort of sins as he did of me, though I was younger. I desire that as sin abounded in both, so grace may abound in me, as it did in him since, even to the last. Who would think that the same vain, filthy, lewd thoughts should be in both of us! It may be 'tis more general, but that men conceal them, and my father wrote down his thoughts. I have confessed them to God, but I dare not make them known. The Lord pardon them, as he hath done to my father! I could not have thought that ever such things had been in his heart, who even before, and then, was a gracious, sincere Christian. I did not think any had been so bad that way as myself; and think so still, for though the same was in him, yet he delighted not in them, but mastered them, which I could or rather would not a great while. I hope that I shall, as he, take more heed while I live. Amen.

Cambridge University Library, MS Add. 8499, f. 134.

70 THE DEATH OF SAMUEL JEAKE Sr DESCRIBED BY HIS SON SAMUEL, 1690

⟨October 3 Friday⟩ About 8h p.m. my dear father Samuel Jeake Senior died (being sixty-seven years of age lacking but six days) after a languishing of above three months, being first taken ill June 25 [*a detailed account of his illnesses and their complications follows*] . . . All which dying symptoms still increased till at last his speech failing him October 3 about noon (his sense continuing till the last) and about 8h p.m., having no breath left, he quietly slept in the Lord. In all this long time of sickness he never had the least murmuring expression against the conduct of Providence towards him. But several times in the evening, when I signified to him my fear that he would not live till morning, his usual answer was 'What God will': and that with a vigour in the expression. October 2 about 8h p.m. I took my leave of him, not knowing how soon he might die, and told him I doubted not but he was going to a better place, and that I was glad he died in peace, in his habitation, notwithstanding the malice of his enemies,[1] and that God had restored the liberty of the Gospel before he died; and that we were not driven from our dwellings by foreign invasion. He replied, 'I die the common death of all men.' And to others that spake of his departure, he said 'I go to my Father', lifting up his hand. At the time before mentioned, he would have me take out his watch and put it into his hand; which being done, he delivered it to me again, and said 'I deliver you this in name of possession of all that I have which I had not

---

[1] He had suffered persecution, together with other nonconformists in Rye, and had been compelled to leave the town between 1682 and 1687.

given you before, so that you may be in possession actually of it and need not take administration.' When I said 'Farewell, dear Father,' and kissed his dying lips, he answered 'Farewell, my dear lamb, the Lord bless thee, and prosper all that thou undertakest.'

Though I was actually possessed of all that my father had long before his death, he putting it into my hands about nine years ago in the persecuting times; yet I still esteemed him as proprietor of such part thereof as he gave me not before or upon my marriage, but would have kept in his own hands had he not been forced from Rye, returning the profits of it or what he desired me to send him to London etc. So that what he left me at his death though already in possession was by computation about £540.

Hunter and Gregory (eds.), *An Astrological Diary*, pp. 206–8.

71   DUDLEY RYDER AND HIS PARENTS, 1715–16

[1715] *Sunday, June* 19. Concerned to see my mother so peevish and fretful, continually saying some ill-natured thing or other to my father or the maid. I will endeavour if possible not to have a fretful uneasy wife. How easy it is to observe the faults my mother is guilty of in contradicting another, though I am too apt to be guilty of the same kind of peevishness myself. I have too much of her temper, but I am resolved to endeavour to quell at its first rise every secret resentment and uneasiness that comes upon me. . . .

Monday, June 27. Went to Father's shop and desired some money of him. Found him in a very good humour, told him what a good husband[1] he was and how little company I kept for fear of spending money. He is very willing to let me have money. If I could but use an agreeable forwardness with him of telling my circumstances to him I should never have him grumble when he gives me money. Nothing is more agreeable to me and

---

[1] Meaning 'how thrifty'. Should the following pronoun really be 'I' rather than 'he'?

more affecting to me than when I see my father give me money with willingness and readiness. He gave me £12.

Saturday, July 9. . . . Came to Hackney. Found Father there and in a very good humour, very kind and full of tender expressions of his love to me. He is indeed a very fond father to me and loves me very well. My mother also expressed herself very kindly to me. But what makes me uneasy is to see that my father and mother sometimes cannot agree in any[*thing*] else but in loving me. Mother is mighty apt to be touchy and see everything my father says in the worst light and take in the worst sense; continually little differences arise in which my mother seems to be chiefly and generally in fault by a cross peevish way of talking. Not but that these differences pass over in a moment and they are the next moment as loving together as ever. From this example I will endeavour to check every hot rising of my passions if ever I should be married, especially keep the furthest possible from little offences, anything that may give uneasiness to my wife, pass by every little failing.

Wednesday, September 14. . . . The afternoon passed away in walking about the garden and these ladies' company. [*Ryder was visiting Westbrook Hay in Bovingdon, Herts., his brother Richard's residence. The ladies were Mrs Cowley, a young widow, and her mother Mrs Jermyn.*] The young widow is indeed a fine lady. What troubled me most was a fear I had a stinking breath and it was perceived. This makes me of late very uneasy in company. I am resolved as soon as possible to find out the truth of it, and though I think to ask my mother that question it sounds so odd to ask whether my breath stinks that I don't know how to ask it. . . .

Tuesday, September 27. . . . Father proposed to the coachman to bring us to the foot of the Hay Hill and then to send for horses of Richard Clerk to help him uphill, upon which I said he would not be willing to let his horses that had been tired at work in the ground all day go again to labour. My father upon this was very angry with me and expressed it more than I have known him a great while that I should be always contradicting him and finding difficulties to whatever he proposes. . . .

[1716] *Sunday, March* 18. Going to meeting with Father, Mr Lacy overtook us. Father told him that I had discovered some mistakes in Mr Barker's sermon and began to enter upon the question and difficulty which I had started at dinner. I was very much concerned to hear my father give such a handle to have it said that we went to meeting only to find fault, so I put it off as well as I could, but Father, fond to show his son's parts and capacity, would still push it on. My father is too apt to be betrayed into great imprudences from the vanity he has to show my parts. . . .

Monday, March 26. Father spoke to me about his circumstances, that they were but indifferent. He mentioned Brother William, that he did not put himself forward in business and was afraid he would not be fit for business. I might have had a pretty good opportunity of talking with my father about Brother William's manner of living and extravagance, but I was afraid to mention it before I had well considered the matter. I know it will be an inexpressible grief and concern to him to have such a thing put into his head and may perhaps do him a great deal of harm. . . .

Monday, June 11. . . . When I and my father and brother walked to London in the morning, my father mentioned Brother William and was very much concerned at his behaviour. He said he had no head for business nor thought about it. He said he was continually out at night, but what he did or where he went he could not tell, and if he asked him he always had a lie ready to tell. He said he heard also that there was some intrigue carrying on between him and Mr Keniston's (a man that works at the shop) daughter. . . .

Monday, July 16. Father this morning at Hackney told me he would give me some certain allowance out of which I should keep myself entirely with clothes and everything, and asked me what he should allow me, whether £50 a year would not be enough, and after some time said he would allow me £80 per annum, which I thought full little enough to provide clothes and everything. . . .

Saturday, August 4. . . . Went to Mr Powell's to breakfast. Our conversation with his father and mother was nothing extraordinary, but I find young Mr Powell treats his parents in a very familiar way and talks to them as his equals and upon a level. . . .

Friday, August 10. I have been all this afternoon with Father in Smithfield in order to buy a horse but could not get one. He is extremely afraid of venturing upon any horse and distrusts his own judgement and suspects everyone he sees, whether he has reason or no. . . . Brother William is very uneasy about his mistress. He has told my father of it, who promised to inquire about her fortune, but I don't know my father has done it yet. He is strangely dilatory.

Sunday, August 12. Rose at 7. My father this morning took notice of some very little trifling things. I have sometimes wished I had been brought up in my father's business when I look upon the difficulties that meet me in the way of a lawyer, but then it has presently come to my mind that I could not tell how to have led a life constantly under my father's eyes. It would have tired me of life to have had him always teasing me with faults in trifles. It has been much happier for me to be absent. I have enjoyed all the pleasure and love and affection of a kind and loving father without any of the uneasiness that arise from his peculiar temper. If ever I shall have children I will endeavour to guide them with a much more even and steady hand, never to regard very little faults or, if they are such as may be of ill consequence, to do it in such a manner as not to be disagreeable to them. It wearies out a child of spirit to be always blamed. . . .

Saturday, August 18. . . . After dinner went with Sister to Aunt Billio's. Mother went part of the way with us but she went in so scandalous a gown that I could not help taking notice of it to her and in such a manner as made her a little angry and she would not go. Indeed I do think I did not do well in talking so much as I did about it to her in something of a harsh manner. But my mother is very much to blame in wearing clothes that make her friends blush for her and ashamed of being seen in her company. . . .

Saturday, September 1. . . . At supper Father and Mother had some little dispute, as they generally have every time they meet at table. I have been thinking which is in fault, my father or mother, but indeed they are both very much in fault, my mother for saying everything in a cross way and taking everything ill, and my father for continuing the matter that gave offence and pushing it on. When he sees my mother peevish and fretful, instead of endeavouring to put an end to it he loves to say the thing over again that made her uneasy.

Monday, October 8. . . . My father and I came to Hackney alone in the coach, and upon the road he talked to me very gravely about my brother and his affairs. But my father chiefly talked to me about his own affairs, said he had entangled his affairs very much. . . . He took an opportunity to advise me about my management of myself in the world, said he observed a very generous temper in me that might lead me into many inconveniences and therefore warned me not to be too good-humoured. My father told me he had done his estate prejudice by too hasty counsels and management; he had been apt to do things without due consideration, which he thought was my temper pretty much and advised against it.

Tuesday, November 27. To Father's in order to see an account of his whole estate as he promised to show it me, and he did so. He appears to have £500 per annum chiefly in houses, and, all his debts paid, about £1,000 personal estate. He advised with me about Brother William's affair and seemed to be in great perplexity what to do. However, at last he was very pleased with the proposal that if she had £1,500 he would settle £100 per annum in houses upon him and her instead of an estate in money equivalent, since her £1,500 would be sufficient to employ in trade. This matter has given me a good deal of trouble, for though I perceive my father seems to have my interest at heart, yet he does not seem much to understand it, for he does not propose to give me anything at all till after his death and after Mother's death about £220 per annum. But this is what I cannot be pleased with at all, since it will quite destroy my prospect of marrying and keep me low as long as he and Mother live.

Matthews (ed.), *Diary of Dudley Ryder*, pp. 38, 43–4, 49–50, 97, 109, 199, 206, 255–6, 276, 288, 292–3, 298, 311, 343–4, 369–70.

VII

Other Kinsfolk

The 'nuclear' or elementary family upon which this anthology has focused so far was set in a much larger network of relationships. The individual's recognition of kinsfolk outside his or her elementary family and the strength of the bonds between them varied greatly. They were influenced by the individual's social status, by his or her place of residence, and by whether he or she was married or single, among other things. Some of our diarists mentioned few relatives, though even those writers of whom this is true usually had one or two kinsfolk who played a significant part in their lives. The passages included in this section all come from the diaries of people who recorded numerous and significant contacts with relatives, but they were not chosen in the belief that they represented the 'typical' experience of Tudor and Stuart England. Such was the variety and complexity of kinship patterns that it would indeed be hard to say what was 'typical'.

It is sometimes quite difficult to ascertain whether particular individuals mentioned by Tudor and Stuart diarists were related to them, or, in the case of those acknowledged as relatives, exactly what the link was. Identification is made harder by the vagueness of English kinship terminology. In these extracts the terms which occur most frequently are 'brother' and 'cousin'. 'Brother' was commonly used of a wife's brother or a sister's husband (brothers-in-law); it could also be applied to a son-in-law's father, a wife's sister's husband, or even a sister's husband's sister's husband. 'Cousin', besides being used in its most common modern sense of a parent's sibling's child, was also employed, without qualification, to describe many more distant relatives, including (for example), first cousins once removed, and second cousins. It was also the term which Adam Winthrop usually applied to his nephews and nieces (72).

Some fundamental features of English kinship are clear enough to form the bases of fairly confident generalizations. In the first place it was (as it still is) bilateral, so that the individual regarded himself as related to his mother's as well as his father's blood relatives, and often had strong links with them. Secondly, kinship established by marriage ('affinal' kinship) could be very important. Thirdly, kinship reckoning was 'ego-focused'; in other words the individual identified his kindred on the basis of their relationship to himself, not their common membership of some larger group. All these characteristics are illustrated in the following section.

First comes a selection of passages from three years in the register of events kept by Adam Winthrop of Groton in Suffolk (72). In the first of these years, 1597, Winthrop, then in his late forties, lost his father-in-law, while in the last, 1605, two of his children were married. He and his wife between them had many sisters, and a number of these women's husbands and children figure prominently in Winthrop's diary. Winthrop's mother and father and he himself all married twice, and he kept in touch with John Still, bishop of Bath and Wells, his first wife's brother, as well as his own stepbrothers and stepsisters. Among Adam's relatives were some linked to him twice over. A good example is Thomas Mildmay of Barnes, mentioned in all three years, with whom Adam seems to have maintained a particularly cordial connection. Mildmay was both Adam's stepbrother (son of his stepfather by another marriage) and brother-in-law (husband of his sister). A prosperous landowner in middle age, Winthrop was well placed to give help and hospitality.

Nicholas Assheton's social status as a member of a long-established middle ranking Lancashire gentry family was higher than Winthrop's. Entries selected from the first year (1617–18) of what survives of his journal (73) describe some of the many contacts with relatives which he recorded during that time. We glimpse the often strenuous social and sporting activities of a young gentleman. Links with paternal kindred are much more prominent than in Winthrop's diary, and the range of recognized kinsfolk mentioned is larger. The Asshetons were a family of

several different branches, among which the Asshetons of
Whalley, represented by his first cousin, and the more distant
senior line of Middleton, both bulk large in Nicholas's diary.
Numerous affinal relatives and some kinsfolk whose precise
relationships with the diarist are somewhat obscure also make
their appearance. Nicholas was still a junior member of his widely
ramifying kindred; social pleasures and duties played a large part
in his life, but he was not yet in a position to act as a major
patron or broker of opportunities.

Samuel Pepys's (74) recognized relatives were exceedingly
numerous, spanning several degrees of kinship and many social
ranks. The fact that many of them lived in London or had
occasion to visit it helped the diarist to keep in touch with them.
Paternal kinsfolk made up the majority; they included a number
of people potentially useful to Pepys (e.g. Roger Pepys and
'Uncle Wight') as well as others are more likely to look to him
for help (e.g. John Angier). His mother's kinsfolk, a much
smaller group, were also of relatively humble social status, and
appear here as recipients of Pepys's help or hospitality; his diary
shows that his attitude towards them was somewhat ambivalent.
It also reveals quite clearly his desire to keep to a minimum his
involvement with his wife's impoverished father and his family
– though Pepys was later, albeit with some misgivings, to help
advance his brother-in-law, Balthasar St Michel. Calculation,
affection and a sense of duty were finely balanced in the young
administrator's attitudes towards his kinsfolk. He had no wish
to allow his humbler relatives to hamper his rapid social ascent.
Space allows the inclusion of no more than a tiny assortment
from the vast number of passages referring to his kinsfolk, and
this selection from the years 1663–4 cannot be fully representative.
Lord Sandwich, who launched Pepys on his career, does not
appear here (though in a previous section we have seen Pepys
performing an important and delicate task for his kinsman and
patron (3)).

From the diary of Oliver Heywood (75), a recently ejected
nonconformist minister, come descriptions of two of the many
preaching journeys he undertook into his native Lancashire from
his home near Halifax. In response to the new laws passed against
dissenters not long before Heywood set out in December 1666

on the first of the journeys recorded here, his ministry had assumed a peripatetic and largely clandestine form. Meetings in private houses played a key part in it, and his hosts included a number of his kinsfolk. His brothers-in-law and father-in-law, John Angier, himself an eminent dissenting minister, were prominent among them.

The favourite diversion of the aged Derbyshire yeoman Leonard Wheatcroft (76) during the last years of the seventeenth century was to visit relatives. The departure of most of his large brood of children had left him with increased leisure, and he was as yet sufficiently hale to walk considerable distances. The majority of the kinsfolk he visited were brothers, sisters and brothers-in-law, but they also included a nephew and an uncle, and in August 1693 he joined in a meeting of no fewer than twenty-five kinsfolk. His remarks about his mother, who died the same year at the venerable age of eighty-eight, illustrate the way in which old people acted as links between large numbers of descendants.

The extracts from Mrs Freke's journal (77) are unlike the others in this section in that they illuminate two particular relationships. Many other women got on badly with their daughters-in-law, and indulgent, even doting, grandparents are not hard to find, but as in so many other situations, Mrs Freke's experience and behaviour were alike extreme.

Effective relationships among kin depended on the three main pillars of pleasure or affection, perceived obligation and expected advantage. They manifested themselves in activities ranging from enjoyable conviviality to the performance of arduous, sometimes hazardous services. From Nicholas Assheton's extensive cousinage were drawn a high proportion of his companions in drinking, hunting, fishing or going to the fair. Hospitality, in one of its many forms, ranging from a drink or a meal to accommodation for days, weeks or even months, appears in all these extracts. Attendance at the rites of passage – christening, marriage and burial – was very important in bringing relatives together. Connected with birth and death respectively were duties which relatives were often called upon to assume: godparenthood and the execution of wills. Help in finding employment or a spouse were other services quite frequently performed by kinsfolk. They were less likely to act as employers themselves, though Samuel

Pepys served his distant cousin Lord Sandwich as his secretary, and Leonard Wheatcroft found masters for some of his children among his close relatives. In general, people were loath to assume the burden of supporting kinsfolk outside their elementary families for a long time. But help in emergencies – in the shape of gifts or loans, the use of influence, or simply the offer of strong arms and a broad back – might reasonably be expected from relatives. Nicholas Assheton's involvement in what came close to being a private war on behalf of his beleaguered Aunt Robinson in June 1617 was nevertheless exceptional at that date.

72   ADAM WINTHROP: 1597, 1603 AND 1605

[*Italicized passages not in square brackets have been translated from Latin.*]

1597 A register of the deaths of my friends, and of other things which have happened since the feast of the Nativity, anno 1596.

The viiith day of January being Saturday my father Henry Browne died, of th'age of seventy-six years, and was buried in Prittlewell Church in Essex.

The xvith day of April Mr Gawen Harvey, the youngest son of Mr George Harvey, high shreve[1] of Essex, came to my house, and the xixth day he and my nephew Henry Mildmay departed toward Springfield in Essex.

The 27 day my Sister Hilles came to my house for that her husband had beaten her face and arms grievously.

The xth day of May I did ride to my Brother [*Thomas*] Mildmay's and returned the xvith of the same and Charles came to dwell with me.

The same day my cousin E[*dmund or Edward*] R[*aven*] did fall in my garden.

The xviiith day of May my Cousin [*William*] Alibaster came to my house.

---

[1] Sheriff.

The xxixth day of May my Cousin Bulwer came to my house.

The second day of June I was at my Cousin [*Joan*] Muskett.

The ixth day [*of July*] I received a letter from my brother out of Ireland sans date. . . .

The xith my Cousin [*William*] Alibaster came to my house.

The xiiith day my Cousin [*William*] Alibaster *confessed himself to be a papist*, the xiiiith we did ride together to London, and I returned home the xxiith.

The same day my daughter Anna came home from my Brother [*Thomas*] Mildmay's.

The xxith day of July my cousin Johane Muskett died *in the year of her age* 59.[2]

The first of August my Cousin [*William*] Alibaster departed to Cambridge from my house, and the third day after Priscilla his sister came to me.

The iiiith of August my brother-in-law William Hilles died.

The xxiith of August I did write unto my brother in Ireland by George Mawle.

The last of August my Cousin [*William*] Alibaster departed to Cambridge.

The viiith day of September Johane Hilles, my wife's natural sister, died, and made me her executor.

The first day of October . . . John Sare, my Lord of Bath's steward, came to me.

1603 The iiith of January I rode to Springfield and the vith I dined at Danbury with Mr Humfrey Mildmay, and I returned home the viith.

The xth I dined with Mr Dr Johanes at my Brother [*John*] Snelling's.

The xvth day of January my Cousin [*William*] Firmyn came to my house and his son with him to board with me. ⟨*Came 14 January, departed 4 March.*⟩

The xxiith day William Hilles did come to Groton and told me that he and my Brother [*Abraham*] Veysie had bargained for the wheat in his barn.

---

[2] So it is uncertain whether she was actually fifty-eight or fifty-nine according to our reckoning.

The ixth of February I received a letter from my brother [*John*] out of Ireland by James [*Elwell*] his man.

The 23th of February my cousin Walter Mildmay came to board with me and departed the xxxth of March.

The 2 of March my son [*John*] went to Cambridge, the same day James [*Elwell*] departed from Groton.

The iiiith day I sealed an obligation of *Cli* to Janet [*Winthrop*] for to pay lv*li* the iiiith day of March anno 1603[*4*] at her house.

On Friday the xith of March my cousin Adam Winthrop's wife [*Jane*] departed from my house in Groton.

The xith of April I and my wife did ride to Bocking, to the christening of my Cousin [*William*] Firmin's child, who was named Joseph.

The xiiiith day of April my Brother [*Roger*] Weston came to my house and I paid him iii*li* for Elizabeth Hilles board.

The xviith day of April I received a letter from my brother [*John*], dated from Asmore the 23 of February 1602[*3*], and also another from James Elwell written from London the xiiiith of April.

The xi of May I sent to Hacwell and writ letters to my Lord Bishop of Bath.

The 22 of May a subpoena was served upon me at the suit of my cousin Adam Winthrop and Johane his wife in my house at Groton.[3]

The 14 [*of June*] my Cousin Bulwer's wife came to my house and told me that my cousin T. M.[*'s*] child was born at Wetherden and named Honor.

The vth of July I sent for a gelding to my Cousin [*William*] Firmin of Bocking in Essex.

The 23th day of July my Brother [*Thomas*] Mildmay was made knight at Whitehall; my son [*John*] came from Cambridge.

The vi of August my cousin Nathaniel Still rid to Cambridge.

⟨August.⟩ The first I dated my letter which I sent to Wells.

The iiiith of September my Cousin [*Humphrey*] Munning came to Groton, and I gave him five books of Lewes Granatensis.[4]

---

[3] There is a pointing hand in the margin at this place.

[4] Possibly *The Flowers of Lodowicke of Granado* . . . or *The Paradise of Prayers* by the same author; see Redstone, 'Diary', p. 82 n. 42.

The xvth of September I set up a house for Adam Podde my godson by the pond in neithe Peryfilde.[5]

The xxith my Cousin [*William*] Alibaster came to my house and showed me his pardon dated the xth of September.

The 28 . . . my Brother [*Roger*] Alibaster received vii*li* for his son . . .

⟨T⟩he viiith of October my cousin Henry Mildmay came to my house.

The [*blank*] day of October Sara my Cousin Frost's wife died . . .

The xxxth of October I was witness to William Hilles son at Holton named Peter who was born the xviiith day of this month.

The xviith day [*of November*] my Cousin [*Humphrey*] Munning came to my house.

The xxvth Father Hilles came a wooing to Johane Bettes my maid. The same day my Cousin Winthrop rid to Brettenham.

1605 The xii of January I delivered a state[6] to John Alibaster. The same day Mr John Forth came to my house.

The xiiiith of January Cousin Nathaniel Still came to Groton.

The xxth of January Mr [*Thomas*] Fones came to Groton.

The xv of February my cousin William Mildmay's late wife died in the Tower of London.

The xxiiith Thomas Fones came to Groton and was married to my daughter Anne the xxvth and they departed toward London the xxviith day of February 1604[5].

The xiiiith [*of March*] I and my son viewed over Mr John Forth's land at Kersey[7] and Hadleigh.

The same day [*15 or 19 March*] I received a letter from my brother [*John*] out of Ireland dated 2 *of March* 1604.

The xxvith of March I and my son [*John*] did ride to Mr John Forth's of Great Stambridge in Essex.

The xxviiith day my son was solemnly contracted to Mary Forth by Mr [*Ezekiel*] Culverwell, minister of Great Stambridge in Essex, *with the consent of parents.*[8]

---

[5] An unidentified location: possibly 'Nether Perryfield' in modern spelling.

[6] Or estate: a right in or title to land.

[7] *Carsey.*

[8] Pointing hand with bracket in the margin at this place.

The vth [*of April*] my brother [*John*] came to Groton after his return out of Ireland and departed the ixth of June.

The ixth my son did ride into Essex.

The xvith of April he was married at Great Stambridge by Mr Culverwell *in the seventeenth year of his age, three months and four days completed.*[9]

The viiith of May my son and his wife came to Groton from London and the ixth I made a marriage feast when Sir Thomas Mildmay and his lady my sister [*Alice*] were present.

The same day my sister [*Mary*] Veysye came to me and departed on Friday the 24 of May.

My daughter [*Anne*] Fones came the viiith of May and departed home the xxiiith of May.

The viiith [*of June*] my Cousin [*Anne*] Duke was delivered of her first son before her time.

The ixth I did ride with my Brother [*John*] Winthrop into Essex and returned the xviith.

The xxith my brother [*John*] departed from London towards Ireland.

The last of June Mr John Forth came to Groton.

The first of July my cousin Walter Mildmay and his wife [*Bridget*] came.

⟨T⟩he xxiiiith of July I and my wife [*Anne*] with my son [*John*] and his wife [*Mary*] did ride to the baptizing of John Hilles, the son of William Hilles of Holton.

The next day my son and his wife did ride to her father's in Essex.

The first of August my son [*Thomas*] Fones came to Groton from London. The same day my Cousin Humphrey Munnings preached at Boxford a very godly and learned sermon upon the v chapter of Genesis v. 1.2.3.

The third day I delivered an estate to my son-in-law Thomas Fones and Anne his wife in Quick's tenement in Edwardstone.

The xvth my Brother [*John*] Forth and his daughter came to [*Groton*].

[*September 30*] . . . I did ride to Stambridge and returned from thence the iiiith of September [*October*].

[9] Born in January 1588, John was already seventeen.

The ixth I was [*at*] Brettenham at my Cousin [*Humphrey*] Munnings.

[*October 21*] . . . My Cousin [*Humphrey*] Munning preached at Boxford.

The vith of November my Brother [*Roger*] Alibaster came to me and bound Thomas his son for a year from the i of the same month with Cook the shearman of Boxford. ⟨iiii*li* per annum.⟩

British Library, MS Add. 37419, ff. 21ᵛ–22ᵛ, 26ʳ–29ʳ, 31ᵛ–33ᵛ. Names added to the text supplied from Redstone (trans.), 'Diary of Adam Winthrop' in *Winthrop Papers*.

73 NICHOLAS ASSHETON OF DOWNHAM: FROM A YEAR OF HIS DIARY, 1617–18

[*1617*] May 12th. Father Greenacres, Mother, Aunt Bess, John, wife, self, at ale. Spent iv*d*.

June 4th. This evening came Sir Thomas Medcalfe with forty men or thereabouts, at sunset or after, to Raydale[1] House in Wensleydale, with guns, about half a score bills, picks,[2] swords, and other warlike provision, and beset the house, where was my Aunt Robinson and three of her little children, which went forth, shutting the door. My aunt left the children and went to Sir Thomas, desiring to know the meaning of that force; if for possession of the house and land, and by what authority; and if better than her husband's, who was now at London, she would avoid with all hers quietly. He answered that he would not so much satisfy her: his will was his law, or authority for that time; so they would not suffer her to go into the house for her stockings and head-dressing and shoes, which she wanted, but she was forced to go a long mile with her little children to a town called Busk,[3] and thence a foot to Worton,[4] two miles thence. This night was the house shot at many times and entered, but rescued.

[1] *Raydall.*
[2] pikes?
[3] Stalling Busk.
[4] Consistently misspelt *Morton* in text.

June 5. To Mr Middleham's[5] and Sir Arthur Daykins, two justices; she could get no remedy, but went to York, double-horsed, to the Council.[6] She left in Raydale House three of her sons, John, William and Robert Robinson, and seven servants and retainers, one Thom. Yorke of Knaresborough, a boy newly come with a letter, and two serving maids. These, with great courage, maintained the possession, in great danger, against a lawless, rude and unruly company, desperate and graceless in their actions and intents.

A messenger came to me with letters from Worton; found me at Downham, and my aunt desired me to come to assist her in that action, so we resolv[ed?] to go the next Monday.[7]

June 6. To Gisburn, Newsholme,[8] Hellifield, Swinden, Otterburn, Kirkby Malghdale;[9] there we drunk. Kettlewell, then dined; so to Starbotton,[10] Buckden Rake, first house in Worton; there light and enquired, and resolved to go to Sir Thomas at Busk, to move him to forbear further violence. So to Busk: my Lady there, but not he; gone to Marsett.[11]. Found him drunk, and some half a score or thereabouts of his followers likewise. There met us one George Scar, his man, with divers well furnished with weapons. This fellow being in drink gave us many insolent respectless speeches, such as, if he or his company had been sober, or we any whit equal in numbers and provision, we had not [*gap in text*] with such patience.

Neither could we be suffered to go to the house to spake [*sic*] with them; therefore we went back to Worton, quickening, to see Sir Thomas in the morning.

This evening, about sunset or after, was shooting at the house, and one James Hodgson, one of the rash barbarians of Sir Thomas, coming upon the house, was shot and slain.

June 7. No speech to be had with Sir Thomas, but my aunt came. She gave very few speeches to us, but only that the sergeant of mace and pursuivant were coming from York, and

---

[5] *Midlom's.*
[6] I.e. the Council of the North.
[7] In fact they set out on Friday.
[8] *Newsham.*
[9] *Malham?*
[10] *Tarbotte.*
[11] *Marrett.*

she went to Raydale House, but in the way she was stayed and unmercifully used. Presently the sergeant and pursuivant and Mr Middleham, the justice of peace, came to Raydale, and there those officers took Sir Thomas with some five or six of his company (the rest dispersed, every one a sundry way), and went to the house and set them at liberty.

Whitsunday, 8. We four to Kettlewell, to Kirkby Malghdale,[9] dined; to Gisburn, drunk wine. Spent in this journey vi*s*.

Ditto 17. I and Brother Greenacres to Portfield (rain), then to Whalley: foxhunting. To the pond; a duck and dog. To the abbey: drunk there. Home.

June 27. Coz.[12] J. Assheton, self, Father, Brother Sherborne, fished with two wades[13] up to the bridge; sent some fish to the parsonage. Dined at parsonage. Spent vi*d*.

June 30. Self, Father, Parson, John Assheton, *cum aliis*, a fox-hunting to Harden, up to Scout Stones; set the greyhounds; found fox; a fine [*gap in text*]; lost him in the holds.

July 22. Magdalen[14] Day. To Browsholme[15] to dinner. Father, Brother, Parson, to Clitheroe Fair. Coz. Assheton there; Coz. Ralph Assheton, of Middleton. Spent xviii*d*. To Worston to supper; so to Downham. Late to our beds.

August 24 (Sunday). Word came, as I was going to church, that Coz. Thomas Starkie's wife was dead this morning, about two o'clock, and he desired me to come to him, and my father and mother, to the burial. So to church; Parson preached. Father, Mother, self, Fogg and Carryer to Downham. I to Twiston;[16] a heavy house. Back to Downham.

August 25. . . . To Twiston. Tom Starkie, Mills his father-in-law, Coz. Giles Parker and myself carried forth the corpse; so to church. Mr Raufhe preached; text, Romans viii. 12, 13. So she was buried, and dinner forty mess[17] provided for. Dined in the hall.

---

[12] *Cooz* (and elsewhere).
[13] Sieves.
[14] *Maudlin*.
[15] *Broxholme*.
[16] Thomas Starkie's residence. Raines was unable to trace any relationship between Starkie and Nicholas Assheton; *Journal*, p. 51 n. 2.
[17] Either a portion of food, or a group of four people sitting together and helped from the same dishes.

October 29. Riding to Worston. Brother Houghton and Coz. Henry hawking; lost their hawk.

November 25. St Katharine's Day. To Downham. There an exercise. To Worston. Tom Starkie etc. very merry, and well all. All at supper. We were all temperately pleasant, as in the nature of a festival day.

December 24. I, my wife and Fogg to Whalley, to keep Christmas with my Coz. Assheton.

St Stephen. Word came that Sir Richard Assheton was very dangerously sick.

December 27. St John's Day. I with my Coz. Assheton to Middleton. Sir Richard had left his speech, and did not know a man. Had not spoken since morning. His extremities began two or three days since. He departed very calmly about eight at night. No extraordinary sorrow, 'cause his death was so apparent in his sickness. Presently upon his death there was enquiring after his will, which was showed by Mr John Greenhalgh of Brandlesome and Sir Richard's second son Ralph Assheton, who, with my Lady, were executors, and Coz. Assheton of Whalley, supervisor. My now Coz. Assheton of Middleton, Richard, began to demand the keys of the gates, and of the study for the evidence, and to call for the plate, upon cause his brother John had some part in them. There was some likeness of present falling out of him and the executors, which certainly had been had not my Coz. Assheton of Whalley so [*gap in text*] as was little or no discord. The reason was former unkindness between Sir Richard and his son, to which Sir Richard was moved by my Lady, and those that were of her faction;[18] but now all well, praised be God, which I pray God to continue.

December 30. To Whalley ward. . . . Stayed all night at Abbey; very merry all with dancing.

[*1618*] January 3. A hunting with Coz. Assheton, Richard Sherborne, etc. With Coz. Braddyll to Portfield; eat, drunk wine, and was merry, and to the field again. . . .

January 15. I had a black sent from Middleton, but because I heard my Coz. Assheton had none, I sent word to Mr Greenhalgh that they should give mine to Cousin Radcliffe. Sir Richard

---

[18] *faccon.*

Assheton's funeral; a great company; I a mourner in my own old cloak. Parson of Middleton, Mr Assheton, preached, text 90 Psalm 12. Divers knights and many gentlemen there. All the gent.[s] to Middleton to dinner.

March 15. I early to Portfield. There was Coz. Millicent Braddyll delivered of a son and heir about 4 or 5 o'clock in the morning. Mr Richard Shuttleworth of Gawthorpe came by, and Coz. Braddyll and I went with him to Whalley. There light at the abbey. Coz. Assheton went with us. All to wine; then all to Lancaster. Charges too much: idle expenses, in all xxxs. Judge Bromley, Judge Denham. Eleven executed. Coz. Edward Braddyll, the priest, came to the bar, and was indict for seducing the king's subjects, but had not judgement. . . .

April 5. Easter Day. To Downham, to church. After dinner some argument about Mr Leigh's ministering the sacrament with the surplice,[19] between my Brother Sherborne and my father. They differed so far as that my father came to Downham, and would go no more back to Dunnow to remain. . . .

April 12. Sunday. John Greenacres to be godfather to Richard Sherborne's child. Parson of Slaidburn[20] was asked to be the other, but by reason of my sister's[21] popish disposition would not; and so, in want of one, I was taken.

April 28. We with many others to Middleton with the corpse and hearse of Coz. Susan Assheton. Coz. Assheton of Slaidburn preached: 1 Thessalonians iv. 13, 14. . . .

Raines (ed.), *Journal of Nicholas Assheton*, pp. 1, 9–15, 19, 29, 51–2, 66–74, 77, 84–6, 88–9, 91–4.

74 SAMUEL PEPYS, 1663–4

[*1663, May*] 25. Up; and my pill working a little, I stayed within most of the morning; and by and by the barber came, and Sarah Kite my cousin, poor woman, came to see me and to borrow

---

[19] *Cirploise.*
[20] *Sladeborne.*
[21] Dorothy, Nicholas's sister, who had married Richard Sherborne.

40s of me, telling me she will pay it at Michaelmas again to me. I was glad it was no more, being indifferent whether she pays it me or no; but it will be a good excuse to lend her nor give her any more; so I did freely, at fist[1] word, do it and gave her a crown more freely to buy her child something – she being a good-natured and painful wretch, and one that I would do good for, as far as I can that I might not be burdened. . . .

27. . . . Here [*Westminster Hall*] I met with my cousin Roger Pepys and walked a good while with him; and among other discourse, as a secret he hath committed to nobody yet but myself, he tells me that his sister Claxton now resolving to give over the keeping of his house at Impington, he thinks it fit to marry again; and would have me, by the help of my Uncle Wight or others, to look him out a widow between thirty and forty year old, without children and with a fortune, which he will answer in any degree with a jointure fit for her fortune. A woman sober and no high flyer as he calls it. . . .

[*June*] 4. . . . At last, by coach I carried her [*Mrs Pepys*] to Westminster Hall, and they two to Mrs Bowyer, to go from thence to my wife's father's and Ashwell to hers. And by and by, seeing my wife's father in the Hall and being loath that my wife should put me to another trouble and charge by missing him today, I did employ a porter to go, from a person unknown, to tell him that his daughter was come to his lodgings. And I at a distance did observe him; but Lord, what a company of questions he did ask him; what kind of man I was and God knows what. So he went home . . .

[*December*] 21. . . . So called with my coach at my wife's brother's lodging, but she was gone newly in a coach homewards; and so I drove hard and overtook her at Temple Bar, and there paid off mine and went home with her in her coach. She tells me how there is a sad house among her friends. Her brother's wife proves very unquiet, and so her mother is gone back to be with her husband and leaves the young couple to themselves; and great trouble, and I fear great want, will be among them; I pray keep me from being troubled with them. . . .

---

[1] First?

31. . . . At present, I am concerned for my Cousin Angier of Cambridge, lately broke in his trade. And this day am sending his son John, a very rogue, to sea. . . .

[*1664, April*] 17. *Lord's day*. . . . I slept soundly all the sermon; and thence to Sir W. Penn's, my wife and I, and there sat talking with him and his daughter; and thence with my wife walked to my Uncle Wight's and there supped; where very merry, but I vexed to see what charges the vanity of my aunt puts her husband to among her friends, and nothing at all among ours. Home and to bed. . . .

26. . . . My wife gone this afternoon to the burial of my she-Cousin Scott – a good woman. And it is a sad consideration how the Pepys's decay, and nobody almost that I know in a present way of increasing them. . . .

[*September*] 9. Up, and to put things in order against dinner, I out and bought some things; among others, a dozen of silver salts. Home and to the office, where some of us met a little; and then home and at noon comes my company – *viz.*, Anth. and Will Joyce and their wives – my Aunt James newly come out of Wales, and my cousin Sarah Gyles – her husband did not come, and by her I did understand afterward that it was because he was not yet able to pay me the 40s she had borrowed a year ago of me. I was as merry as I could, giving them a good dinner; but W. Joyce did so talk, that he made everybody else dumb, but only laugh at him. I forgot, there was Mr Harman and his wife. My aunt a very good harmless woman. All their talk is of her and my two she-Cousin Joyces' and Will's little boy Will (who was also here today) [*going*] down to Brampton to my father's next week – which will be trouble and charge to them; but however, my father and mother desire to see them, and so let them. They eyed mightily my great cupboard of plate, I this day putting my two flagons upon my table; and indeed, it is a fine sight and better than ever I did hope to see of my own. Mercer dined with us at table, this being her first dinner in my house. . . .

18. *Lord's day*. Up and to church, all of us. At noon comes Anth. and W. Joyces (their wives being in the country with my father) and dined with me, very merry as I can be in such company. After dinner walked to Westminster (tiring them by

the way, and so left them, Anthony in Cheapside and the other in the Strand) and there spent all the afternoon in the Cloister, as I had agreed with Jane Welsh; but she came not, which vexed me, staying till 5 a-clock; and then walked homeward and by coach to the Old Exchange, and thence to my Aunt Wight's and invited her and my uncle to supper. And so home; and by and by they came and we eat a rare barrel of oysters Mr Povey sent me this morning, and very merry at supper; and so to prayers and to bed.

Last night it seems my Aunt Wight did send my wife a new scarf, laced, as a token for her many givings to her. It is true, now and then we give them small toys, as oranges, etc. – but my aim is to get myself something more from my uncle's favour than this.

Latham and Matthews (eds.), *Diary of Samuel Pepys*, vol. IV, pp. 154–5, 159, 173, 429, 439; vol. V, pp. 125, 134, 266, 273–4.

75   OLIVER HEYWOOD, 1666–7 AND 1670

[*1666*] On the latter end of it, viz. December 31, I went into Lancashire, where I had not been of a quarter of a year. I baptized a child at Halifax as I went, preached at Rochdale at night where I lodged, and though I was very sick immediately before, yet God helped me sweetly through. 1667: the Tuesday I went to Little Lever, preached on Wednesday at my Brother Whitehead's, the house wherein I was born. On Thursday I joined with my Cousin Bradshaw at Ralph Leaver's and the same day joined with my Brother Heywood at my brother Thomas Crompton's; on Friday we preached together at my brother Samuel Bradley's, on Lord's Day at Brother William Whitehead's, where we had a multitude of auditors. On Monday I went to Bolton, and at night up to High Horrocks where I preached on Tuesday all day; at night came to Bolton and preached at George Holt's. On Wednesday I preached at Thomas Mason's in Little Lever, and at night at Peter Heywood's. Thursday we spent as a solemn fast at William Whitehead's, and though the Lord sweetly affected

my heart when some others were at duty, yet I found not the
usual assistance my soul is wont to have in those duties: the Lord
show me the cause thereof and humble me. Upon Friday I went
to Manchester, preached at night at my lodgings (Mr James
Hulton's house); the day after came to Denton, preached there
in public upon the Lord's Day, being January 13 1666–7. Upon
Monday, being requested, I accompanied my Mother Angier to
the funeral of old Mistress Robinson at Mobberley in Cheshire
(my Grandmother Moseley's sister); lodged at Knutsford that
night at the house of one Mr Antrobus[1] who used us exceeding
courteously. On Tuesday we returned to Denton, and visited
some friends by the way. On Wednesday we observed a fast in
my Father Angier's house, and oh it was a sweet day, a token
for good. On Thursday I returned homewards, dined at Mr
Ran's house at Ashton-under-Lyne; lodged at Chadwick Hall at
my cousin Edmund Hill's, where I preached that night. On
Friday I came home, visiting some friends by the way.

[*1670*] On Wednesday September 7 I went for Lancashire; lodged
that night with Mr Horton at Sowerby. The day after went to
Rochdale; lodged with Cousin Edmund Hill at Chadwick Hall.
On Friday went to Manchester, on Saturday to Denton; heard
Mr Eddleston and Mr Hickenbottom, two conformists. On
Monday night I lodged at Captain Hulton's in Droylsden, on
Tuesday night at Manchester. On Wednesday I went to Denton;
there we kept a day of thanksgiving. Oh what a sweet day was
it! Returned that night to Manchester. On Thursday we went to
the funeral of Cousin James Crompton of Clifton at Eccles; Mr
Usherwood preached. On Saturday we were at the funeral of
Mr Birch, one of the fellows at Manchester; that night I went
to Little Lever; preached at Brother Whitehead's the day after,
had a large auditory, good help. On Monday went back to
Manchester; sent a messenger to Denton about business. On
Tuesday my Father Angier came and dined with us; after that
we sealed some writings referring to my father. On Wednesday
morning we went to Little Lever, kept a fast there for my own
father; my Brother Heywood preached that night. On Thursday

---

[1] *Antribus.*

I went with him as far as Deane Church, where I had some business with Brother Angier, Mr Tilseley; so returned to Crompton Fold. On Friday we had a fast at Brother Thomas Crompton's; at night I preached at Brother Laurence Crompton's. Saturday I studied a funeral sermon; preached it at night at Cousin Adam Greenhaugh's. Lord's Day, Mr Sutton preached at Cockey, whom I heard all day with comfort; at night I preached at Crompton Fold. On Monday I went to Bolton; there despatched visits and business. On Tuesday I went to Little Lever; preached a funeral sermon for James Mason's wife; returned to Bolton; spent some time in the evening with that sad widow Cousin Hanna Crompton. On Wednesday morning looked through Mr Parke's excellent library; went to Crompton Fold, into Little Lever. On Thursday we came homewards to Rochdale; on Friday got home, September 30 70; found all well, blessed be God.

British Library, MS Add. 45965, ff. 30^v–31^r, 56^{r-v}

76   LEONARD WHEATCROFT, 1693–1700

Soon after, my own mother fell sick; she then had been blind above four years. She died March 12 1692[3]. She was of age fourscore and eight. She had nine children: six sons and three daughters, and when she died she was mother to six of them and grandmother and great-grandmother to fourscore and three.

[*Not long after this, Wheatcroft had a bad fall.*]

And when it pleased God I did recover of my fall, I was resolved to sojourn[sic] again, and to visit all my brothers and sisters. First I went to my Brother Samuel's. Then to Solomon Sheldon's, who married my Sister Mary, May 6 '93. Then to my sister Sarah Chadwick's, where I had not been of five years before; this was in July 4 1693.

My next travel was to my Winster brother's, Robert Hawley of Winster.[1] There I stayed one night, July 7 1693.

---

[1] His brother-in-law.

Again, August 21, Brother William, Brother Samuel, myself and several more of my relations to the number of twenty-five met at one of my relations near Sheffield, whose name was Edward Gill, where we was rarely[2] entertained, the next day to Sheffield; there were we all civilly[3] merry with more of our relations for the space of two days. . . .

[*In 1697 Wheatcroft and his daughter Sarah went to visit his daughters Anna and Elizabeth in Yorkshire, returning on 28 June*].

But we had not long rested at home but we were both invited to a welcoming unto my cousin Samuel Billings, who had married my Sister Sarah[*'s*] daughter, by whom he had one child, called John; he was born May 21 1697. But the welcoming was not till July 1. There was we all very merry for two days and, blessed be God, did safe return.

After that [*a visit to Chesterfield on 17 July*] I went to several places up and down to see my relations. But above all I and my Brother William went to Morton to see an uncle of ours who married my father's sister, whom we had not seen of many years, nor he us, for he had been blind seven years; and no little was he comforted to hear of us at that time, which was May 31 '99. The next day did I return to my family in good health, blessed be my God.

And again June 5 in the same year I went to a christening at Cowhouse Lane to my cousin John Benbrig who had married James Brough[*'s*] daughter Mary [etc?]. There and at my Sister Chadwick's I stayed two nights; from thence I safely returned, blessed be my God, but very ill tired.

And October 9 '99 I went to Brother Solomon's, where I met with Brother William; there did we three brethren spend the day very merrily, and, blessed be God, I got home very well that night.

And upon January 1 I went to Winster, to my Brother Robert's,[4] where I tarried five nights, and with him to [High Grooves?] and seeing good store of ore, I bought of him a 12

[2] *raryly.*
[3] *sivily.*
[4] *Robard's.*

part of a new tacker call[ed] by the name of Shelldon Mere, or [*blank*].[5]

Then I rested at home till I went to my Brother William's, which was their wakes, where I was two nights.

[*Wheatcroft made one more recorded visit to a relative, his brother-in-law at Winster, in March 1701.*]

Matlock, Derbyshire Record Office, MS D2079/F1.

77 MRS ELIZABETH FREKE'S DIFFICULT RELATIONSHIP WITH HER DAUGHTER-IN-LAW, AND HER GRANDSON'S DEATH, 1704–5

[*1704*] Saturday November the 18: my dear son, his wife and my two dear grandchildren and their three servants came to Bilney after they had been near four months in England, my dear son loaded with his dropsical humour and grown so big and fat with it I hardly knew him.

⟨1704/5⟩ January the first, I begged of Mr Freke to give my dearest son fifty pounds and a year's interest for a New Year's gift, which he gave him, and I gave him ten pounds for a New Year's gift. E.F.

⟨2d⟩ The next day Mr Freke and I, in my chamber, speaking of it by ourselves, only my maid, who had lived a great while with me [*being present*]; my daughter in her own chamber stood hearkening at the door, flew into the chamber to us and told Mr Freke her father-in-law he might be ashamed to speak of such a trifle as that gift before my servant, and she said she had a good mind to kick her downstairs, and said she would begone [*herself*] if I did not turn her out of doors. So after I were forced to discharge her and take a stranger about myself after she had lived

---

[5] Wheatcroft had purchased an interest in lead workings. *Higroufes* (reading uncertain) may perhaps be rendered 'High Grooves': a groove was an entrance to a lead mine. A tacker, from 'tack' or 'take', was probably a mining lease, of which Wheatcroft was buying a twelfth part or share. A mere or meer was an underground working. See Daniel Defoe's description of the Derbyshire lead mines and miners in his *A Tour through the Whole Island of Great Britain* (Dent, London, 1962), vol. II, pp. 159–65.

three times with me, and the last time two years want one month. My daughter was near two month [*at Bilney*] and never said to her father or me good night or good morrow.

Monday the 7 of May my dear son, his wife, and my two dear grandchildren left me alone at Bilney and went away for London, Mr Freke carrying them all up at his charge as he did [*entertain?*] eight of [*them?*] here half a year. In which time I often begged of my daughter the youngest children [*sic*], her son John, finding him no favourite, and I loved him to my soul because he was the picture of my dearest son. But she as cruelly denied him to me and carried him away from me, which turned me to a violent sickness for above six week; I though[t] [*it*] would have been my last.

⟨May 10⟩ Notwithstanding this and several other cruelties to me, I sent my daughter up to London (paid on sight by my cousin John Freke) a hundred pounds to ease their expenses in London; for which and their half year being with me at Bilney, eight of them, servants and horses, and all manner of bills, pothecaries, letters, smiths, near twenty pound in cord etc., five asses and a horse to drive them to Bristol, all which never deserved thanks from them.

White Monday, the 27 of May, I writ to this my said daughter for God sake to carry my two dear grandchildren out of London, for else there I should lose them, since she would not be so kind to trust me with either of them (so long as till she went for Ireland); but were never thought fit to be answered by letter or otherways, it being near two month since.

June the tenth, Sunday, about two a clock, my dearest grandchild I had so often begged for, being like my own dear son, near four years old (and in my eyes the loveliest child was ever seen by me), by name Mr John Freke, he, with his brother Mr Percy Freke, and Mr Molson their landlord[*'s*] two sons where they lodged, where Tom Molson found my son's pocket pistols charged and primed, and so left by his man Perryman, which pistol the lad took, and discharged by accident in the head of my dearest and best beloved grandchild, Mr John Freke; the bullet went in at the eye, and though all the means of London was used, yet no help, so that on Wednesday the thirteenth of June about 5 a clock in the morning, my dear babe gave up his soul to my God, who would not have taken root and branch from me had it been left by my cruel [children?];[1] but God forgive them[2] and I shall ever lament it, for I had set my whole heart on it, which it has broke, that and me, for any comfort in this life: E. Freke.

Monday June the eighteenth, my dearest grandchild Mr John Freke was brought down from London in a hearse to me, to be here interred in Bilney chancel, where he lies at the upper end, and where, God willing, I will lie by him as fast as I can get to him. I lost my child to show their undutifulness and cruelty to me, which God forgive them.[2] E. Freke.

British Library, MS Add. 45718, ff. 63ʳ–64ʳ.

---

[1] *daughter* deleted.
[2] *her* deleted.

Diarists and Diaries: Biographical and Bibliographical Appendix

This appendix lists in alphabetical order the diarists and other writers represented in this anthology. Each entry includes biographical details, a brief description of the source, its present location where known, the most useful printed edition of it, if one exists, and any other works drawn upon in the compilation of the entry, apart from the *Dictionary of National Biography*. The main aim in selecting biographical information has been to provide the facts necessary to an understanding of the passages in the anthology.

The writer's name, the word 'diary', 'memoirs' etc., and details of the version of the source used in the compilation of this anthology, are given in **bold** type.

In those cases where I have been able to compare passages in the original manuscript with a printed edition, I have included an assessment of the quality of the latter as follows: (A) excellent; (B) reliable in the main; (C) unreliable, either because substantial portions have been omitted without warning, or because of mistakes in transcription.

Abbreviations: b. born; d. died; da. daughter; m. married; s. son; BL British Library.

Isaac Archer, b. 1641, son of William (d. 1670), lecturer at Halstead and Colchester, and Mary Woolnough. Studied at Trinity College, Cambridge; BA 1661, MA 1664. In 1662 a reluctant and ambivalent conformist, against his father's wishes; ordained deacon and priest. Presented to his first living, Chippenham (Cambs.) soon afterwards. M. in 1667, without his father's full consent. His wife's maiden name was Peachey. Nine children, of whom all but one died in infancy or early childhood. William Archer drew up a will designed to prevent his son's gaining control of his estate. Isaac was deeply distressed, but his father's dispositions were largely overturned as a result of subsequent legal proceedings.

Diary or autobiography: 1641–1700. He began to keep what he called 'an account of my life in writing' in 1659. The surviving MS contains a series of entries written at different times. Handwriting deteriorates badly towards the end.

Cambridge University Library, MS Add. 8499.

Nicholas Assheton (*c*.1590–1625) of Downham (Lancs.), son of Richard and Margaret Hulton. M. Frances, da. of Richard Greenacres. They had five children.

Diary: May 1617–March 1619. A record of his social life.

MS: whereabouts unknown.

F. R. Raines (ed.), *The Journal of Nicholas Assheton of Downham, in the County of Lancaster, Esq.*, Chetham Society, old series, 14 (1848).

Katherine Austen (1629–83) of London, da. of Robert Wilson, m. Thomas Austen (d. 1658). Bore him at least three children (one da., two s.).

Diary: *c*.1664–8, largely consists of memoranda, reflections and meditations.

BL, MS Add. 4454.

See also B. J. Todd, 'The remarrying widow: a stereotype reconsidered', and S. H. Mendelson, 'Stuart women's diaries and occasional memoirs', both in M. Prior (ed.), *Women in English Society, 1500–1800* (Methuen, London and New York, 1985), pp. 76–7, 184, 199, 202.

Edward Barlow, b. 1642, seaman, son of George Barlow, husbandman of Prestwich, Lancs. M. Mary Symans, 1678. Apprentice to chief master's mate of *Naseby*, 1659. Travelled all over known world in royal and merchant ships. Took command of East Indiaman *Septer* (Sceptre?) on death of her captain in Indian Ocean, 1697. Last voyage 1703.

Journal: vivid and magnificently illustrated journal of his voyages, 1659–1703, prefaced by autobiographical sketch. Apparently begun in 1673.

Greenwich, National Maritime Museum, MS JOD/4.

B. Lubbock (ed.), *Barlow's Journal of his Life at Sea in King's Ships, East & West Indiamen & Other Merchantmen from 1659–1703*, 2 vols (Hurst and Blackett, London, 1934) (B).

Nicholas Blundell (1669–1737) of Little Crosby near Liverpool, son of William (d. 1702) and Mary Eyre; member of long-established recusant family. Educ. Jesuit College, St Omer. M. Frances, da. of Marmaduke, third Lord Langdale of Holme, 1703. They had two das.
Great Diurnal: July 1702–April 1728, the most outstanding of all the records begun or maintained by Nicholas. Touches on every aspect of his family, social and business activities. Transcribed from a series of smaller notebooks and scraps of paper.
MS in possession of Blundell family.
F. Tyrer (trans. and annot.), J. J. Bagley (ed.), *The Great Diurnal of Nicholas Blundell of Little Crosby, Lancashire*, 3 vols, The Record Society of Lancashire and Cheshire, 110, 112 and 114 (1968, 1970 and 1972).

Countess of Bridgewater, *see under* **Egerton**.

Sir Walter Calverley, Bart (1670–1749) of Esholt (Yorks.), son of Walter, Esq. (d. 1691) and Frances Thompson. M. Julia, da. of Sir William Blackett of Newcastle-Upon-Tyne, in 1707. Bart. 1711. He left one da. and one s.
Diary and Memorandum Book: 1663–1749 (but few entries after 1718), covering social life and estate and family matters, particularly their financial aspects.
BL, MS Add. 27418.
S. Margerison (ed.), 'Memorandum Book of Sir Walter Calverley, Bart', in *Yorkshire Diaries and Autobiographies in the Seventeenth and Eighteenth Centuries*, Vol. II, Surtees Society, 77 (1886 for 1883), 43–148 (B).

William Carnsew, d. 1588 or 1589. Lord of the manor of Bokelly in St Kew (Cornwall), son of William, M. Honor, da. of John Fitz of Tavistock, who bore him at least five children: Richard, Matthew, William, Frances and Grace. All died without issue. JP; active in mining ventures.
Diary: January 1576–February 1577, concise daily record of family and social life, reading, weather and estate management.
London, Public Record Office, SP 46/16, ff. 37–52.
N. J. G. Pounds (ed.), 'William Carnsew of Bokelly and his Diary, 1576-7', in *Journal of the Royal Institution of Cornwall*, new series, vol. VIII, part 1, 1978, 14–60 (A).
See also A. L. Rowse, *Tudor Cornwall: Portrait of a Society* (Jonathan

Cape, London, 1941), pp. 55–9, 426–33, and idem, *Court and Country: Studies in Tudor Social History* (Harvester Press, Brighton, 1987), pp. 136–80.

Lady Anne Clifford, Countess of Dorset, Pembroke and Montgomery (1590–1676). Da. (heir) of George Clifford, third Earl of Cumberland (d. 1605), by Margaret Russell. M. Richard Sackville, Lord Buckhurst and Earl of Dorset (d. 1624) in 1609; secondly, Philip Herbert, Earl of Pembroke and Montgomery (d. 1650), in 1630. By Dorset she had two das, Margaret (b. 1614) and Isabella (b. 1622) who survived to adulthood, and three sons who died in early childhood. Her father left his lands to his brother and £15,000 to Anne. She and her widowed mother (to whom she was deeply attached) resisted these provisions tenaciously and insisted on the estate coming to Anne, and Anne refused to accept even James I's award of the estates to her uncle in 1617. Dorset, anxious to receive the money, was angered by Anne's obstinacy. Anne at last gained the old Clifford lands when her cousin died without a son in 1643. During the period of her diary she was usually resident at Knole (Kent). For a short account of her life, see R. T. Spence, 'Lady Anne Clifford, Countess of Dorset, Pembroke and Montgomery (1590–1676): A Reappraisal', *Northern History*, 15 (1979), 43–65.

Dairy: January 1616–December 1617; January–December 1619, preceded by short sketch of events in 1602–3. Her pastimes and family and social life.

Maidstone, Kent Archives Office, MS U269. F48/1–3 (a much later – eighteenth century? – copy of now lost original diary).

V. Sackville-West (ed.), *The Diary of the Lady Anne Clifford* (William Heinemann, London, 1923), a transcript of the above copy, then at Knole (A).

William Coe (1662–1729), farmer of Mildenhall (Suffolk), described as 'gent.', in the burial register. M. at least twice: his second wife was Sarah Hatfield. He had had ten children by 1709: Judith (b. *c.*1688), Anne (b. by 1692), Betty (b. by 1693), William (b. April 1694), Sarah, Susan, Barbara, Henry, Thomas (b. *c.* 1705) and James (b. *c.*1709).

Diary: 1680–1729, register of his participation in holy communion, of sins noted when preparing himself and at other times, and of notable mercies received, especially narrow escapes from serious accidents.

Cambridge University Library, MS Add. 6843.

'The Diary of William Coe of Mildenhall, Suffolk, A.D. 1680–1729', in *East Anglian*, new series, 11, 12 (1905–8) (A).

Anthony Ashley Cooper, first Earl of Shaftesbury (1621–83), eldest son of Sir John Cooper and Anne, da. of Sir Anthony Ashley. M. in 1639 Margaret, da. of Lord Coventry (d. 1649); secondly, in 1650, Lady Frances Cecil (d. 1654); thirdly, in 1655, Margaret, da. of Lord Spencer, who outlived him. His first wife was pregnant four times but bore no live children. One of the two sons of his second marriage survived to succeed him. He fought first for King, then for Parliament, 1643–6; sheriff of Wilts., 1646–8. His subsequent career in national politics culminated in his leadership of the exclusionist cause, 1679–81.
Diary: January 1646–July 1650. For the most part brief jottings about journeys, social visits, financial and estate transactions, local government.
London, Public Record Office, Shaftesbury Papers, 30/24 8.
W. D. Christie, *A Life of Anthony Ashley Cooper, First Earl of Shaftesbury, 1621–1683* (2 vols., Macmillan, London and New York, 1871), I, pp. xxxii–lv (A).

John Dee (1527–1608), mathematician and astrologer, son of Rowland, gentleman sewer to Henry VIII. His first wife (m. 1575) d. 1576. M. in 1578 Jane (1555–1605), da. of Bartholomew Fromonds, who bore him eight children: Arthur (13 July 1579), Katharine (7 June 1581), Rowland (28 January 1583), Michael (1585?), Theodore (28 February 1588), Madinia (5 March 1590), Frances (1 January 1592), Margaret (14 August 1595). At St John's College, Cambridge; BA 1545; original fellow of Trinity College, 1546; MA 1548. Travelled widely in Europe; longest journey abroad (1583–9) included a stay in Bohemia. Warden of Manchester College, 1595–1604.
Diary: Notes of important events in his work and family life entered in contemporary almanacs, where any possibly relevant movements of heavenly bodies were apparent. Greek characters used for intimate or secret matters.
Oxford, Bodleian Library, MSS Ashmole 487–8.
J. O. Halliwell (ed.), *The Private Diary of Dr John Dee*, Camden Society, old series, 19 (1842) (C).
See also C. F. Smith, *John Dee (1527–1608)* (Constable and Co., London, 1909).

Lady Elizabeth Delaval (1649–1717), da. of Sir James Livingston, Viscount Newburgh (d. 1670) and Lady D'Aubigny. Brought up by father's sister Lady Stanhope at Nocton (Lincs.), and by her grandmother, Lady Gorges, while Newburgh was in exile during the interregnum. Maid of the Privy Chamber to Catherine of Braganza, c.1663. After being courted by Count Dohna, a relative of William of Orange, and James Lord Annesley, eldest son of the Earl of Anglesey, ultimately consented, against her will, to marry Robert, eldest son of Sir Ralph Delaval (1670). Robert d. 1682; she m. Henry Hatcher in 1686. She went abroad in 1689 or 1690, probably because of involvement in Jacobite plotting, and (save for brief visit to England in 1703) remained on the continent till her death.

Meditations and prayers: c.1662–c.1671, arising out of her own sins and other distressing or instructive experiences. She apparently copied them out, probably in later life, with some revisions and autobiographical additions.

Oxford, Bodleian Library, MS Rawlinson D. 78.

D. G. Greene (ed.), *The Meditations of Lady Elizabeth Delaval, written between 1662 and 1671*, Surtees Society, 190 (1978, for 1975) (A).

Elizabeth Egerton, Countess of Bridgewater (1626–63), second da. of William Cavendish, first Duke of Newcastle, m. in 1641 John Egerton, Viscount Brackley, who succeeded as second Earl of Bridgewater in 1649. She bore nine children and died in childbed. Her third daughter Katherine ('Keatty') must have been born in or after 1657. Her funeral inscription in Little Gaddesden Church pays tribute to her beauty, accomplishments and moral qualities. It mentions her occasional meditations and prayers, 'full of all the holy transports and raptures of a sanctifyed soule'.

Book of occasional meditations and prayers: c.1648–63.
BL, MS Egerton 607.

See also *Dictionary of National Biography,* under Egerton, John; R. Clutterbuck, *The History and Antiquities of the County of Hertford* (3 vols., London, 1815–27), vol. I, pp. 392, 399.

John Evelyn (1620–1706), second son of Richard Evelyn of Wotton. M. Mary, da. of Sir Richard Browne, ambassador to France, in 1647, after a period at Balliol College, Oxford (1637–40) and extensive continental travels. They had eight children, three of whom survived to adulthood. Settled in 1652 at Sayes Court, Deptford, his wife's family home, where he spent most of the rest of his life. Wrote on subjects ranging from coins to tree cultivation; one of the earliest members of the Royal Society. Sat on various commissions.

Diary: runs from his birth to within a month of his death, but was not begun in its present form till 1660, and until c.1684 is a transcription of older notes and diaries. It records public events, E's family and social life, scholarly interests, travels, and (especially in later years) the sermons he heard.

MSS in the library of Christ Church, Oxford; they belong to the Evelyn family.

E. S. De Beer (ed.), *The Diary of John Evelyn* **(6 vols, Clarendon Press, Oxford, 1955).**

Adam Eyre (1614–61) of Hazlehead (Yorks.), yeoman, but described on burial as gent. M. Susanna Mathewman in 1640 (no children). Served in parliamentary army during first civil war, returning home with arrears of £688 8*s* owing to him.

Diary: January 1647–January 1649; describes management of estate, involvement in parish administration, relations with neighbours and kin, financial problems and difficulties with his wife and tenant, who apparently shared his house.

MS has vanished.

H. J. Morehouse (ed.), 'A Dyurnall or Catalogue of all my Accions and Expences from the 1st of January 1646', in *Yorkshire Diaries and Autobiographies in the Seventeenth and Eighteenth Centuries***, Surtees Society, 65 (1877 for 1875), 1–118.**

Elizabeth Freke (1641–1714), da. of Ralph Freke (d. 1684) of Hannington (Wilts.). M. her second cousin Percy Freke (d. 1706) in 1671, without her father's consent. Her one child, a son, Ralph, b. 1675. Percy's improvidence and her deep-rooted distaste for living in Ireland, where he wanted to build up an estate, helped to make the marriage an unhappy one. Elizabeth retained strong ties with her father and sisters and from 1686 onwards, with some interruptions, made her home at West Bilney (Norfolk), an estate bought with her father's help.

Memoirs: Two drafts survive. The first, written at intervals, ends in February 1714, two months before Mrs Freke's death. Extracts in this anthology are taken from this manuscript. The sequence of precisely dated entries suggests that the manuscript was based on an earlier diary or memoranda. A revised version goes down to 5 May 1713.

Some Few Remembrances of my Misfortuns [which] haue Attended me In my unhappy life since I were marryed: which was November the 14: 1671. **BL, MSS Add. 45718, 45719.**

Mary Carbery (ed.), *Mrs Elizabeth Freke Her Diary 1671–1714* (Cork, Grey and Co., 1913). Lady Carbery conflated elements of both manuscripts in her edition (C).

John Greene (1616–59), son of John, sergeant-at-law, was educated at St John's College, Cambridge, and Lincoln's Inn. M. Mary, da. of Philip Jermyn, sergeant-at-law, in 1643. Eight of their eleven children survived infancy; Mary d. in childbed, together with the eleventh child, four weeks after John's death. He was Recorder of London in 1658.
Diary: in a series of almanacs, 1635–57, jotted observations concerning public affairs and descriptions of professional, social and family events. Eleven volumes were extant in 1928.
MSS belong to the Festing family.
E. M. Symonds (ed.), 'The Diary of John Greene (1635–57)' in English Historical Review, 43 (1928), 385–94, 598–604; and 44 (1929), 106–17.

Edmund Harrold (d. 1721), wig-maker of Manchester, m. in 1702 Alice Bancroft (d. 1703 or 1704); secondly in 1705 Sarah Boardman (d. 1712) and thirdly in 1713 Ann Horrocks. By April 1713 he had lost five children, including Sarah (November 1712–April 1713). Two daughters, Anna and Esther, are known to have survived. His third wife bore another, Mary, in September 1714.
Diary: June 1712–June 1716, describes deaths of second wife and daughter Sarah, courtship and marriage of third wife, his work, recreation and social life, heavy drinking, periods of repentance and extensive reading.
***Edmund Harrold his book of Remarks and observations*, Manchester, Chetham's Library, MS Mun. A.2.137.**
J. Harland (comp. and ed.), *Collectanea relating to Manchester and its Neighbourhood at Various Periods*, Chetham Society, old series, 68 (1866), 172–207 (C).

Oliver Heywood (1630–1702), son of Richard, of Little Lever (Lancs.) and Alice Critchlaw. At Trinity College, Cambridge, 1647–50; BA 1650. Ordained at Bury classis, 1652. Presbyterian minister of Coley Chapel (Halifax) till ejected in 1662, and thereafter continued an active, largely itinerant ministry from his home near Halifax. M. in 1655 Elizabeth (d. 1661), da. of John Angier, minister of Denton (Lancs.). They had three sons: John (b. April 1656), Eliezer (b. April 1657), both of whom survived childhood and entered the ministry, and Nathaniel (b. and d. August 1659). Heywood m., secondly, Abigail, da. James Crompton of Breightmet in Bolton, in 1667. They had no children.
Among Heywood's copious writings are his **autobiography** (to 1666), **diaries** (1666–73, 1677–80) and sundry **event and note books**. His

main concerns were to record the workings of divine providence and monitor the performance of his own duties towards God; he included much information about his ministry, family and kinsfolk.

BL, MSS Add. 45963–9 (except for item 38 in this anthology, taken from Horsfall Turner).

J. Horsfall Turner (ed.), *The Rev. Oliver Heywood, B.A. 1603–1702: his Autobiography, Diaries, Anecdote and Event Books* (4 vols, Brighouse, 1882–5) (A).

Lady Margaret Hoby (1571–1633), only daughter and heir of Arthur Dakins of Linton (Yorks.) and Thomasine Guy. Brought up in strongly puritan household of third Earl of Huntingdon. To this she owed her marriages to Walter Devereux, brother of second Earl of Essex (1589–91) and secondly to Thomas Sidney (1591–5). In 1596 m. Sir Thomas Posthumous Hoby (d. 1640), whose suit had been supported by his uncle Lord Burghley. The couple, who had no children, lived at Hackness, an estate purchased for Margaret and Walter Devereux.

Diary: August 1599–July 1605. Records daily activities of a pious puritan gentlewoman, notably her devotional round and the management of her household and estate.

BL, MS Egerton 2614.

D. M. Meads (ed.), *Diary of Lady Margaret Hoby, 1599–1605* (George Routledge and Sons, London, 1930) (A).

Thomas Isham (March 1657–July 1681), son and heir of Sir Justinian, Bart, (d. 1675), of Lamport (Northants.) and Vere Leigh. His father, a royalist who had been imprisoned in 1655 and 1658, was a member of the Cavalier Parliament. He was also a gentleman scholar keenly interested in his children's education.

Diary: 1 November 1671–30 September 1673. Written in Latin. Sir Justinian had as early as November 1667 written Thomas a letter in which he suggested that his son keep an account of happenings in the house and neighbourhood with a view to turning it into Latin. He corrected the diary himself till December 1672. Records happenings in the family and locality, news of relatives and neighbours, some national events.

Thomae Ishami Commentarii Patris Jussu Inchoati Novembris Primo 1671, Northampton, Northamptonshire Record Office, Isham of Lamport MSS, I.L. 527.

N. Marlow (trans.), Sir G. Isham (ed.), *The Diary of Thomas Isham of Lamport, 1671–1673* (Gregg International, Farnborough, 1971). Contains Latin text and translation (A).

James Jackson, bailiff of the manor of Holme Cultram (Cumberland), m. Jane Currey. They had at least seven children: Richard (b. Feb. 1648(9?)), William (b. Oct. 1651), Isabel (b. Oct. 1653), John (Sept. 1655–June 1656), Joseph (b. Oct. 1657), John (b. Nov. 1659) and Daniel (b. Feb. 1661(2?)).
Memoranda and accounts: 1650–83, relating to family, farming and manorial business.
MS in possession of Mr J. C. W. Atkinson of Abbey Cowper. Microfilm in Cumbria Record Office, Carlisle, JAC 257, section TL/702.
F. Grainger, 'James Jackson's Diary, 1650–1683', *Transactions of the Cumberland & Westmorland Antiquarian and Archaeological Society*, new series, 21 (1921), 96–129 (B).

Samuel Jeake (1652–99), merchant of Rye, puritan, astrologer, son of Samuel Jeake (d. 1690), with whom he enjoyed a particularly close relationship. M. Elizabeth Hartshorn in 1681. They had six children, one of whom died after eight days.
Diary or autobiography: 1652–94; begun in its present form in 1694, it nevertheless clearly rests in large part on earlier materials. The main purpose of the diary is well described by its full title *A Diary of the Actions and Accidents of my Life: tending partly to observe & memorize the Providences therein manifested; and partly to investigate the Measure of Time in Astronomical Directions, and to determine the Astrall Causes, &c.* Particularly interesting accounts of his economic activities, family life, reading and illnesses.
Los Angeles, University of California, William Andrews Clark Memorial Library, MS J43M3/D540.
M. Hunter and A. Gregory (eds), *An Astrological Diary of the Seventeenth Century: Samuel Jeake of Rye 1652–1699* (Clarendon Press, Oxford, 1988).

Thomas Jolly (1629–1703), son of James, clothier of Gorton (Lancs.) and parliamentary army officer, and Elizabeth Hall. At Trinity College, Cambridge. Married and lost three wives between 1651 and 1656; his fourth wife, whom he married some time after the Restoration, died in 1675. He had two sons by his first wife, another son by his third, and two daughters by his fourth. All survived childhood, but all save his third son and one of his daughters predeceased him. Appointed pastor of Altham Chapel in 1649, he was ejected in 1662 and suffered frequent imprisonments, but established a congregation at his house at Wymondhouses.

Abstract of diary: 1671–93. Recorded especially his pastoral work, retirements for prayer, and outstanding family events.

The MS was lent to H. Fishwick for the preparation of his edition of extracts from it, but has since disappeared.

H. *Fishwick (ed.)*, **The Note Book of the Rev. Thomas Jolly, A.D. 1671–1693, Chetham Society, new series, 33 (1895) (extracts).**

Ralph Josselin (1617–83), son of John. At Jesus College, Cambridge, between 1633 and 1637 (BA 1636–7, MA 1640). M. Jane Constable in 1640. They had ten children; those whose dates of death are given here predeceased Josselin: Mary (12 April 1642–27 May 1650), Thomas (30 December 1643–15 June 1673), Jane (b. 25 November 1645), Ralph (11–21 February 1648), Ralph (5 May 1649–2 June 1650), John (b. 19 September 1651), Anne (20 June 1654–31 July 1673), Mary (b. 14 January 1658), Elizabeth (b. 20 June 1660), Rebecka (b. 26 November 1663). Vicar of Earl's Colne (Essex) from 1641 till death. Supporter of Parliament during the civil war, moderate reformer in religion; reluctantly accepted the use of the Prayer Book in 1662.

Diary: After preliminary autobiographical sketch, covers years 1644–83, with entries growing less frequent after 1665. Divine mercies and chastisements his main concerns, but recorded many details of his ministry, economic activities and family life, especially births, illnesses and deaths.

MS in possession of Colonel Richard Probert, Bevills, Bures, Suffolk. Partial transcript and microfilm in Essex Record Office, Chelmsford, T/B 9/1, 2.

A. Macfarlane (ed.), The Diary of Ralph Josselin, 1616–83, British Academy Records of Social and Economic History, new series, 3 (Oxford University Press, London, 1976).

Lady Elizabeth Livingston. See under Delaval.

Roger Lowe (d. before 22 April 1679), shopkeeper of Ashton-in-Makerfield (Lancs.); described as husbandman at head of his probate inventory. Apprentice till November 1665. Married Emma Potter in March 1668.

Diary: some entries for every month, January 1663–October 1667; a few further entries till March 1674. Vivid picture of courtships, companionable drinking, sports, attendance at funerals and weddings and participation in meetings held by ejected Presbyterian ministers.

Wigan Record Office, Leigh District Office, MS D/DZ A58.

W. L. Sachse (ed.), The Diary of Roger Lowe of Ashton-in-Makerfield, Lancashire, 1663–74 (Longmans, Green, London, 1938).

Claver Morris (1659–1727), physician, son of William, rector of Bishop's Caundle (Dorset), matriculated at New Hall (Oxford) in 1676, became an extra licenciate of the Royal College of Physicians in 1683, MD (Oxon.) in 1691. M. in 1685 Grace Green (d. 1689); secondly in 1696 Mrs Elizabeth Jeans (d. 1699); thirdly in 1703 Molly Bragge (d. 1725). By his first wife he had one shortlived da.; by his second his beloved da. Betty (b. 1697), by his third two children, including one son who survived him. From 1686 he lived in Wells, where he built up an extensive practice and later held various offices. In 1718 he was deeply angered by Betty's clandestine marriage to John Burland.

Diaries: four volumes of Morris's diaries and account books were still extant in the early twentieth century, including diaries covering March 1709–March 1710 and June 1718–August 1726. Most of the published entries deal with Morris's family and social life, some with his professional and official work.

MSS belong to Mr Paul Hobhouse of Hadspen House, Somerset. The diaries are not at present available for consultation.

E. Hobhouse (ed.), *The Diary of a West Country Physician, A.D. 1684–1726* (Simpkin Marshall, London, 1934).

Henry Newcome (1627–95), fourth son of Stephen, rector of Caldecote (Hunts.), and Rose Williamson. At St John's College, Cambridge (1645–7). In 1648 took his BA, married Elizabeth Mainwaring, and was ordained. Had five children: Rose (b. April 1649), Henry (b. May 1650), Daniel (b. October 1652), Elizabeth (b. April 1655), Peter (b. November 1656). Rector of Gawsworth (1650–7) and then assistant at the Collegiate Church in Manchester (1657–62). Ejected in 1662, he continued a largely itinerant nonconformist ministry until the 1687 Declaration of Indulgence allowed the safe establishment of a Manchester Presbyterian congregation.

Diary and Abstract: One original diary, 1661–3; a substantial abstract of the diaries which he kept from 1646 until death, prefaced by short autobiographical memoir.

Manchester, Chetham's Library, MSS Mun.A.2.140 and Mun.A.3.123.

T. Heywood (ed.), *The Diary of the Rev. Henry Newcome, from September 30, 1661, to September 29 1663*, Chetham Society, old series, 18 (1849) (B); R. Parkinson (ed.), *The Autobiography of Henry Newcome, M.A.*, 2 vols, Chetham Society, old series, 26 & 27 (1852) (C).

Sir Richard Newdigate, 2nd Bart (1644–1710), of Arbury (Warwickshire), son of Sir Richard, 1st Bart (d. 1678). M. in 1665 Mary Bagot (d. 1692), da. of Sir Edward, of Blithfield (Staffs.), who bore him

fifteen children; secondly in 1704 Henrietta, da. of Capt. Thomas Wigginton of Ham (Surrey). Extravagant, eccentric and irascible; affectionate but sometimes overbearing towards his family. Kept a series of 'colossal' account books and some diaries.
Fragments of diaries of the 1680s have been used here.
Warwick, Warwickshire Record office, Newdegate of Arbury MSS, CR 136/B 1307.
Lady Newdigate-Newdegate, *Cavalier and Puritan in the Days of the Stuarts* (Smith, Elder & Co., London, 1902), contains copious extracts.

Sir John Oglander (1585–1655), of Nunwell, Isle of Wight, son of Sir William, m. Frances (d. 1644), da. of Sir George More of Loseley. He had at least seven children; his eldest son George predeceased him, to his lasting grief, and he was succeeded by his second son William. Was lieutenant governor of Portsmouth garrison, deputy lieutenant of the Isle of Wight, justice of the peace and sheriff of Hants. (1637–8). A strong royalist.
Copious memoranda, memoirs and anecdotes about himself and his family, estates and neighbours on the Isle of Wight, some written in account books.
MSS belonging to the Oglander family are at present in the custody of the Isle of Wight Record Office, Newport, MS Og/AA/26–31. **A photographic copy is in the National Register of Archives (London), no. 9841.**
F. Bamford (ed.), *A Royalist's Notebook: The Commonplace Book of Sir John Oglander Kt. of Nunwell* (Constable and Co., London, 1936) (C).

Samuel Pepys (1633–1703) of London, eldest son of John, tailor, and Margaret Kite. His career was founded on his acquaintance with his father's cousin Edward Mountagu, later first Earl of Sandwich (1625–72), probably made through his uncle Robert Pepys, Mountagu's bailiff. Pepys became Mountagu's London secretary and agent after taking his degree and leaving Magdalene College, Cambridge (1654). Mountagu, a general-at-sea (1656) brought Charles II back to England (1660). Clerk of the acts to the navy board (1660–73), secretary to the admiralty commission (1673–9) and secretary for admiralty affairs (1684–9), Pepys was one of the chief architects of a professional navy. M. in 1655 Elizabeth St Michel (d. 1669), daughter of a Huguenot refugee. They had no children. It was a love match, but, despite their continuing mutual affection, they had frequent quarrels, to which Elizabeth's lack of connections, boredom and intermittent ill health contributed, together with Samuel's possessive jealousy, fear of extravagance, strong sexual appetites and sometimes insensitive assertion of his husbandly authority.

Diary: 1 January 1660–31 May 1669. In shorthand. Very full record of public and private events. Begun in response to momentous political developments, it was kept up partly as a means of self-discipline, partly for private enjoyment. In honesty, variety and exuberant vitality it is probably without equal among English diaries.

MS in Pepys Library, Magdalene College, Cambridge.

R. Latham and W. Matthews (eds), *The Diary of Samuel Pepys: A New and Complete Transcription* (11 vols, Bell and Hyman, London, 1970–83).

Elias Pledger (b. 1665), apothecary, of St Mildred Poultry. From Little Baddow; of London from 1680 (when apprenticed). M. in 1690; his wife Elizabeth d. in 1709. Had two children: Elizabeth (September 1691–September 1695) and Elias (b. November 1692).

Diary: apparently began his 'account of God's various providences to me, and my carriage to Him' in 1683, prefacing it with an autobiographical memoir. An intermittently kept spiritual log book which also records major family events. Last entry, after long gap, 1725.

London, Dr Williams's Library, MS 28.4.

See also D. V. Glass (introd.), *London Inhabitants within the Walls, 1695*, London Record Society, 2 (1966), p. 234.

Mary Rich, Countess of Warwick (1625–1678), da. of Richard Boyle, first Earl of Cork, m. in 1641 Charles Rich, younger son of the Earl of Warwick, despite her father's initial opposition. She came to see her later misfortunes as punishments for this undutifulness. They had two children, both of whom predeceased them: the death of their twenty-year-old son Charles of smallpox in 1664 caused them especial anguish. Her husband, who succeeded to the earldom in 1659, was racked by gout for many years before his death in 1673 and often lost his temper with Lady Warwick.

Diary: 1666–78; sombre and detailed record of her daily religious observances and spiritual vicissitudes.

BL, MSS Add. 27351–6.

Memoir of Lady Warwick . . . also her Diary from A.D. 1666 to 1672 . . . (Religious Tract Society, London, 1847). Extracts only; those printed here were not included.

See also C. F. Smith, *Mary Rich, Countess of Warwick (1625–1678): Her Family and Friends* (Longmans, Green and Co., London, 1901), which contains some extracts, including many of those printed here.

John Richards Esq. (d. 1721), merchant of London, son of John, of Abbotsbury, bought the manor of Warmwell (Dorset) in 1687 and settled there. Had at least four children; his wife Alice d. in 1723.

Diary: 1697–1702. Short entries on family, household, social life, estate and parish affairs. Some, especially those concerning his wife, in Italian.
Dorchester, Dorset Record Office, MS D. 884.
'Extracts from the Diary of John Richards Esq., of Warmwell, in Dorsetshire; from March 1697, to March 1702', *Retrospective Review*, new series, 1 (1853), 97–101, 201–5, 408–18 (B). Miss Margaret Holmes is preparing a full edition.
See also J. Hutchins, *The History and Antiquities of The County of Dorset*, 3rd edn. corrected by W. Shipp, J. W. Hodson (4 vols, London 1861–70), vol. I, pp. 430, 434; vol. II, p. 499.

Richard Rogers (1551–1618), son of a Chelmsford carpenter, was at Christ's and Caius Colleges, Cambridge, and took his MA in 1574. Became lecturer at Wethersfield (Essex). M. twice; six of his children were alive when he died.
Diary: a spiritual journal spanning 1587–90 with some long gaps between entries.
London, Dr Williams's Library, MS 61.13.(17).
M. M. Knappen (ed.), *Two Elizabethan Puritan Diaries* (American Society of Church History, Chicago, 1933), pp. 53–102 (A).

Dudley Ryder (1691–1756), second son of Richard, linen-draper of Cheapside and Hackney, and his second wife Elizabeth Marshall. Educated at the dissenting academy in Hackney, the universities of Edinburgh and Leyden (where he studied civil law) and the Middle Temple (where he was admitted a student in June 1713). His career culminated in his appointment as Lord Chief Justice of King's Bench (1754). Knighted in 1740; his death interrupted the process of his elevation to the peerage as Baron Ryder of Harrowby. M. Anne Newnham in 1734.
Diaries: June 1715–December 1716 and 1746–56; in shorthand. The earlier diary gives very full picture of Ryder's studies, social life and relations with his family (with whom he still regularly spent weekends). Intended to monitor and assess his own behaviour and aptitudes, the diary is unusually frank.
MS in the archive of the Earl of Harrowby at Sandon Hall, Staffs.
W. Matthews (trans. and ed.), *The Diary of Dudley Ryder, 1715–1716* (Methuen, London, 1939). (Selected passages.)

Sir Henry Slingsby, Bart (1601 or 2–1658), son of Sir Henry (d. 1634), m. Barbara Bellasyse (d. 1641), da. of Viscount Fauconberg, in 1631. He left three children. Fought for the King during the civil war and was executed for his part in a royalist plot.

Diary: 1638–49; an occasional journal of reflections, pen portraits and vivid descriptions of incidents in domestic, social and military life. MS has vanished.

D. Parsons (ed.), **The Diary of Sir Henry Slingsby, of Scriven, Bart. (London, 1836).**

Mrs Alice Thornton (1626–1707), da. of Christopher Wandesford (d. 1640), briefly Lord Deputy of Ireland in 1640, and Alice Osborne. M. William Thornton (d. 1668) in 1651. She bore nine children (dates of death included for those who predeceased her): First child (b. and d. – unbaptised – 27 August 1652); Alice (b. 3 January 1654), Elizabeth (14 February 1655–5 September 1656), Katherine (b. 12 June 1656), William (b. and d. 10 December 1657), William (17–28 April 1660), Robert (19 September 1662–4 June 1692); Joyce (23 September 1665–26 January 1666) and Christopher (11 November–1 December 1667). The couple lived with Alice's beloved mother at Hipswell (Yorks.) till her death in 1659, and from 1662 at a newly built house at East Newton, where Alice spent her widowhood.

Meditations and reminiscences: she is known to have left at least four volumes, written at different times, with some overlapping and duplication of material. I have traced only one volume, a slender autobiography, now in the Yale University Library, much less detailed than the MSS on which the published selection of her writings was based.

C. Jackson (ed.), **The Autobiography of Mrs Alice Thornton of East Newton, Co. York, Surtees Society, 62 (1875 for 1873).**

Nehemiah Wallington (1598–1658), turner, of St Leonard's Eastcheap, London, son of John, m. Grace Rampaigne. They had five children: Elizabeth (October 1622–October 1625), John (January 1624–April 1626), Nehemiah (December 1625–November 1628), Sarah (b. December 1627) and Samuel (February 1630–October 1632). Wallington was deeply pious and an active Presbyterian.

Notebooks: seven are known to survive of the fifty he left. Concerned above all with the divine mercies and judgements experienced by the nation and by individuals, including himself, they also included sermons, letters and resolutions. Passages printed here come from **A Record of the Mercies of God: or A Thankfull Remembrance, London, Guildhall Library, MS 204.**

R. Webb (ed.), *Historical Notices of the Reign of Charles I* (2 vols. London, 1869) (extracts). See also P. S. Seaver, *Wallington's World: A Puritan Artisan in Seventeenth-Century London* (Methuen, London, 1985).

Alice Wandesford. *See under* **Alice Thornton**

Countess of Warwick. *See under* **Mary Rich.**

Leonard Wheatcroft (1627–1707) of Ashover in Derbyshire, eldest son of Leonard (d. 1648) and his wife Anne, m. Elizabeth Hawley (d. 1689) in 1657. They had at least nine children (dates of birth in brackets): Leonard (30 May 1659), Anna (29 July 1661), Ester (16 November 1663), John (14 June 1666), David (30 March 1668), Elizabeth (25 June 1670), Solomon (3 May 1673), Sarah (2 October 1675) and Titus (20 May 1679). Wheatcroft not only followed his father's craft as a tailor, but also acted at various times as parish clerk, sexton, school teacher, alehouse keeper, tree planter and carpenter, and wrote a large amount of occasional verse.

Autobiography or chronicle of his life: down to 1701, continued by his son Titus. Describes not only his own work and travels, but also the major events in the growth and dispersal of his family.

MS belongs to Dr Philip Riden: at present in the custody of the Derbyshire Record Office, Matlock, D2079/F1.

C. Kerry (ed.), 'The Autobiography of Leonard Wheatcroft', in *Journal of the Derbyshire Archaeological and Natural History Society*, 21 (1899), 26–60 (B). Dorothy Riden is preparing a new edition, to be published by the Derbyshire Record Society. See also G. Parfitt and R. Houlbrooke (eds), *The Courtship Narrative of Leonard Wheatcroft, Derbyshire Yeoman* (Whiteknights Press, Reading, 1986). My probably erroneous statement ibid, p. 8, that the Wheatcrofts had *eleven* children was due to reliance on Kerry, 'Autobiography', 41, which omits the words 'for she twise miscarried' after the description of Titus as the 'eleventh' child.

Adam Winthrop Esq., (1548–1623), son of Adam. Auditor to St John's and Trinity Colleges, Cambridge; Lord of the manor of Groton (Suffolk). M. in 1574 Alice Still, sister of John, master of Trinity College and later Bishop of Bath and Wells. She died in childbed of a stillborn son in 1577. He married secondly, in 1580, Anne Browne. She bore Anne (b. and d. 1582), Anne (1586–1619), John (1588–1649), governor of Massachusetts, Jane (b. 1592) and Lucy (1601–1679).

Diary: 1595–1610. Records his visitors, journeys and business, and events in the lives of his neighbours and kinsfolk.

BL, MS Add. 37419.

L. J. Redstone (trans.), 'The Diary of Adam Winthrop', in *Winthrop Papers, vol. I, 1498–1628* (Boston, Massachusetts Historical Society, 1929), pp. 64–105 (A).

Mary Woodforde, née Norton (d. 1730), second wife of Samuel Woodforde (q.v.). She bore him at least seven children: Anne, Mary, Samuel, John, Robert (b. 1675), William (b. 1680) and Jane.

Diary: 1684–90, largely devoted to the activities of her husband, children and other close relatives.

Oxford, New College Archive, Steer 9507

D. H. Woodforde (ed.), *Woodforde Papers and Diaries* (Peter Davies, London, 1932), pp. 12–25 (extracts) (C).

Samuel Woodforde (1636–1701), son of Robert, steward of Northampton. At St Paul's School, Wadham College, Oxford, and the Inner Temple. His great uncle Edmund Heighes left him the manor of Westcotte, near Binstead (Hants.), on condition that he obey his grandmother and aunt, especially in choosing his wife. He apparently did not obtain his aunt's consent before he m. Alice Beale (d. 1664) in 1661. She bore him two children, Alice and Heighes, grandfather of James Woodforde, the eighteenth-century diarist. Samuel abandoned his intention of making the law his profession and entered the Church. He became prebendary of Chichester (1667) and of Winchester (1680). In 1667 he married Mary Norton (q.v. under Woodforde).

Diary: 1663–5; a full and vivid domestic record, written in the shadows of litigation, of his uncle's and aunt's disapproval of the manner of his first marriage, and of the death of his beloved first wife Alice.

Oxford, Bodleian Library, MS Eng. misc. f. 381.

See also D. H. Woodforde (ed.), *Woodforde Papers and Diaries* (Peter Davies, London, 1932), pp. 4–11 and genealogical table at end.

Some Further Reading:
A Short List

DIARIES IN GENERAL

B. Didier, *Le journal intime* (Presses Universitaires de France, Paris, 1976).

W. Matthews, *British Diaries: An annotated Bibliography of British Diaries Written between 1442 and 1942* (University of California Press, Berkeley, Los Angeles and London, 1950).

A. Ponsonby, *English Diaries: A Review of English Diaries from The Sixteenth to the Twentieth Century* (Methuen, London, 1923).

—— *More English Diaries: Further Reviews of Diaries from the Sixteenth to the Nineteenth Century* (Methuen, London, 1927).

RECENT STUDIES OF FAMILY RELATIONSHIPS OR OF PARTICULAR FAMILIES OR INDIVIDUALS LARGELY BASED ON DIARIES

K. Hodgkin, 'The Diary of Lady Anne Clifford: A Study of Class and Gender in the Seventeenth Century', *History Workshop Journal, 19. (1985)*.

A. Macfarlane, *The Family Life of Ralph Josselin, a Seventeenth-Century Clergyman: An Essay in Historical Anthropology* (Cambridge University Press, 1970). Contains useful discussion of diaries as sources.

S. H. Mendelson, *The Mental World of Stuart Women: Three Studies* (Harvester Press, Brighton, 1987). Chapter II is devoted to Mary Rich, Countess of Warwick.

L. A. Pollock, *Forgotten Children: Parent–Child Relations, 1500–1900* (Cambridge University Press, 1983).

P. S. Seaver, *Wallington's World: A Puritan Artisan in Seventeenth-Century London* (Methuen, London, 1985).

R. Spalding, *The Improbable Puritan. A Life of Bulstrode Whitelocke, 1605–1675* (Faber, London, 1975).

THE FAMILY

Two surveys presenting different views of their subject, Lawrence Stone's *The Family, Sex and Marriage in England 1500–1800* (Weidenfeld & Nicolson, London, 1977) and my own *The English Family, 1450–1700* (Longman, Harlow, 1984), contain substantial bibliographies. The following are a few of the more important books and articles which have appeared during the last five years.

L. Bonfield, R. M. Smith and K. Wrightson (eds), *The World We Have Gained: Histories of Population and Social Structure. Essays Presented to Peter Laslett on his Seventieth Birthday* (Basil Blackwell, Oxford, 1986).

P. Crawford, '"The Sucking Child": Adult Attitudes to Child Care in the First Year of Life in Seventeenth-Century England', *Continuity and Change*, 1(1), 1986. ·

D. Cressy, 'Kinship and Kin Interaction in Early Modern England', *Past and Present*, 113 (1986).

V. Fildes, *Breasts, Bottles and Babies: The History of Infant Feeding* (Edinburgh University Press, 1986).

A. Fraser, *The Weaker Vessel: Woman's Lot in Seventeenth-Century England* (Weidenfeld and Nicolson, London, 1984).

M. Ingram, *Church Courts, Sex and Marriage in England, 1570–1640* (Cambridge University Press, 1987).

V. Larminie, 'Marriage and the Family: The Example of the Seventeenth-Century Newdigates', *Midland History*, 9 (1984).

A. Macfarlane, *Marriage and Love in England: Modes of Reproduction, 1300–1840* (Basil Blackwell, Oxford, 1986).

L. A. Pollock, *Lasting Relationship: Parents and Children over Three Centuries* (Fourth Estate, London, 1987).

M. Prior (ed.), *Women in English Society, 1500–1800* (Methuen, London, 1985). Contains S. H. Mendelson's useful discussion of 'Stuart Women's Diaries and Occasional Memoirs'.

M. Slater, *Family Life in the Seventeenth Century: The Verneys of Claydon House* (Routledge and Kegan Paul, London, 1984).

R. Smith, *Land, Kinship and Life-Cycle* (Cambridge University Press, 1984).

L. Stone and J. C. Fawtier Stone, *An Open Elite? England 1540–1880* (Oxford University Press, 1984).

Index

Diarists and other writers appearing in this anthology are indicated by an asterisk. Two or more people of the same names are usually distinguished by their relationships to the diarist, specified in brackets.